SEXUAL DIVISIONS IN LAW

LAW IN CONTEXT

Editors: Robert Stevens (Haverford College, Pennsylvania),
William Twining (University College, London) and
Christopher McCrudden (Lincoln College, Oxford)

ALREADY PUBLISHED

Accidents, Compensation and the Law (Third Edition), P. S. Atiyah
Company Law and Capitalism (Second Edition), Tom Hadden
Karl Llewellyn and the Realist Movement (reissue), William Twining
Cases and Materials on the English Legal System (Fourth Edition), Michael
   Zander
Computers and the Law, Colin Tapper
Tribunals and Government, J. A. Farmer
Government and Law (Second Edition), T. C. Hartley and J. A. G. Griffith
Land, Law and Planning, Patrick McAuslan
Landlord and Tenant (Second Edition), Martin Partington
How to do Things with Rules (Second Edition), William Twining and
   David Miers
Evidence, Proof and Probability (Second Edition), Richard Eggleston
Family Law and Social Policy (Second Edition), John Eekelaar
Consumers and the Law (Second Edition), Ross Cranston
Law and Politics, Robert Stevens
Obscenity, Geoffrey Robertson
Labour Law (Second Edition), Paul Davies and Mark Freedland
Charities, Trusts and Social Welfare, Michael Chesterman
The Law-Making Process (Second Edition), Michael Zander
An Introduction to Law (Second Edition), Phil Harris
Sentencing and Penal Policy, Andrew Ashworth
Law and Administration, Carol Harlow and Richard Rawlings
Legal Foundations of the Welfare State, Ross Cranston
British Government and the Constitution, Colin Turpin

Sexual Divisions in Law

KATHERINE O'DONOVAN
Senior Lecturer in Law at the University of Kent

WEIDENFELD AND NICOLSON
London

For my daughter, Julia
'Segui il tuo corso, e lascia dir le genti'

George Weidenfeld and Nicolson Ltd
91 Clapham High Street, London SW4 7TA

British Library Cataloguing in Publication Data

O'Donovan, Katherine
    Sexual divisions in law.—(Law in context)
    1. Women—Legal status, laws, etc.—Great Britain
    I. Title   II. Series
    344.1061'34   KD734

    ISBN 0–297–78664–4 cased
    ISBN 0–297–78665–2 paperback

Filmset by Deltatype, Ellesmere Port
Printed in Great Britain by Butler & Tanner Ltd, Frome and London

CONTENTS

Foreword   ix

PART ONE   *DEFINITION AND HISTORY OF*
           PUBLIC AND PRIVATE   1
   1 Divisions and Dichotomies   2
       Dichotomies   2
       Conceptions of Privacy   5
       The Distinction Between Private and Public
       in Legal Discourse   8
       The Unregulated Family   11
       State Intervention   14
       The Feminist Critique of the Private   15
       The Importance of Law   19
   2 From Feudalism and Patriarchy to
     Market Society   21
       Patriarchy   22
       Access to Land Through Inheritance   24
       Gifts and Maritagium   25
       Purchase of Land   28
       Married Women's Property   29
       The Natural Order of Status and Gender   30
       Transformation and Separation of Work and
       Home   35
       Bastardy   40
       Forms of Marriage   42
       Regulation of Marriage   44
       Legal Regulation of Divorce   50
       Separate Spheres and the Cult of Domesticity   53
       Conclusion   56

PART TWO   *DIVISIONS BETWEEN THE SEXES AND*
           THE PUBLIC/PRIVATE SPLIT   59
   3 Legal Construction of Sex and Gender   60
       The Distinction Between Sex and Gender   60

The Social Consequences of Error in Sex
Classification   62
Legal Definitions of Sex   64
Legal Definitions of Sex Applied   70
Gender as a Socially and Legally Con-
structed Category   73
Eliminating Sex Classification from Law   76

4 The Boundary Between Private and
Public   81
Boundaries   81
Contraception   83
Abortion   87
Infanticide   92
Sexuality   99

5 The Private Relationship of Marriage   107
Contracts or Agreements Between Spouses   108
Finances   109
Property   112
Sexual Relations   119
Violence   122
Behaviour   125
Divorce   127
Private Regulation of Marriage   130

6 Public Law from the Private Perspective   135
Taxation   136
Social Security   142
Equal Treatment   145
Pensions   148
Is Marriage an Economic Unit or an
Aggregate of Two Individuals?   150
Women's Work   153
Conclusion   157

PART THREE   CROSSING THE DIVIDE: REFORMIST
POSSIBILITES   159

7 Reforming the Public: Why Can't a
Woman Be More Like a Man?   160
The Demand for Equality   161
Protective Legislation: A Problem?   163
Motherhood: A Source of Discrimination?   166
Equal to Whom?   173

Equality Reconsidered   176
Conclusion   180
8 Reforming the Private: Why Can't a
  Man Be More Like a Woman?   181
Regulation   181
Legalisation   187
Informal Justice   194
Privatisation   197
Legal Withdrawal?   198
*A System of Principles or Market-place
Values?*   201
What are the Alternatives?   205

Afterword   207
References   209
Suggestions for Further Reading   226
Index of Cases   234
Index of Statutes   236
General Index   240

Foreword

This book is about current and past ideas and beliefs concerning the relationship of women to men as reflected in the law. It is also about social justice. It began with an attempt to describe in a straightforward way the distinction made by law between the sexes. The first task was to specify instances when this occurs. Accumulating examples revealed a mass of confusing and contradictory legal rules and decisions. Questions about the necessity for and justification of differential treatment of women and men arose. Deeper enquiry seemed to produce particular but no general answers. There was evidence that other writers in Anglo-American law who had gone over this ground had settled for writing conventional legal textbooks laying down the law, but making no effort to offer a general theoretical framework. The reasons for this lie in the diffuse and complex nature of legal provisions which do not carry within themselves their reasons for existence.

Explanations for legal differentiation between women and men were sought in the structure for pre-industrial English society, in the material facts of biological reproduction, and in the organisation of home and work in modern industrial society. The unity of the book as a whole remained elusive over a long period of work. But certain themes did emerge with clarity. I realised that a major division in society corresponding to, and related to, the division between women and men is the division between private and public. So I decided to elaborate on that as an explanatory hypothesis.

The difficulties faced in writing a book of this kind are both literary and intellectual. Women's invisibility in traditional academic writing has been emphasised in recent years; redressing the balance remains a problem. For the search must take place among materials which have already been defined as defective. Legal materials seem to tell you everything except what you are seeking. As Milsom remarked on legal history: 'it is what was assumed that we need to know, not what was said.'[1]

Women's legal manifestation has been that of a special case, a different category, separate from the male norm on whom the spotlight falls. The law's silence on major aspects of women's existence, on the private, meant that there were research difficulties. But this silence, and the invisibility of women, are significant. Chapter 2 of the book investigates this issue.

The account presented here of sexual divisions in law not only concerns an analysis of legal provisions, but also advances a certain political thesis. That thesis posits that it is the split between what is perceived as public (and therefore the law's business) and private (and therefore unregulated) that accounts for the modern legal subordination of women. Differential treatment does not necessarily mean subordination, and there may be societies where that is not its effect, but in English society, at least, that is what it has come to mean.[2]

This is a book about law rather than a law book.[3] Legislation, decisions in cases, judicial and official pronouncements, administrative arrangements, are the source materials from which arguments are made. In relying on these sources I am not suggesting that law is the only, or even the primary, evidence for the thesis advanced. On the contrary I am confident that other materials also support the thesis. I am a lawyer and I believe that the institutional arrangements of a society, and its laws, reflect pretty accurately the nature of that society, so law is my chosen source. It is also a fairly reliable indicator of some forms of sexual differentiation.

In its assertion of a political thesis this book is concerned with values. The explanatory hypothesis of the movement of Western society from a hierarchical feudal society to market society involves investigation of the values contained in such typologies. This has been variously explained by Maine as the movement from status to contract, by Tönnies as the contrast between societies which correspond to the ideal types *Gemeinschaft* and *Gesellschaft*. What is implicit in these terms is a comparison between the values of community and individualism.

The enquiry undertaken by the book is directed partly at social change. The model that underpins this analysis is a model of social change in which there is a movement from a community-based society, where kinship and property determine rights, to an individualistic society. This is accompanied by a separation of life as experienced by people into two major aspects: the private and the public. It is suggested that the values of altruism which were part of kinship and community in the past have adhered to the private sphere. The public is characterised by freedom of contract, the economic market, and the values of competition and individualism, according to which persons are dealt with neutrally and equally.

Written in the 1980s this book proceeds on egalitarian assumptions concerning the relation of women to men. This is not just a matter of personal preference, but also reflects official policy and public rhetoric on the subject. It does not assume that this is a value that is, or always has been, accepted in English society. On the contrary, as the analysis of hierarchy and separate spheres for the sexes will make clear, dominance and subordination are accepted by some men and women as the natural relationship of the sexes. Law plays an important part in the internalisation of beliefs about the natural in social relationships. Part of the book's enquiry is directed at uncovering how law constructs beliefs about gender roles, the family, home and work, and how these categories define each other by opposition and contrast.

Since the book's thesis is that the root of inequality of the sexes lies in the dichotomy between private and public and the clash of values involved, it might seem that a prescription of merging these two spheres follows. However, as the book demonstrates, this is fundamental to the way people live, not only in England, but in market societies generally. Simple prescriptions do not cure complex problems. The first step is to analyse the institutional arrangements and laws under scrutiny, in order to reveal the contradictions between official rhetoric and actuality.

If official policies favouring sex equality and the elimination of sex discrimination are to be taken seriously, legal principles implementing these policies must follow. It is not enough for legislation to be passed regulating the public sphere; if the private sphere remains unaffected and if the belief that it is women's separate sphere continues, then nothing will change. As a minimum this book advocates a fundamental legal principle recognising the equal rights of all human beings to dignity and respect in both private and public.

My use of the terms 'gender' and 'sex' in this book should be clarified. Gender denotes legal, social and economic distinctions that follow from biological difference. Sex denotes the biological classification of human beings into two categories. I am aware that in using these terms I am also creating dichotomies, but the distinction between the social and the biological is crucial to the book's argument.

This book was conceived five years ago. Since then I have become a mother, moved home many times, and spent two years teaching law at the University of Malaya. Throughout this time my old friend and mentor William Twining has continued to give me intellectual stimulation and support. Chris McCrudden's trenchant criticism and positive suggestions have made this a better book. Niki Lacey reassured me that the effort was worthwhile and her comments on the manuscript helped me enormously. In addition I am grateful to the Women Law Teachers Group for providing a forum for discussion, to the University of Kent for six months' study leave, and to the Institute of Advanced Legal Studies for the hospitality of the library and the common room.

PART ONE
Definition and History of Public and Private

Liberal philosophy has developed the ideas of public and private as separate areas of life. Both concepts are used in a variety of ways. In seeking to define the private I shall concentrate on its nineteenth-century use. Central to liberalism is the concept of privacy as a sphere of behaviour free from public interference, that is, unregulated by law. The interest of an account of traditional usage of the concept of the private is not merely definitional. It is the prelude to an explanation for the divisions between women and the men in law.

In a sense the private has no history. The purpose of a chapter on herstory here is not merely 'a search for origins'. It is to explain how the patriarchal family form, which flourished in medieval and early modern European culture, survives today in another guise. This is accounted for, in large part, by the unregulated private.

I
Divisions and Dichotomies

'The realm of life and work in *Gemeinschaft* is particularly befitting to women; indeed, it is even necessary to them. For women, the home and not the market, their own or a friend's dwelling and not the street, is the natural seat of their activity.'

FERDINAND TÖNNIES

Dichotomies

The liberal conception of the private refers to behaviour and activities unregulated by law. For Mill, 'the only part of the conduct of any one, for which he is amenable to society, is that which concerns others. In the part which merely concerns himself, his independence is, of right, absolute. Over himself, over his own body and mind, the individual is sovereign.'[1] Mill argues for a sphere of action in which society has only an indirect interest. This 'appropriate region of human liberty' covers matters of conscience, thought, opinion, expression. It also covers 'liberty of tastes and pursuits; of framing the plan of our life to suit our own character; of doing as we like subject to such consequences as may follow'.[2]

In liberal philosophy privacy is central to individualism as an area of life not subjected to the power of society. The importance of this area has grown in recent times, for as Benjamin Constant observed, 'nearly all the enjoyments of the moderns are in their private lives: the immense majority, forever excluded from power, necessarily take only a very passing interest in their public lives.'[3] Steven Lukes, in his review of privacy as a core idea of individualism, concludes that

the idea of privacy refers to a sphere that is not of proper concern to others. It implies a negative relation between the individual and some wider 'public', including the state – a relation of non-interference with, or non-intrusion into, some range of his thoughts and/or action. This condition may be achieved either by his withdrawal or by the 'public's' forebearance.[4]

An outcome of this is that law as regulator or non-regulator is a crucial expression of the limits of state intervention. Law's role in maintaining a boundary between private and public has not always been recognised by philosophers. Yet as Lukes notes: 'liberalism may be said largely to have been an argument about where the boundaries of this private sphere lie, according to what principles they are to be drawn, whence interference derives and how it is to be checked.'[5] This statement might be thought to suggest that law is discounted as a mere boundary divider. It will, however, be argued throughout this book that law is not only central to the concepts of private and public, and to the division between the two, but also plays an important part in the construction of that division.

This book uses the concepts of private and public to distinguish between areas of activity and behaviour unregulated or regulated by law, as in the classical liberal fashion. In legal discourse privacy is more often used as a concept concerned with the protection of individuals from an overly intrusive corporate state prying into personal secrets. Clearly privacy as a concept concerns itself not only with social regulation but also with data protection and evidentiary matters of access to information. This relates to the boundaries of law, for in some cases law enforcement depends on evidence as to behaviour normally classified as private. Further difficulties of definition arise because in recent writings the concepts private and public stand for a variety of referents. 'Public' may be used to denote state activity, the values of the market-place, work, the male domain or that sphere of activity which is regulated by law. 'Private' may denote civil society, the values of family, intimacy, the personal life, home, women's domain or behaviour unregulated by law. The confusion is increased in legal discourse which calls legal relations between state and citizens public and those between individuals private.

If the private is identified as the unregulated zone of life this poses problems which are neither discussed nor recognised in liberal political philosophy. Those areas such as the personal, sexuality, biological reproduction, family, home, which are particularly identified socially as women's domain, are also seen as private. It can be argued that social differentiation between women and men in the gender order has its counterpart in the general social distinction between private and public. A simple summary is: 'the public sphere is that sphere in which "history" is made. But the public sphere is the sphere of male activity. Domestic activity becomes relegated to the private sphere and is mediated to the public sphere by men who move between both. Women have a place only in the private sphere.'[6] This argument raises issues about power in personal relations and in the organisation of the private; these issues are considered throughout this book.

The importance of the distinction between private and public lies in its influence on our perception of the social world and the maintenance of the distinction in law. Scholars of the medieval period agree that the pre-industrial household was a centre of production and consumption. Life was not experienced as compartmentalised into separate categories. It is true that a hierarchical order divided human beings according to status, and that gender was a crucial determinant. This was experienced as natural. Living conditions in the past, the presence of servants and kin, meant that most, if not all, behaviour was open to comment and control. With the revolution in production and the change of mentality that accompanied it, 'life would now be experienced as divided into two distinct spheres: a "public" sphere of endeavour governed ultimately by the Market; and a "private" sphere of intimate relationships and individual biological existence.'[7]

In traditional sociological theory the term *Gemeinschaft* has been used to sum up the values associated today with the private sphere. The term originates with the German sociologist, Ferdinand Tönnies, writing in the late nineteenth century. *Gemeinschaft*, or community, is represented by pre-modern, organic, pre-capitalist societies, usually agrarian, where everything was produced within the household. Here individuals were regulated according to status but their interactions were mediated by love, duty and a common understanding and purpose. The emphasis is on regulation as expressing internalised norms, traditions and the will of the organic community. There is little or no distinction between public and private, between formal law and other forms of regulation. Social status and gender are primary determinants of the expectations of individuals for themselves and of others.

The *Gemeinschaft* conception of justice 'elevates social harmony and subordinates both conflict resolutions and resource allocation to a conception of the total social order'.[8] It is not a description of an actual social order but rather a Weberian ideal type which enables us to understand historical ideologies of how people should live. Although *Gemeinschaft* is sometimes used as an alternative for a concept of 'the good', it has to be recognised that this type of society is status- and gender-based with a consequent subordination, for the sake of the community, of women and lower-class men. That this lesser status is seen as natural and therefore internalised does not detract from the point. Modern writing which idealises the values of community often overlooks the hierarchical and dependent relationships traditionally associated with self-abnegation for the sake of others.

Tönnies contrasted *Gemeinschaft* with the modern commercial market society, the *Gesellschaft*. This represents the world of striving for profit by isolated persons. This world develops as a protest against status society and with the growth of individualism. In this atomistic market-place the general good is seen as derived from individual competition for material advantage. A free market promoted by the liberal theory of possessive individualism enables the pursuit of self-interest through the instrument of contract. The *Gesellschaft* conception of justice emphasises formality, neutrality of adjudication, precision, rationality and predictability. Individuals are seen as abstract right- and duty-bearing entities. The distinction between law – that which is formally regulated – and the private is sharply pronounced. Contract is the model for all law, an exchange between equal individuals, the *quid pro quo* of commercial dealings.

Gesellschaft is sometimes used as a synonym for 'the bad', but it can be argued that the neutrality and equality of the market is preferable to hierarchical society. Von Ihering illustrates the advantages of contractual independence by comparing a land without hotels but general hospitality, with a land with a supply of paid accommodation. On reflection he prefers to retain his personal freedom and independence and to pay for his lodging. He argues that our moral as well as our economic independence depend on exchange.[9]

Conceptions of Privacy

Legal discussions of privacy distinguish between the definition, content and zone of privacy on the one hand, and a notion of the right to that privacy on the other. Lack of agreement about the area to be delimited has prevented a right of privacy from being enacted in English law. However, a leading American authority has shown four areas of interests in privacy that are protected by law. These are intrusion into seclusion or private affairs; public disclosure of embarrassing private facts; false publicity; appropriation of name and likeness.[10] It is noticeable that these areas which are protected concern relations between individuals. The issue of state intervention has hardly been raised yet. This may be because it is open to the state to define what is public and what is private, and the boundary between.

Lack of agreement about a zone of privacy in English law has not prevented courts from ruling on specific instances. But, as yet, the case law deals only with disputes between individuals. In *Prince Albert* v. *Strange* an injunction was issued to prevent the publication of photographs of the royal family. According to the court the interest to be protected was the privacy of domestic life from 'an unbecoming and unseemly intrusion – an intrusion not alone in breach of conventional rules, but offensive to that inbred sense of propriety natural to every man – if intrusion, indeed, fitly describes a sordid spying into the privacy of domestic life, – into the home (a word hitherto sacred among us)'.[11]

An individual can sue another family member for breach of confidence in order to prevent disclosure of personal information. This was done in the *Argyll* case where disclosure of matters revealed in marital confidence was restrained by the court.[12] This is not always so, however. For the courts distinguish matters or relationships which they call private from those which are the subject of public gossip and knowledge. Thus in *John Lennon* v. *Cynthia Twist* Lord Denning refused an injunction to Lennon to restrain his former wife from revealing details of their married life on the ground that 'the relationship of these parties has ceased to be a private affair. . . . [Neither of them] has had much regard for the sanctity of marriage.'[13] So what is initially private can become public and unprotected by law through undue publicity.

An attempt to arrive at a legal definition of the area of privacy through case analysis is unsatisfactory. There are few cases and they do not make clear where the lines are drawn. Yet the idea of privacy does affect perceptions of the social world and social policy, even if not translated into legal concept. Furthermore the desire for privacy has grown in the recent past, probably as a reaction to market society. As the Younger Committee pointed out:

The modern middle-class family of two parents and their children, relatively sound-proofed in their semi-detached house, relatively unseen behind their privet hedge and rose trellis, travelling with determined reserve on public transport or insulated in the family car, shopping in the supermarket and entertained by television, are probably more private in the sense of being unnoticed in all their everyday doings than any other sizeable section of the population in any other time or place.[14]

Privacy, then, has various dimensions of which being unnoticed, not having one's seclusion intruded upon, and controlling information and knowledge about oneself, are only aspects. Those instances where privacy is regarded as having been violated largely concern individuals. The issue of state intrusion is more difficult. It is for the state to decide how, where, and in what manner it will regulate individuals' lives. Zones can be mapped out as being inside or outside the state's purview. The placement of an aspect of life inside or outside the law is a form of regulation. Legal acknowledgement of its existence defines and constitutes it. So regulation may take a form within or without the law.

It has already been stipulated that the term private is used in this book as synonymous with non-regulated. This requires further elaboration. There is a distinction between areas of privacy that are unrecognised and invisible and those that are specifically delimited as private. With the non-existence or invisibility model there is no public reference to the private zone. Not being referred to, it is not brought into existence, defined or constituted. A comparison of the legal regulation of male homosexuality with the non-regulation of female lesbianism shows the creation and circumscription of areas of privacy in relation to the former by contrast with the invisibility of the latter.

Where the state recognises the existence of a private zone or behaviour it draws a boundary between what is private and what is to be regulated. In so doing it constitutes both. For instance prostitution which is off the streets and does not fall within the terms of the Street Offences Act 1959 is unregulated, whereas the same conduct on the streets is a crime. Yet both forms of behaviour are controlled. Control may occur through circumscription of behaviour or through the state's reliance on other agencies, such as the family.

A deliberate policy of non-intervention by the state may mask a passing of control to informal mechanisms. For instance the legal doctrine of the unity of spouses serves as a justification for state policy of non-intervention in marriage. As Michael Anderson observes: 'family behaviour has become the most private and personal of all areas of behaviour, almost totally free from external supervision and control.'[15] Who then controls the family? It can be argued that non-intervention by law may result in the state leaving the power with the husband and father whose authority it legitimates indirectly through public law support for him as breadwinner and household head. A deliberate policy of non-intervention does not necessarily mean that an area of behaviour is uncontrolled.

The Distinction Between Private and Public in Legal Discourse

The idea that private and public can be distinguished is imbued in legal philosophy and informs legal policy. 'One of the central goals of nineteenth-century legal thought was to create a clear separation between constitutional, criminal, and regulatory law – public law – and the law of private transactions – torts, contracts, property and commercial law.'[16] This division is not confined to distinguishing relations between individual and state from relations between individuals. It also draws a line dividing the law's business from what is called private. Although this boundary between the private and public shifts over time, the existence of the distinction and the notion of boundary are rarely questioned.

The dichotomy between private and public as unregulated and regulated has its origins in liberal philosophy. The seventeenth-century liberal tradition as represented by Locke posits a distinction between reason and passion, knowledge and desire, mind and body. This leads to a split between the public sphere in which individuals prudently calculate their own self-interest and act upon it, and a private sphere of subjectivity and desire. As Roberto Unger describes it: 'In our public mode of being we speak the common language of reason, and live under laws of the state, the constraints of the market, and the customs of the different social bodies to which we belong. In our private incarnation, however, we are at the mercy of our own sense impressions and desires.'[17] The liberal conception is of man as a rational creature making rational choices and entering the political sphere for his own ends.

Nineteenth-century liberal thought, as expressed by John Stuart Mill, continued the tradition of the private/public split. In his feminist work *On the Subjection of Women* the solution for Mill was the grant to women of full equality of formal rights with men in the public sphere. From public equality, he believed, would follow a transformed family, a 'school of sympathy in equality' where the spouses live 'together in love, without power on one side or obedience on the other'. Yet he did not propose the merging of the two spheres but rather sanctioned the division of labour in which women remain in the realm of subjectivity and the private. Thus he argued: 'When the support of the family depends, not on property but on earnings, the common arrangement, by which the wife superintends the domestic expenditure, seems to me in general the most suitable division of labour between the two persons.'[18] Women's role was to remain that of loving and softening men in the domestic realm. Mill's views on household management overlooked the connection between economic power and dominance in the home. Economic inequality leads to an imbalance of power. The division of labour whereby one spouse works for earnings and the other for love encapsulates the public/private split.

The Wolfenden Committee Report on Homosexual Offences and Prostitution provides an excellent example of the implementation in law of the liberal view of the distinction between public and private. The committee accepted as unproblematic the idea of 'private lives of citizens'. It stated that the function of criminal law in relation to homosexuality and prostitution was 'to preserve public order and decency, to protect the citizen from what is offensive and injurious, and to provide sufficient safeguards against exploitation and corruption of others'.[19] Individual freedom of choice and action in 'matters of private morality' was upheld in the report:

Unless a deliberate attempt is to be made by society, acting through the agency of the law, to equate the sphere of crime with that of sin, there must remain a realm of private morality and immorality which is, in brief and crude terms, not the law's business. To say this is not to condone or encourage private immorality. On the contrary, to emphasise the personal and private nature of moral or immoral conduct is to emphasise the personal and private responsibility of the individual for his own actions, and that is a responsibility which a mature agent can be properly expected to carry for himself without the threat of punishment from the law.[20]

This is a classic statement of liberal philosophy.

Faced with a question of defining 'the public', the judiciary have attempted to elaborate the distinction between private and public. In *Charter* v. *Race Relations Board*[21] the House of Lords was called upon to interpret s.2(1) of the Race Relations Act 1968, which made it 'unlawful for any person concerned with the provision to the public or a section of the public ... of any goods, facilities or services to discriminate' on grounds of colour, race, ethnic or national origins 'against any person seeking to obtain or use those goods, facilities or services by refusing or deliberately omitting to provide him with any of them'. The East Ham South Conservative Club had refused membership, on the chairman's casting vote, to a Mr Shah, who was born in India. It was alleged that the chairman was opposed to Mr Shah's membership on the ground of his colour. The question at issue was whether the club provided its facilities and services 'to the public'. If the members and their guests did not constitute a public, then the club's action was not unlawful.

Counsel for the Race Relations Board accepted that the Act 'is not intended to interfere with people's domestic lives'; and their main argument was that the Act 'seeks to contrast not public and private but public and domestic so that the family in the narrow sense is admittedly without the scope of the Act but private associations of individuals not connected by family ties or perhaps household ties are within the ambit'.[22]

The majority in the House of Lords approached the issue on the assumption that 'the antithesis of "public" is "private" and the enquiry there is as to who is fitted by the cap "private".'[23] Thus the board's suggestion that the word 'public' in the Act was in contradistinction to 'domestic' was rejected. 'Private' in the context of a club covered a pesonally selected group of people meeting on private premises, where the club which they constitute does not provide facilities or services to the public or a section thereof. Screening or selection for membership was emphasised by the majority as a feature of the private role of belonging to a club. Therefore it was held (Lord Morris of Borth-y-Gest dissenting) that the club was private and had not acted unlawfully.

That private is the antithesis of public and covers a wider area of personal choice than domestic life was the view of the majority of the court. Only Lord Morris, in his dissent, accepted the board's argument that the Act is confined to exempting only the domestic family circle from its operation. In his view the club held itself open to application from all male Conservatives over eighteen and therefore it was open to a section of the public, as laid down in the Act.

The interest of this case is that both parties and all the members of the court accepted that domestic matters are private and outside the purview of the Act. This was never at issue. In the judicial opinions the domestic family area was held up as the paradigm case of a sphere set aside from the public arena. In Roman law the family household was the sacred area of the *paterfamilias*. He had *patria potestas* (power) over all other household members and they had no independent recourse to law. In effect he made the law for them. In medieval England this power was explained in terms of patriarchy. In both systems, intervening in a man's family affairs was seen as an invasion of his private personal sphere.

Two reasons were put forward in the judgments of the House of Lords for the exclusion of discrimination in private from the ambit of the Act. One was the inviolability of personal preferences of the head of a household; the other was the inference that 'the legislature thought all discrimination on racial grounds to be deplorable but thought it unwise or impracticable to attempt to apply legal sanctions in situations of a purely private character.'[24] Thus respect for status combined with pragmatic arguments about the limits of law in order to defeat judicial views of ethical behaviour.

The elaboration in legal discourse of a private domain of subjectivity, morality and the personal as 'not the law's business' has inevitably led to non-intervention in domestic life. Legal ideology views the private as a domain 'in which the King's writ does not seek to run, and to which his officers do not seek to be admitted'.[25] One implication is that those confined to the domestic sphere need not look to law to rectify any power imbalance resulting from the division of labour.

The Unregulated Family

The retreat of the family from society in the eighteenth century has been described by Philippe Aries. A zone of private life developed, not just for the nobility, but for the middle class and eventually for all. 'The family began to hold society at a distance, to push it back beyond a steadily extending zone of private life,'[26] and became a place of intimate relations, in which it was safe to be oneself, where personalities were enlarged and expressed. This development mirrored and was part of the location of paid work outside the home. In the nineteenth century the public sphere, which had earlier been a place in which men realised their social and cultural being, now became identified with the market for commodities. This change in the public sphere has led the family to be regarded as the last outpost of *Gemeinschaft*.

The values of *Gemeinschaft* are those of self-sacrifice in the interests of the community but the context in which these are expressed is one where social roles are ascribed according to gender. Men who pass freely between public and private, but who are primarily located in the public, are socially expected to act as rational, calculating, economic individuals, whose actions are guided by self-interest. Women, who are seen primarily in the context of reproduction, home and family are expected to retain the values of *Gemeinschaft*. The private, regarded in legal ideology as unsuitable for legal regulation, is ordered according to an ideology of love.

The thesis to be elaborated in this book is that ideas of privacy established in legal decisions preclude intervention in the family. The common law assumption that 'the house of everyone is his castle'[27] is an early and useful bulwark in the defence of civil liberties. But it may also conceal a power struggle within the family. This remains unrecognised and the judicial posture is one of defence of freedom, as the following passage makes clear:

I for one should deeply regret the day, if it ever came, when Courts of Law or Equity thought themselves justified in interfering more than is strictly necessary with the private affairs of the people of this country. Both as regards the conduct of private affairs, and domestic life, the rule is that Courts of Law should not intervene except upon occasion. It is far better that people should be left free.[28]

Free for what? is the question. Insofar as this type of rhetoric involves upholding the values of liberty and the restraint of police powers it is no doubt admirable. But it also masks physical abuse and other manifestations of power and inequality within the family.

In discussions of the privacy of marital relations or of the boundaries of state intervention, the home, the family and the married couple remain an entity that is taken for granted. The couple is a unit, a black box, into which the law does not purport to peer. What goes on inside the box is not perceived as the law's concern. The belief is that it is for family members to sort out their personal relationships. What this overlooks is the power inequalities inside the family which are of course affected by structures external to it. This ideology of privacy and non-intervention has been articulated by legislators, by the judiciary and by legal scholars.

The reluctance of Parliament to legislate on areas of family life denoted private can be illustrated from a wide variety of materials concerning relations between the spouses and those between parent and child. Twentieth-century debates on equal ownership of the matrimonial home have foundered on Parliament's unwillingness to lay down a legislative principle of equality. In 1980 when a Law

? Mat. Homes Act

Commission Bill on co-ownership of the matrimonial home was introduced in the House of Lords, the Lord Chancellor made it clear that there was no government support.[29] Nineteenth- and early-twentieth-century debates on child protection and incest demonstrated a great reluctance on the part of parliamentarians to legislate on 'that d—d morality' which was regarded as a private, internal and domestic affair.[30]

The judiciary also have repeatedly expressed reluctance to intervene in the private. Lord Evershed, a former Master of the Rolls, expressed his view thus:

It was in the year 1604, not far removed from the date when Shakespeare wrote the lines from the Taming of the Shrew that, according to Coke's report of the judgement in Semayne's Case, it was judicially laid down that the house of everyone is to him as his castle and fortress. More than three centuries later Atkin L.J., in a famous judgement, said: The parties themselves are advocates, judges, courts, sheriff's officer and reporter. In respect of these promises each house is a domain into which the King's writ does not seek to run, and to which its officers do not seek to be admitted.[31]

The Shakespearian lines referred to express a husband's ownership of his wife. Petruchio: 'I will be master of what is mine own; she is my goods, my chattels; she is my house, my household stuff, my field, my barn, my horse, my ox, my ass, my anything.' The promises regarded by Atkin L.J. as internal to each house were promises of financial support made by a husband to his wife. The case in question stands as legal authority for the non-enforcement of promises made by spouses, and probably by immediate members of the family, unless sealed and witnessed.[32]

This legal ideology is described as follows by a legal scholar: 'English practice has been to refrain from formulating general principles as to how families should be managed.'[33] The view is that the ongoing family and marriage should be left alone, so long as conflict does not cause breakdown. But some scholars extend their opinions to prescription:

The normal behaviour of husband and wife or parents and children towards each other is beyond the law – as long as the family is 'healthy'. The law comes in when things go wrong. More than that, the mere hint by anyone concerned that the law may come in is the surest sign that things are or will soon be going wrong.[34]

State Intervention

It is a standard liberal view that intervention by the state in family life is to be avoided if at all possible. The Victorians believed that 'to undermine parental responsibility was to undermine family stability and thus the stability of society itself.'[35] The 'sanctity of the domestic hearth' was not to be invaded by law or state. Family law continues to be imbued with a belief in non-intervention. But discussions of non-interference whether expressed in legal ideology or in state policy usually refer only to direct intervention. What is overlooked is that structures external to the family have a significant effect on it, and that state policy in areas such as employment, taxation and social security affects what goes on in the family. Furthermore, informal mechanisms of intervention through education, medicine, psychiatry and welfare policies have existed since the Tudor Poor Laws.

Elizabethan Poor Law legislation created a public responsibility for support of the poor which was placed on the parish as an official duty. State concern became that of minimising the cost of this expenditure to the parish. The liability of the immediate family for the maintenance of relatives was legally established and defined. This state intervention constructed new ideas about family and community responsibility. On the one hand it defined what a family is and its rights and duties of financial support. But it also changed the ideas about mutual community aid which had once devolved not only within the household but also upon a wider circle of kin and neighbours: what had been done out of sympathy and neighbourliness now became a legal duty which was resented. It has been suggested that this change symbolised a weakening of personal and kin ties outside the immediate family.[36]

This early example is intended to show that, although the state is reluctant to intervene directly, policies in areas which impinge on the family and which are expressed in legislative, judicial and administrative provisions construct a particular family form. The nuclear family in which there is a division of labour between wife and husband is an expression of these policies.

Conventional academic discussion of state intervention in family and personal life is based on the premise that legislation which directs the management of these areas is not only a problem, but the only problem. The effects of formal legal intervention are said to be the undermining of the stability of the family, the weakening of family bonds, the atomising of individual family members, and the destruction of the family as a political bulwark against excess of state power.[37] Critics of the state hold the family up as a universal good. What they overlook is that the nuclear family which they so admire reflects a particular culture within a particular set of social relations: it is the family form of the nineteenth-century bourgeoisie. 'People everywhere and for all time have not participated in market relations out of which they have constructed a contrastive notion of the family.'[38]

An even more serious omission in the analysis of direct state intervention as unmitigatedly bad is that it ignores the influence of state policy in areas which impinge on the private. Policies on employment, welfare, housing, education, medicine, transport, production, planning, crime, in fact on almost everything, influence family life. How could it be otherwise? The whole fabric of the personal life is imprinted with colours from elsewhere. Not to acknowledge this, and to pretend that the private is free, leads to a false analysis.

The Feminist Critique of the Private

The anthropologist Michelle Rosaldo has argued that the assignment of women to the domestic sphere and of men to the public sphere is characteristic of all societies. This provides a thread linking all known human societies, from the most primitive to the most complex, and which underlines the universal oppression of women, despite the variety of forms this takes in different societies.[39] Although Rosaldo later suggested that 'gender is not a unitary fact determined everywhere by the same sort of concerns, but, instead, the complex product of a variety of social forces,'[40] her analysis provided a universal explanation. All cultures, she argued, distinguish between male and female, and assign appropriate behaviour and tasks to each as a sexual division of labour. No matter what form this takes, men's tasks and roles are given importance, authority and value, whereas those assigned to women are of lesser significance. 'Men are the locus of cultural value.'[41]

According to Rosaldo's analysis cultural value is attached to activities in the public sphere, whereas the domestic sphere is differentiated as concerned with activities organised immediately around one or more mothers and their children. Although advanced and capitalistic societies are extreme in this regard, the dichotomy between domestic and public is found in all societies. Male authority is based partly on an ability to maintain distance from the domestic sphere. Those societies that do not elaborate the opposition of male and female seem to be the most egalitarian. 'When a man is involved in domestic labour, in child care and cooking, he cannot establish an aura of authority and distance. And when public decisions are made in the household, women may have a legitimate public role.'[42]

Although this analysis locates women's subordination in culture, it permits a foundation of that culture in an interpretation of biology. The radical feminist, Shulamith Firestone, offered 'a materialist view of history based on sex itself'.[43] Using Friedrich Engels's original insight that the first division of labour was that between men and women, and that the first expropriation of labour was by men of women's reproduction of the species, Firestone reinterpreted materialism to signify the physical realities of female and male biology. The substructure is biology, the superstructure is those political and cultural institutions which ensure that biological differences determine the social order. Firestone acknowledged that these differences did not necessitate the domination of females by males but asserted that reproductive functions did. She identified four elements of biological reproduction which lead to women's subordination: childbirth, dependency of infants, psychological effects on mothers of child-dependency, division of labour between the sexes based on 'natural reproductive difference'. Her revolutionary project was to abolish current methods of biological reproduction through the substitution of artificial methods and the socialisation of child-care.

Subsequently feminist theorists criticised Firestone for misappropriating the term materialist and for failing to examine women's relationship to economic production. It is generally agreed, however, that her insistence on the ideological association of women and the private sphere as a major source of women's subordination was an unique contribution to feminist theory.

The insistence on the idea that women belong in the private sphere is part of the cultural superstructure which has been built on biological foundations. Identifying these elements and disassembling the whole gave rise to the important insight that gender is socially constructed. Conceptually the distinction between sex and gender brought out the distinction between biological sex and social and cultural expectations and roles based on gender. Feminist analysis, relying on medical research into gender identity, broke the link between biology and culture by showing that one is not necessarily connected to the other.

The focus on the social construction of women's difference from men had an immediate consequence in terms of law. Feminists and liberals were agreed in questioning differential treatment of women and men in legislation. In particular, in the United States, a whole series of challenges to gender-based legislative classifications took place. Each court success, and there were many in the 1960s and 1970s, was regarded as a victory for women.[44] Since social attitudes of employers and those providing such services as credit, housing and education were perceived as denying women equal opportunity, legislation was passed in Britain and the United States making discrimination on grounds of sex illegal.[45] The aim was to eliminate women's differences as a source of subordination so far as possible by opening up the public sphere and assimilating women to men. But in their alliance with liberal reformers feminists seemed to forget that element of the analysis of difference that identified the private sphere as the location of women's oppression. See Smart p. 82

With the focus on sexual division came the celebration of women's difference. The woman-centred analysis which developed from the mid-1970s studied women's culture, held up by some as a model for all persons. This meant an examination of mothering, of women's virtues, of female sexuality, of female experience as values for the culture as a whole, and a critique of masculinity. Celebrating women's difference as a source of strength rather than of oppression became an accepted mode of analysis. Important and perhaps even essential though this stage in the development of feminist theory was, it seemed to lose contact with the major early feminist dissection of the myths surrounding gender.

There is a curious similarity between the positions of the feminist theorists of the 1960s and early 1970s who focused on eliminating women's differences and those from the mid-1970s onwards who celebrated difference. Both streams accepted the dichotomy between public and private. The first group favoured eliminating the differences between women and men, but not necessarily the division between private and public. The second group celebrated women's private existence.

Yet there is within feminist analysis a slogan 'the personal is political' which emphasises the falsity of the public/private dichotomy. Male hegemony has been identified as a continuum in relations between the sexes in all spheres. In the private arena, according to this analysis, relations of domination and subordination are masked by the ideology of love. In the public sphere economic and cultural factors hide the reality. Gender relationships are power relationships.

This account of the feminist critique of the private thus far is a résumé of radical feminist thought since the mid-1960s. There is also within feminist theory a marxian analysis which places class alongside gender in its account of women's oppression. This tradition has been stronger in Britain than the United States. Within marxian feminism what I have presented as a public/private dichotomy is designated as the sexual division of labour. Relationships within the family are on a material site 'located in the relations of production of capitalism and their private, intensely individual character draws on the ideology secured by the bourgeoisie as well as pre-capitalist notions of gender and sexuality'.[46] Marxian analysis correctly identifies notions of the private with the capitalist mode of production and the separation of work and home, for as Marx said of the alienated worker: 'he is at home when he is not working, and when he is working he is not at home.'[47] Yet the historical evidence is that gender divisions pre-dated capitalism, and these were socially constructed by feudal law.

Recently a series of questions about the state have been raised by the feminist lawyer Catharine MacKinnon. Pointing out that feminism has a theory of power but no theory of the state, she argues that the 'state's formal norms recapitulate the male point of view on the level of design'.[48] Her view is that the liberal state's claim to objectivity rests on its allocation of public matters to itself to be treated objectively, and of private matters to civil society to be treated subjectively. 'But feminist consciousness has exploded the private. . . . To see the personal as political means to see the private as public.'[49] MacKinnon criticises both marxism and liberalism for transcending the private and for failing to confront male power and its expression in state and law.

The meaning of the slogan 'the personal is political' has not been examined in detail in relation to law. Although feminists have produced a literature depicting the relative powerlessness of women as a sex category, this insight has not been documented in relation to law, although some work has begun in the United States.[50] Feminist legal analysis in Britain has been content with the liberal position of opening up access for women to the public sphere through sex-discrimination legislation.[51] The importance of the private has not been recognised, perhaps because lawyers cannot see that not regulating is as significant as regulating. Yet we need a detailed understanding of how the particular gender/social order is constituted by law.

The Importance of Law

Feminist analysis has largely succeeded in disassembling the structure of current gender arrangements, if not on a universal basis, at least in the West. What has been lacking however has been an account of how various social, economic and legal structures combine in creating, ordering and supporting the present system. In particular law has remained resistant to analysis. Because it appears immanent, that is embedded in the seemingly natural, law's role is difficult to isolate. Understanding how existing legal structures appear natural and necessary is not a process of justification; rather it is essential to a full analysis of the gender order.

Unravelling law's part is not easy. It is not just external and institutional but also has an internal aspect whereby it forms part of individual consciousness. In its external aspects law may be coercive, but legal institutions also structure, mould and constitute the external world. Law influences the world as well as responding to it. In my view law is historically and culturally contingent. The form it takes depends on the particular conditions in which it occurs. A generally accepted theory is that the law adapts to and reflects shared social values. This ignores the active part played by law in shaping perceptions of these values.

In an essay published in 1971 Professor Robert Summers identified law as a set of techniques for the discharge of social functions. He gave examples of five basic techniques used in modern law. These are the penal, which serves the function of crime prevention; grievance-remedial, which is designed to provide compensation for injury; administrative, which is for regulation; public-benefit-conferral, which is for distributive ends; and private, which is for arranging to facilitate personal choice.[52] Of these only the penal is obviously coercive. Summers's typology enables us to see how law is not merely coercive but takes on a number of different guises in its construction of the social order. The limitation of this account is that it takes a purely instrumental view of law. This ignores the symbolic or ideological aspect, which is also important.

The internal aspect of law is its acceptance by individuals as natural and necessary in the form it takes and the values it expresses. It is internalised and most people are unconscious of its contingency. This helps to explain why the current social/gender order is accepted by those subordinate within that order. Here law as ideology plays an important part. In using the term ideology I am referring to the symbolic statement a particular legal principle or rule makes. In popular consciousness this is generally accepted as a statement of what is fair, or at least what is unchangeable. Teasing out the content of a particular principle or rule is not easy. As the immanent critique of the apparently natural character of law shows, the infusion of law in the social fabric makes isolation difficult. The term ideology stands also for those beliefs that legitimate or justify legal statements of values and perspectives, and consequent practices. Making explicit the implicit content and premises is what the analysis of law as ideology attempts.

How does the immanent critique and the analysis of law as ideology relate to a dissection of current gender arrangements in Britain and the United States? In constructing legal distinctions on biological differences law constitutes both gender and the social order. In relation to the issues explored in this book law rarely shows its coercive side. Yet its external and instrumental techniques, other than coercion, order the regulation of gender categories, sexuality, marriage, taxation, social security and the mapping out of a private zone.

Although I have used the Summers typology to show how law functions, I do not share his instrumental views. For me the great significance of law is that it addresses the ineluctable problems of what people are and how they live, and it prescribes answers.[53] These answers reveal a great deal about the kind of society prescribed. Law is not autonomous. It is part of the social order whose functions it serves. But it is also symbolic. We need to know what it means in people's lives.

This book is part of an attempt to dislodge law as something natural and necessary. Several efforts converge here: unpicking ideology, filling in the feminist account of gender structures, and understanding law's meaning for women. In order to achieve this I must acknowledge that although law is not exogamous to society it does have its own internal rules and logic. To fail to account for these would be to provide an incomplete analysis. So a degree of autonomy for law must be recognised.

2

From Feudalism and Patriarchy to Market Society

'I found that law did not keep politely down to a "level", but was at *every* bloody level; it was imbricated within the mode of production and productive relations themselves (as property-rights, definitions of agrarian practice) and it was simultaneously present in the philosophy of Locke; it intruded brusquely within alien categories, reappearing bewigged and gowned in the guise of ideology; it danced a cotillion with religion, moralizing over the theatre of Tyburn; it was an arm of politics and politics was one of its arms; it was an academic discipline, subjected to the rigours of its own autonomous logic; it contributed to the definition of the self-identity both of rulers and of ruled; above all, it afforded an arena for class struggle, within which alternative notions of law were fought out.'

E. P. Thompson

This chapter puts forward a series of propositions about feudal law and the transition to market society. These propositions are not new and are generally accepted by historians. Because I am concerned to illustrate ideas rather than to document the past, the material is condensed.[1] The object is to depict the controlling and shaping of lives in a gender order by the twin systems of feudal law and patriarchy, and to explain state intervention in family life and its limits. Law was fundamentally constitutive of social relations in feudal society and it differentiated person according to status and gender. These legal relations are described because they defined the place of persons, the limitations of their position, and the terms of relationships within the social order. Looking at the question of access to and control of land as the major form of wealth under feudalism, illustrates the constitutive nature of law.

The concept of patriarchy is used here to encapsulate the idea of a gender order which is dominated by males. Feudal law in its provisions on inheritance, marriage, wardship assumed a natural subordination of women. Thus it bolstered patriarchy as a family form and as a political belief. Women internalised the feudal and patriarchal order as natural.

Patriarchy

The term patriarchy can be explained by reference to *Patriarcha* by Sir Robert Filmer, published in the seventeenth century.[2] This historical document reveals the strength and persistence of a particular family form in European culture. The patriarchal family is marked by the supremacy of the father, the subordination of women, laws which differentiate between the sexes, and the rule of primogeniture in inheritance. Filmer's thesis was based on an assumption of natural inequality. Patriarchal authority in the household was exercised not only over women but over lesser males and servants. Such households, justified by biblical authority, made up the patriarchal order of society. The *paterfamilias* in each household considered himself in a line of descent from Adam and authorised by the Bible to control the members of his household. Rules of law, particularly those on property, reinforced his position. These rules privileged the eldest son as his father's heir and the future successor or *paterfamilias*. This system of property rights, known as primogeniture, subordinated women's property interests to those of men. Younger sons, although less privileged than the heir, were preferred to daughters by the law of succession. Primogeniture was concerned with posterity and the family lineage, but it also enabled the accumulation of wealth.

Patriarchy is a term in political science. It is used to describe a stable, hierarchical, authoritarian order of male dominance. A feature of such an order is that it affects the psychology of those who live under it. Women in medieval England will have perceived patriarchal authority as natural, accepting their inferior place within it. Not only were there no other ways of seeing the social order, but patriarchy was reinforced by feudal law and by religious beliefs.

The social system dubbed 'feudalism' by historians restricted land-holding in the thirteenth and fourteenth centuries to a feudal class whose tenants performed services in return for their tenure. Rules and customs surrounding feudalism have been investigated by legal writers and historians, and it is to these that we owe our knowledge of the system. Their accounts when pieced together give a picture of restrictions placed on land-holding by women as belonging to a subordinate sex, rather than as members of a particular feudal class. Thus the sex/gender system of patriarchy existed alongside the socially stratified feudal structure. Both systems took inequality for granted as part of the natural order.

Feudal society was characterised by hierarchy. Members of the society could recognise the status of others by the work performed and by differences in dress, speech, manner and bearing. The major status distinctions were between men and women, and between freemen and serfs (who were unfree). There were other status definitions. Although the common law administered by the king's courts governed the rights of the feudal class, the tenants of a manor or village were dealt with by custom administered by their local lord.

The beliefs, or social ideology, produced by feudal society emphasised respect for established rights, the treatment of persons according to their sex and their station in life, and the mutual dependence of members of household or manor. Medieval Christianity preached that men were called to a position in life whose obligations they should fulfil. Patriarchal duty was to provide for those over whom authority was exercised. Justice was respect for those legal rights which accorded with station in life. Law enforcement, public order, the preservation of the status quo were seen by medieval canonists as justice. Christianity did not challenge the social hierarchy or the sex/gender system of patriarchy. Egalitarian ideas were not promulgated. 'Under feudalism justice is understood, first, as the obligation to respect established rights, and, second, as the obligation to help the needy, within the limits of one's social position.'[3]

Position within the hierarchical structure of feudalism depended on rank. Access to property, and therefore to wealth and independence, was restricted for the mass of the population. Women's access was also affected by their sex. Not all women were subjected to identical rules. Whether or not a woman was married was a crucial factor. At common law a wife's control of her property passed to her husband, whereas a single woman had control. Although she was postponed in the canons of inheritance, with her property interests secondary to those of men, the unmarried woman was under no legal restriction in her holding of land. The picture painted by some writers is of medieval women who were entirely powerless under common law. At least for single women this was not so. Although the bonds of patriarchy and feudalism restricted their independence they had sufficient legal rights to enable them to manoeuvre within their feudal class. The women of the village governed by customary law were subject to a separate régime; again, it differentiated them from men. As we shall see, however, marriage was the goal for all women and feudal law impelled women with property into marriage. Once wed, economic independence was lost.

Access to Land Through Inheritance

The most usual method of acquiring land in medieval England was by inheritance. At common law, primogeniture being the rule, we would expect to find more male landowners than female. About 20 per cent of families in pre-industrial England had no male heirs, and the property was then partible among daughters.[4] Impartible succession combined with primogeniture meant that provisions had to be made by fathers for daughters and younger sons. By alienating part of their land through subinfeudation, that is by bringing in a tenant, fathers could provide marriage portions for daughters and make provisions for younger sons.[5]

Gaining access to property through a marriage portion was dependent on wedding – whereas inheritance produced a husband. 'The young heiress did not long remain unespoused; her marriage was disposed of at the earliest possible moment; . . . it is rare therefore to find that any large mass of land long remains in the hands of a feme sole,' according to Maitland.[6] This was because the heiress was an attractive economic proposition to a suitor, but above all because her father will have wanted the estate to avoid the onerous duties of the feudal incidents of wardship and marriage. Hajnal has calculated that over half the children in the thirteenth century lost their fathers before they reached their seventeenth birthday.[7] Wardship was a legal institution whereby the crown or feudal lords held the land of the unmarried heir or heiress on the death of the father. The rights included arranging the ward's marriage. There were consider-able profits from the estate and sale of the marriage for the lord. The Statute of Westminster I, c.22, 1275 enacted that if a lord kept an heiress unmarried for two years after her fourteenth birthday she would have an action to recover her land. This was to prevent the lord from keeping the girl unmarried for the sake of his profits from the land. Thus in order to collect the marriage fine the lord will have married her off. Refusal of the lord's match meant that the heiress had to pay its value to her guardian, a penalty which did not apply to male heirs. Thus fathers and then lords had an interest in ensuring the marriage of an heiress. The heiress's person was subordinated to her possessions.

Under medieval customary law both partible and impartible inheritance existed, according to place and form of tenure. Daughters only became heirs in default of sons, either one daughter holding alone or sisters holding as co-parceners. For a village man to marry and found a family, land was necessary. One way to get land was to marry an heiress. Otherwise a non-inheriting sibling could remain in the childhood home on condition of not marrying. 'If there were no sons, one of the daughters inherited the holding, or it was divided between them, and the future for any woman who held land in her own right was secure: she was sure to find a husband. There was no lack of men looking for land and they would marry to get it.'[8]

Daughters might take their portions of their father's goods and go into the world. But unattached women were looked upon with distrust by communities in which they were strangers. So the commonest way for the daughter to leave the holding was to be married from it. Suits before the manorial courts where the daughter's husband sued his father-in-law for the goods promised with the daughter in marriage are evidence of marriage portions, usually in chattels. Custom required such daughters to be excluded from any claim to inheritance, so long as there was another daughter unmarried. The daughter remaining at the hearth, the astrier, was preferred to the daughters who had married out. A daughter who remained unmarried could look to the heir for her subsistence, but only so long as she was unmarried could she remain on the holding. So marriage will have been the normal expectation of daughters of the village.

Gifts and *Maritagium*

The *maritagium* was a gift of land proceeding from the wife's father or other kin, and was granted to her, or to her husband or to both jointly on marriage. Its principal object was to provide for the children of the marriage, and so its continuance after the death of the spouses depended on the issue of the marriage. The idea was to make provision for a daughter and her descendants. So if there were no descendants the property was expected to revert to the wife's kin group. Portions in the form of chattels were also given, but perhaps this was most common in the classes with less land where the father wished to preserve the holding intact.

The English system of marriage in medieval times, at least for the upper classes, thus included the portion, or dowry as it is more commonly called. The portion was the share a daughter received of her father's wealth on marriage. It was a form of anticipated inheritance and gifts on marriage (*maritagium*) were deducted from a daughter's share of inheritance on her father's death. Dower was a gift from husband to wife at the time of marriage to take effect on his death if he predeceased her. Bracton says: 'Dower is that which a free man gives his spouse at the church door on the marriage day, because of the burden of matrimony and the future marriage, for the maintenance of the wife and nurture of the children when they are born, should the husband predecease her.'[9] This was one-third of all lands and tenements of which the husband was seised at the time of his death.

Customary law exercised a push towards marriage for peasant women, just as common law did for the upper classes. A daughter's share of family wealth, generally in the form of chattels, was provided on marriage. This was the critical point of inheritance and departure from home. In the case of villein tenement, if there was no son to inherit the land, daughters could be residual heirs; usually, because the lord resisted partibility, one daughter only received the holding. The astrier, or daughter who remained by the hearth, chose herself.

Marriage portions took a variety of forms. A husband in Belper, Derbyshire, sued his father-in-law in 1312 for failing to provide a house promised on marriage.[10] There are examples of fathers, and grandmothers, giving over a holding when a daughter is about to marry, in return for maintenance on retirement. 'Hugh Coverer, marrying Emma Lord and taking over her father Richard's land', agreed to 'keep the said Richard in board as well as he [Hugh] keeps himself and will give him every year one garment and one pair of shirts and one pair of hose and shoes'.[11]

Dowry has its counterparts at the level of inheritance, and is part of that set. A system which provides dowry for women will usually allow them also to be heirs, with the proviso already expressed, that any takings from the inheritance pot will be taken into account. This does not necessarily mean that siblings are on an equal footing; differential provision for the eldest son, for sons, or for daughters is still possible. And those who have received their portions may be excluded from later inheritance. The testament rules of the Church contained in the acts of the Synod of Exeter (1287) show that sons did not always have to wait until their father's death before getting their share of his goods, but were given their share in his lifetime, and that these were barred from further inheritance. This may be contrasted with the rule in Normandy whereby the father's death cancelled the arrangements made for his children during his lifetime, and the heirs are obliged to restore to the common stock whatever they have received, the whole to be divided amongst the heirs on the principle of equality.[12] The custom which prevailed in the manors of Bray and Cookham was

that if any tenant has three or four daughters and all of them are married outside their father's tenement, save one, who remains at the hearth, she who remains at the hearth shall have the whole land of her father, and her sisters shall recover no part thereof . . . and if the daughters are married after father's death with his chattels, and this without protest, and one of them remains at the hearth, she at the hearth shall retain the whole tenement as aforesaid.[13]

Marriage, then, for women was the time of transmission of property from her own kin. The portion she received was matched with property brought by the husband, the conjugal contributions becoming one whole, to be managed by the husband. The portion received from the wife's kin determined the marriage. Since the portion was tied to marriage, the freedom for the individual woman was limited. On the other hand, if she had to await her father's death for her inheritance she may have been too old for child-bearing, so a society intent on reproducing itself will naturally have allowed anticipated inheritance. Also, given freedom of testation, which developed in the medieval period, the prospective husband may not have trusted the father to include the already married daughter in his will. This adds up to a lack of personal freedom for women, who had little choice other than marriage, the convent or remaining at the family hearth. The words of the well-known ballad, 'Babes in the Wood', indicate a practice by fathers of making provision in their wills for the marriage of daughters:

> The father left his little son
> As plainly did appear,
> When he to perfect age should come,
> Three hundred pounds a year;
> And to his little daughter Jane
> Five hundred pounds in gold,

> To be paid down on marriage-day,
> Which might not be controlled,
> But if the children chanced to die
> Ere they to age should come,
> Their uncle should possess their wealth;
> For so the will did run.[14]

The possibility of daughters preferring to remain single will not have occurred to the medieval man of property, so provision was generally made conditional on and for marriage.

Purchase of Land

It has been argued up to now that legal and customary institutions of feudal society put women under great pressure to marry in the feudal class, and that for the women of the village marriage was a goal. The question arises whether it was possible for the medieval woman to earn sufficient wealth by her labour to purchase land. There was an active market in land in the thirteenth and fourteenth centuries:

On the Glastonbury estates in the second half of the thirteenth century more than a third of the sitting tenants had acquired their holdings by various forms of open or disguised purchase, and sometimes over the heads of the legal heirs whom they bought out. Another, and increasingly common, means of acquiring land was to marry well-endowed women, more especially widows with land . . . . The transmission of land by purchase or by marriage, and the declining proportion of transmission by ordinary inheritance, was merely one of the signs of the increasing land hunger.[15]

Postan refers to manorial tenants in this passage and he found sufficient evidence to satisfy him that 'free land underwent continuous fragmentation because it was fully exposed to the action of the land market.' However, 'the great majority of villeins – perhaps as many as 75 per cent – succeeded to land either by purchase or by marriage to heiresses and widows.'[16] This suggests that, despite the market in land, women acquired land through father or husband and it seems unlikely that a single woman could acquire it by her own labour.

The village women of the thirteenth and fourteenth centuries participated in manual labour. They hired themselves out as workers in field, dairy, estate and house. But their independence was limited to some extent by their sex. Hilton's research convinced him that in certain localities women engaged in the heaviest of agricultural labour alongside men, and were paid at the same rates. But he also admits that full-time female manorial servants were paid less than men. 'Dairymaids, for example, on the Bishop of Worcester's estate got less than male servants,'[17] a picture confirmed by Coulton, who cites evidence that 'women's wages were lower than those of men, even for the same work'.[18]

It is possible, but improbable, that unmarried women labourers purchased land for themselves and worked it, or even hired agricultural help. The *Liber Gersumarum* of Romsey Abbey shows that 'a substantial minority of marriages were independently contracted by bondwomen, generally paying merchet out of their own earned resources and often using this capacity to purchase general licences that would maximise their freedom of choice.'[19] It was marriage that these women used their wages for, not land purchase.

Married Women's Property

Marriage removed a woman from control of her property at common law. Her land or real property, whether through inheritance or *maritagium*, passed immediately into her husband's possession, giving him an interest known as *jure uxoris*, which lasted as long as the marriage or until a child was born. The birth of a child extended the husband's interest to possession for life, even after his wife's death. Glanvill and Bracton recognised the existence of the husband's right to enjoy his wife's freehold lands during the marriage, including those she might acquire by gift, inheritance or otherwise.[20] The husband, having possession, could alienate the property at his discretion, but there was the possibility that the wife could later claim her lands back. The husband's creditors could attach the wife's property.

After the husband's death the wife could claim back her land from those to whom he had sold or given it. But it was a good defence for the present holder to show that the wife had consented to the alienation in the king's courts. For this reason careful purchasers would demand that the wife's consent to the sale be obtained. Early charters show that payment to both husband and wife was common. In any suit in relation to the wife's land she had to be joined as a party. However, there are frequent instances of alienation by husbands of wives' land without consent, 'which she could not gainsay in his life time', and the wife had to wait until her husband's death before she could complain. In the thirteenth century the problem of alienation of land without the wife's concurrence to the consequent disinheritance of the wife's heirs became sufficiently serious for the Statute of Gloucester to be passed in 1278 to protect the heirs. But it was a risky business purchasing a wife's land and probably engaged in by speculators. Nevertheless, 'the frequent efforts by husbands to alienate their wives' inheritance or to deprive them of their dower are by far the most numerous instances of litigation as to warranties during the thirteenth century.'[21]

The wife's real property could be recovered by her on her husband's death but her other property such as leaseholds and chattels became the husband's absolutely on marriage. If the wife did purchase land her title to it could subsequently be challenged as ineffective. The Countess Gundred, whose landholdings and various litigations are the subject of an illuminating study, provides an example.

While married to Earl Hugh, she had bought (for sixty marks) a half knight's fee in Norfolk and had taken the precaution of transacting the matter in the King's court. In 1196, however, her stepson Earl Roger sued her for this land, claiming it as heir of Earl Hugh (his father). Gundred's defence was that she had bought the land herself; and she produced a chirograph made in the King's court to that effect. Earl Roger answered that whilst her husband lived she could not have had any money or other chattels of her own and so could not have made a purchase which would stand valid for herself. This argument prevailed and seisin was adjudged to Roger. The recorded *ratio decidendi* is 'she could have no chattels for herself in the time of her husband which were not her husband's'.[22]

The husband's position was strengthened by the birth of a child to the marriage, for his interest in his wife's property was now to last for his lifetime. He became a tenant-for-life, and his rights after his wife's death were known as 'tenancy by the curtesy'. The theory was that the wife's property was united with the husband's on the birth of a child who was heir to both.

The Natural Order of Status and Gender

A feature of medieval common law which may seem remarkable to the modern mind is that it appeared quite natural that women should have different and lesser rights than men. This was an integral part of the institutions and beliefs of feudal society. In time the propertied classes overcame the difficulties of providing economic independence for their daughters through the trust or use. But for several centuries marriage was civil death for women. The legal concept used to describe this state was couverture, which epistemologically implied that the husband covered his wife's existence. Explanations for the harshness of the common law rules for married women fall into three categories: the ideological, the technical and the economic. Bracton was concerned to classify mankind according to status: the free, the unfree, children, male, female. He says: 'Women differ from men in many respects, for their position is inferior to that of men.' The laws relating to married women are explained by saying that husband and wife 'are of one flesh though different souls', and that they are 'one body and blood. For a woman has nothing which is not the property of her husband.'[23] This language, reminiscent of religious prescription, is the language of ideology and it is used also by Glanvill, who insists on the wife's subjection to the husband.[24] The couple were, in the eyes of the law, united in the person of the male.

An apparently practical account is related to military tenure. According to this argument land was granted by the Norman kings in return for military service and, since women were considered incapable of bearing arms, this led to their subordination. But, as Bracton tells us, a woman could 'marry a husband, who, by himself or by another, can perform the military service'.[25] Since military service often meant no more than the provision of men and horses, or the money equivalent (scutage), and since women could inherit military tenures, this argument is not convincing.

Many examples of ideological explanations can be found in judicial pronouncements and legal writings from the thirteenth century onwards. The early legal texts such as Glanvill or Bracton had great influence on the subsequent development of the law. Their views on married women were used to justify later court decisions denying legal capacity to wives. A common justification was that no precedent could be found to support the claim of women to be treated in the same way as men. Arguments based on women's alleged refinement, delicacy or timidity or on their domestic role and duties became common later.[26]

Technical explanations are given by legal historians and relate to legal institutions and competition between courts. These illustrate the relative autonomy of law. For Maitland the presiding tendency in

English family law prior to the coming of the Normans was one which separated 'the wife from her blood kinsmen, teaching her to "forget her own people and her father's house" and bringing her and her goods more completely under her husband's dominion'.[27] With common law the husband's dominion was mitigated to protection or 'mund'. This mund or guardianship was a source of profit to the husband, as were most guardianships under feudalism. So the wife was, in many ways, a child under the law.

Guardianship as an explanation has appealed to other legal scholars, who find it consonant with the legal aspects of marriage such as a wife's personal subjection to her husband and his rights over her property, the husband's liability for his wife's debts and torts, the wife's right to refuse consent to permanent sale of her land, and the return to her of the land on her husband's death when the guardianship ended.

The second technical explanation for the wife's incapacity is the separation of the royal courts from the ecclesiastical courts. Maitland suggests that at one time the early common law was on the point of creating a community of property between husband and wife but that this development was frustrated by the handing over of matters concerning succession to movables to the tribunals of the Church. There was no consistent view of the effect of marriage. In France community of property started amongst the lower classes but 'in England with its centralised justice, the habits of the great folk are more important than the habits of the small.'[28] The king's courts took the view that all matters of land were within their jurisdiction and that during the marriage the husband had the full rights which have already been outlined.

The competition between the ecclesiastical courts and the king's courts as to jurisdiction over wills and testaments was won by the common law courts. The Church had championed the wife's right to own chattels, to leave them by will on her death. There was also an attempt to preserve for her some of her husband's chattels by limiting his testamentary powers.[29] But the view which triumphed was that 'the wife has nothing of her own while her husband lives, and can make no purchase with money of her own', and that she 'has no property in chattels during the life of her husband'.[30] The king's courts objected to all restraints on the husband's testamentary freedom. This is an important battle, for the germs of community of property and of partnership marriage were defeated. One should add that the Church's partisanship of wives was not disinterested, as there was potential economic gain to it from the wills and intestacy of women.

According to Sheehan the desires of a large part of the population that a wife should keep her own chattels were ignored by the king's courts. Tension between the ecclesiastic view and that of the common law appears. There is evidence of a practice by wives of making wills in the thirteenth century, and the fourteenth century. Although the system of reserving a portion of chattels to wives and children and only leaving the remainder by will was observed by men in the twelfth and thirteenth centuries, by the fourteenth century the implications of the common law had become obvious, and men were disposing of chattels as they wished. The defeat of the Church courts by the common law courts in this matter was to the detriment of women.[31] Alan MacFarlane's thesis that English individualism flourished because of freedom of testation and lack of family property is confirmed in this aspect, but it was a development at the expense of wives and children.[32] From the possibility of a legal form which recognised marriage as a sharing relationship, the law had turned away. Individual control and ownership by men was the chosen form. The importance of this choice and the values it represents in terms of preferring patriarchy to partnership cannot be underestimated. Its significance remains in the legal form today.

Economic explanations locate the subordination of women in the changes in social and economic forms which accompanied human control of the sources of subsistence. For Engels it is the transition to monogamy in marriage form and private property in legal form that is crucial. The subjugation of women was based on the transformation of their socially necessary labour into private service within the family.[33] For Ester Boserup it is the transition to the use of the plough in cultivation of the land and the consequent displacement of women as primary food suppliers and hoers that is significant. The wife then becomes dependent on her husband for economic support and is valued only as a mother. This relates the denial of sexually equal rights in land-holding to procreation. A married woman's fecundity was her greatest asset but it also led to her secondary place in the norms of transmission of land. Since a great part of the married woman's life would be concerned with pregnancy, childbirth and nursing, her husband would effectively control her land. Thus male dominance became institutionalised.[34]

A woman's fecundity was her greatest asset but it was also a source of her subjection. In customary law the pregnancy or marriage of a daughter of the village brought into focus her father's status. The distinction between the freeman and the serf was not made according to land-holding or tenure, but according to personal status. Thus a freeman could hold land in villeinage, just as a villein could hold in freehold. There is some disagreement as to how villein status was constituted, but there is unanimity that the man who paid merchet or a fine for his daughter's marriage was a villein. The antecedents of merchet are unclear but it seems to have been preceded by an earlier fine, legerwite, literally a payment for lying down. Legerwite was a tax on women for 'being deflowered without permission', generally regarded by historians as insignificant. Yet it was a crucial part of the sex/gender system of the feudal period. 'Legerwite was one of the minor profits of Anglo-Saxon law, so humble that they are usually spoken of only collectively as wites, forfeits, or amends. The Leges Henrici, however, specifies legerwite as one of the minor amends paid by villeins "and those of that sort" to their lord, and "for which they sometimes compounded".'[35] The task of reconstruction of these humble fines has not yet been accomplished and legerwite is often referred to as for fornication, which implies that it was exacted from all who enjoyed sexual intercourse outside marriage. But the fine seems to have been levied on women only, although opinion differs as to whether this was for defloration, or for any sexual adventures, or for pregnancy. Childwite was the old fine for unmarried pregnancy and it coexisted in some areas with legerwite. The lord of the manor will hardly have objected to the addition of a villein to the manor even though a bastard, so that fine may have been a mark of ownership of the child.

Eleanor Searle suggests that merchet was a tax on a daughter's marriage portion and that it had the desired effect of forcing peasant dowries to be paid in chattels, less threatening to the lord than dowries in land, and easier to tax. She supports this suggestion with the instructions to the steward of St Albans for holding a court: the steward is to enquire 'whether any bondsman's daughter has married without leave, and what her father has given with her by way of goods'.[36] Further support for this view can be found in the heriot tax which the lord exacted on the death of one of his land-holding villeins. At one time the villein's chattels were all held at the will of the lord and could be taken on death, and although the heriot had become the best beast of the deceased tenant by the thirteenth century, the daughter's pre-mortem inheritance must have been viewed as a threat to the lord's rights.

Merchet was the test of personal status for, as Bracton tells us, 'one who holds in villeinage must give merchet for marrying his daughter but this does not fall on a free man in villeinage.' Merchet determined the right to plead in the king's courts: 'if the exception of villeinage is raised with the addition (among others) that he may not marry his daughter without the payment of merchet, at a fixed or uncertain amount, that will never be proper against a freeman, though he holds by villein customs.'[37] There was resentment against this mark of servility that 'he must buy, he must make ransom for, his flesh and blood.' To be a free person meant that one could leave the manor, that one could marry at will, that one was exempt from many fines, and that one could plead in the king's courts. The elements here of villein status as constituted by a mark on a man's daughter and her position as chattel whose sexuality is controlled by a fine add up to a clear example of ideological representation and law constituting social relations and status. The patriarchal order within the family was reflected in the feudal order outside.

Transformation and Separation of Work and Home

A very influential account of the separation of women and men and of the private from the public is provided by Alice Clark. Her thesis is that the home was the centre of production throughout the medieval period and that all adult members of the household contributed their labour to production. Women also participated in the professions, guilds, trades and craft industries. But with the accumulation of wealth in the hands of a small sector of society in the sixteenth century, a process which was facilitated by the law of primogeniture, women were gradually excluded from trades and industry and the home was separated from work. Clark argues that upper-class women became idle along with the women of the burgeoning mercantile class because the rapid growth of wealth made this possible. Thus with the separation of work and home women were located in the private sphere.

Clark concludes:

As capitalistic organisation developed, many avenues of industry were, however, gradually closed to married women. The masters no longer depended upon the assistance of their wives, while the journeyman's position became very similar to that of the modern artisan; he was employed on the premises of his master, and thus, though his association with his fellows gave him opportunity for combination, his wife and daughters who remained at home did not share in the improvements which he effected in his own economic position. The alternatives before the women of this class were either to withdraw altogether from productive activity, and so become entirely dependent upon their husband's goodwill, or else to enter the labour market independently and fight their battles alone, in competition not only with other women, but with men.

She suggests, 'at this time the idea that men "keep" their wives begins to prevail.'[38]

The interest of Clark's analysis is that she documents closely the process which she describes and she introduces the notion of a wife's dependence upon her husband. Although her account is influenced by economic determinism, and is overly concerned with the gentry, her contribution to feminist history is significant. This account of the separation of work and home serves two functions. Firstly, it idealises the pre-industrial household to which all members made a contribution on a basis of equality. This serves as a model for the sort of household which some feminists would like to see re-created in the future. But this is a modern myth, because feudal society was stratified on gender and class lines. Secondly, separation of work and home in the course of industrialisation serves to account for the position of the sexes in England today, where men are ascribed the role of breadwinner and women the role of dependant. Feminists who regard economic individualism as the solution to dependency rely on Clark's work as an explanation for the origins of the subordination of modern woman.

Alice Clark does not discuss women's work in terms of private and public. Separation of work and home, as a gradual process in the course of the seventeenth century, precedes the creation of a zone of privacy. It is in modern society that the home becomes a private place of emotional refuge from the cold and competitive world of work.

Conventional analysis by legal writers presents a picture of linear progression by emancipated woman out of the private sphere into the public. Emancipation means the acquisition of rights to vote, to control one's property, to custody of children, to enter the professions, to control one's body. Maine's view is much cited:

The movement of the progressive societies has been uniform in one respect. Through all its course it has been distinguished by the gradual dissolution of family dependency, and the growth of individual obligation in its place. The individual is gradually substituted for the Family, as the unit of which civil laws take account . . . . Nor is it difficult to see what is the tie between man and man which replaces by degree those forms of reciprocity in rights and duties which have their origin in the Family. It is Contract . . . . The movement of the progressive societies has hitherto been a movement *from Status to Contract.*[39]

This analysis of progress accounts for legislative developments related to women's rights from the mid-nineteenth century, but it ignores other state interventions which defined and constituted the family as a unit in a manner antithetical to the notion of progress towards the autonomous individual.

This chapter argues that, whilst both analyses outlined above are useful ways of encapsulating tendencies which can be observed from the historical material, both are incomplete. Legal regulation of the family through intervention in the relationships of women and men, of child and parent, created definitions of those relationships which were crucial to the subsequent history of women, both within and without the family. This is not to engage in crude legal determinism and to ignore economic and social forces including beliefs about nature or religion, but I want to highlight a process which was part of the increasing regulation of life by the state and which resulted in the constitution of a particular family form. Clearly this was connected to other economic and social changes which were part of the change in the mode of production. I suggest that the modern family and women's subordination therein is the product not just of the separation of work and home which came about gradually from the seventeenth century, but of processes which were already contained in the regulation of work and wage labouring in the medieval period.

State intervention in the family has been identified by Jacques Donzelot as part of a process of control of poor families. In his *Policing the Family* (*La Police des familles*) he argues that under the *ancien régime* the family was part of a network in which the head of the family, in return for recognition of his position by the state, was accountable for the family members: he had to guarantee the loyalty to public order of those who were part of his household, and to supply services or taxes, in recognition of his own fealty. Beggars and vagabonds not tied into this system acted as disturbers, being dependent on alms which did nothing to integrate the receiver into this sociopolitical order. The head of the family, in return for the responsibility he owed to the authorities that bound him, had virtual *discretionary* power over those around him – power of decision over work, marriage and punishment. Donzelot sums up as follows:

The mechanism was . . . to ensure public order, the state relied on the family for direct support, trading indiscriminately on its fear of discredit and its private ambitions. All this took place according to a very simple scheme of collaboration, with the state saying to families: 'You will keep your people within the rules conforming to our requirements, in return for which you can use them as you see fit, and if they go against your injunctions, we will furnish you with the support necessary to bring them back to order'.[40]

The eighteenth century in France saw the breakdown of this system with a consequent political debate between the 'statists' who proposed the organisation of welfare, work, education and health to all citizens without regard to outmoded family adherences, and the liberals who favoured the organisation of society around the private property of the family. This at least is the classical formulation of the conflict. The way out for the liberal state was to establish a system of philanthropy or public services and facilities at a sensitive point midway between private initiative and the state. However, before assistance was supplied to the poor, they had to be visited and inspected, and the family rehabilitated by bringing to light the moral fault that made a request for aid necessary. 'In this new policy *morality was systematically linked to the economic factor*, involving a continuous surveillance of the family, a full penetration into the details of family life.'[41]

Donzelot is critical of traditional marxist functionalism which argues that the family under capitalism exists because it performs an essential role in the reproduction of the social relations of production, namely the reproduction of labour power. The family, rather than other institutions, performs this function best because the unpaid labour of women as housewives and mothers makes the cost of reproduction lower in the family than elsewhere. For Donzelot the interesting question is how families were persuaded to reproduce labour power and the social order in education and the upbringing of children. He argues for investigation of the family as the target of different social practices such as medicine, law, social work, education and psychiatry. The intervention of these agencies of the state in the family, usually in collaboration with the wife and mother, not only persuaded the family to perform the functions required of it but also dealt with families which were unable or unwilling to do so. The nature of the family was thus transformed and thereby constituted.

If we apply this thesis to the England of an earlier period, we see the same processes at work. Starting with the Statute of Labourers in 1349, the state inculcated values in relation to the work ethic, the responsibility of family members for dependants, and the stigmatisation of those people or families unable to conform (and thus of the indigent poor). This was done gradually over the centuries and finds its clearest expression in the Elizabethan Poor Law. In peasant society control over people's lives, particularly over women, was important to ensure the security of land. This control was transformed to ensure a labour force and the transmission of the work ethic. The notion of family responsibility for dependants was transmitted by the state to the people through legislation on the Poor Law, marriage and bastardy which was compatible with an ideology of female subordination.

The Tudor legislation encapsulated the view that some family members were dependent on others by law. Section 6 of the Poor Relief Act 1601 stated (spelling modernised):

the father and the grandfather, and the mother and the grandmother, and the children of every poor, old, blind, lame and impotent person . . . being of a sufficient ability, shall at their own charges relieve and maintain every such poor person, in that manner and according to that rate, as by the justices of peace of that county, where sufficient persons dwell, or the greater number of them, at their quarter sessions shall be assessed: upon pain that every one of them shall forfeit twenty shillings for every month which they shall fail therein.

Under this Act the Poor Law authorities could intervene in the families of the poor in the following ways: removing the children, if the parents were considered to be unable to maintain them; binding the children to be apprentices; sending the parents to the house of correction if they deserted their children. As TenBroek has said: 'The poor law was thus not only a law about the poor but a law of the poor. It dealt with a condition, and it governed a class.'[42] It also defined and constituted the notions of the family's dependence on wage-earners and the corresponding responsibility of earners for their dependants. Gone were the days of the home as centre of production to which all the members of the household contributed.

Patriarchy was undermined through public intrusion in those families regarded as a threat to social or economic security. Minimising parish expenditure was the object of the legislation, and in pursuance of this goal a particular family form was constituted and behaviour likely to burden the ratepayers was censured. Attempts to control bastardy provide an example.

Bastardy

Bastardy presented a threat to the parish because the unsupported child and mother might become a charge on the rates. From the mid-sixteenth century legislation imposed penalties on the parents for 'defrauding of the Relief of the Impotent and aged true Poor of the same Parish', and required them to reimburse the parish for costs incurred.[43] Those women who had economic support were protected from censure. This is an early legal structuring of women's dependence on men. Yet bastardy seems largely to have been created and constituted by legal provisions. What follows is an explanation of how this came about.

Under the Statute of 1575 (18 Eliz. 1, c.3) the unmarried woman was examined in order to establish who was the father of her child. This could be done at the time of childbirth when the mother's resistance was low, if she initially refused to disclose. The evidence obtained revealed, in many cases, that the woman had become pregnant when she believed herself already married according to Church law. This belief was based on the minimal requirements of canon law for marriage. The sacrament of marriage did not require the presence of a priest. The couple ministered to one another through their mutual promises. In canon law a promise followed by sexual intercourse constituted a valid marriage. This gave rise to a considerable problem of the definition of marriage and of legitimacy.

Hair discusses those who did not marry in church. 'Bastardy was serious because of its social complications. Indeed, it could be argued that the reason for treating fornication as a moral and social offence was that it discouraged bastardy. To bring a child into the world without providing for its maintenance, was unquestionably an anti-social act in a parochial society with very limited resources.' The difficulty with this discussion is that it assumes the couple were not married. 'In the church courts, much effort was put into finding the father and forcing him to maintain the child. Occasionally it was possible to make the parents marry. But presumably most couples who could bring themselves to marry had already done so during the last stages of pregnancy.'[44] Hair does not appreciate that the mother may have considered herself already married, a church celebration merely being a confirmation of that marriage.

This possible explanation of bastardy, long overlooked by scholars, is now being recognised. Some significant figures on prenuptial pregnancy add supporting evidence. Laslett suggests the following figures for prenuptial pregnancy:[45]

1550–99	31%	1700–49	22%
1600–49	23%	1750–99	33%
1650–99	16%	1800–49	37%

One interpretation of these figures is that 'many pregnant spinsters were made "honest women" before the delivery – and in most cases by their seducer.'[46] The use of the word prenuptial, and this interpretation, proceed on the assumption that these couples were not already married. But many may have been and merely went to church to fulfil their religious duty.

Work on Terling confirms this theory. Between 1570 and 1640 prenuptial pregnancy was prosecuted in the Church courts in 40 per cent of cases. The evidence is that the number of prosecutions increased drastically after 1620. Concern with this offence grew with concern over bastardy. There was a dramatic rise in illegitimacy at the end of the sixteenth century. Those prosecuted for bastardy in Terling fall into three groups. About a third are cases of sexual delinquency; in another rough third the circumstances are unknown; and the largest group are cases of 'problems and delays in the process of marriage entry'. An example is Catherine Jackson, presented in 1599 for carrying Richard Chapman's child. Her father explained to the court that 'god willing she and the sayd Richard Chapman intend to semnise matrimony and lyve like man and wyf together.' The marriage was solemnised in 1602.[47]

Perhaps it is refining too much on legal niceties to insist that in cases of marriage contract, or promise, the couple were already married. For it is clear that the Church courts and quarter sessions applied their own definitions of marriage and bastardy. In the years after 1620 churchwardens took a much tougher attitude to prenuptial pregnancy:

Prior to the 1620's pre-nuptial pregnancy was almost never prosecuted if marriage had already taken place. Persons presented were those who had been observed to be pregnant but whose marriage was not yet accomplished and was perhaps uncertain in the eyes of the churchwardens. One may surmise that the essential point of the prosecutions was to hasten the solemnization and avoid adding further to the wave of illegitimacy in the village. After 1620 couples were prosecuted even when long married – some had been married more than eight months when their child was born – someone was keeping a careful count. The churchwardens seem to have discovered an interest in defending the principle that there should be *no* pre-marital sexual relations. They had turned their faces against what had been customarily tolerated.[48]

If a customary form of marriage was to be defined out of existence the power lay with local courts and with those in authority who had mastery not only over people but also over language, in the ability to read and write, and to define. The pregnant woman and the mother of the child defined as a bastard, whether she considered herself married to the father or not, was to be censured if she was likely to burden the parish.

General comparisons of mothers of bastards with other mothers reveal that age of mother at first child is almost the same and that fertility of one group matches the fertility of the other. This again suggests that 'women who had their first child out of wedlock were neither particularly gullible nor exceptionally promiscuous. They were, however, unfortunate. They, unlike the pregnant brides, were left to bear their children alone.'[49] It does not require much imagination to suggest that some of these women believed themselves married, but without the husband's support or witnesses they could not prove it. In Quaife's study six out of ten women prosecuted for bastardy gave as their reason for fornication the agreement of marriage made prior to sexual intercourse: 'In effect for the peasant community there was very little premarital sex. Most of the acts seen as such by church and state were interpreted by the village as activities within marriage – a marriage begun with the promise and irreversibly confirmed by pregnancy.'[50]

Forms of Marriage

Marriage in England until 1753 was privately constituted by the couple to be married and their kin. The theory of marriage promulgated by the Church was that the couple married each other by promises. Contracts or promises to marry were of two kinds. In *spousals de futura* the couple promised to marry at some later time. This promise is often referred to as *per verba de futuro*, and it occurred where the couple used words of the future tense in getting engaged and agreeing to marry after harvest or Lent, etc. But if this promise was followed by sexual intercourse it was binding, and the couple were married. No other ceremony was necessary. In other words, sexual intercourse changed engagement into marriage. The promise could otherwise be broken for good cause.

Spousals de praesenti was a promise to marry immediately, and constituted a marriage without further formalities. The language used was in the present tense, *per verba de praesenti*, and these words performed the marriage. Thus the Duchess of Malfi: 'I have heard the lawyers say, a contract in a chamber. *Per verba praesenti* is absolute marriage.' A contract agreed in words of the present tense constituted, in itself, the marriage bond.

In theory, there was no difference between a contract of marriage and the act by which a complete marriage was initiated. The words of the contract by verba de praesenti were, in J. L. Austin's terminology, performative words, themselves creating the bond of marriage. Deciding whether that bond had been created by the contractual words spoken by men and women was to be the principal task of the courts in marriage litigation.[51]

Where the couple lived together after either form of spousals, and without any formal marriage ceremony, they laid themselves open to punishment by ecclesiastical law, but their union was recognised as a valid marriage by both Church and state. Thus it was possible to contract an irregular or common law marriage which was legal without the intervention of either ecclesiastical or civil authority.

Irregular, formless or common law marriages gave rise to problems for patriarchy, Church and state. The difficulties of proof of marriage have already been discussed in relation to pregnancy. Two reliable witnesses were required. Had the populace conformed to Church practice of publication of banns and marriage before the church door there would have been few problems. As marriage litigation records show, lack of publicity, lack of witnesses and lack of record or registration was the main cause of difficulty. Private marriages were contracted in gardens, in bed, on the highway.[52]

The Church did not insist on the presence of a priest, or banns or publicity for the contracting of a valid marriage. However, the canon law of the Church of Rome changed in the mid-sixteenth century, by decision of the Council of Trent. Thereafter a priest and two witnesses were necessary for a marriage to be valid in the eyes of the Church. But England had broken with Rome so the reforms of the Council of Trent were not implemented. The old law which recognised common law or formless marriage remained good until 1753. Then, with the passing of Lord Hardwicke's Marriage Act, formal or solemnised marriage was necessary for the validity of marriages. A customary and social practice whereby marriage, a legal relationship, was constituted by the couple themselves was eliminated by a state-imposed legal form. What had been a private contract now became publicly regulated.

Regulation of Marriage

The destruction of local custom and of people's autonomy over marriage was finally achieved by legislation in the mid-eighteenth century. This was done by Parliament's passing of Lord Hardwicke's Act in 1753, 'for the better preventing of clandestine marriages'. The Act required all marriages to be celebrated in a parish church or public chapel, unless the Archbishop of Canterbury gave other permission. Persons under twenty-one could not be married validly without parental consent. An entry had to be made in the parish register at the time of marriage, signed by both spouses. Prior to this, banns were to be read or a licence obtained. A clergyman who contravened the new law could be banished to a penal colony for up to fourteen years.[53]

Explanations for state intervention to control marriage can be summarised as stemming from the interests of patriarchy, of the Church and of the state. The metaphysical nature of sacramental marriage, pleasing to notions of privacy and conscience, did cause problems to patriarchy. As Peter Laslett says: 'No hard-headed peasant would have let his daughter get to the point of espousals until a firm agreement had been made between the two families.'[54] Patriarchy's concerns were with controlling the activities of the women of the household and community. But social practice ensured that it was community acceptance that defined a couple as married.

The proponents of the new Act were not concerned about popular common law marriage but about the threat to the propertied classes and to patriarchy of clandestine marriage:

How often have we known the heir of a good family seduced, and engaged in a clandestine marriage, perhaps with a common strumpet? How often have we known a rich heiress carried off by a man of low birth, or perhaps by an infamous sharper? What distress some of our best families have been brought into, what ruin some of their sons or daughters have been involved in, by such means, every gentleman may from his own knowledge recollect.[55]

Not all the Members of Parliament were convinced that the legislature had the power to declare null and void a conjugal promise. Robert Nugent pointed out:

the most pernicious consequence of this Bill will be, its preventing marriage among the most useful, I will not scruple to say, the best sort of our people. The healthy, the strong, the laborious and the brave, I may justly call so . . . . Shall we for the sake of preventing a few misfortunes to the rich and great amongst us, make any law which will be a bar to the lawful procreation of such sort of men in this country?[56]

Several speakers suggested that the cost of a licence deterred many of the poor from marrying in church and that those labourers mobile by trade would be prevented from marrying at all. Parental failure to control marriage among the rich might result in 'a great disappointment to the avarice or ambition of the parents'; but now the poor would be prevented from marriage.

The arguments of patriarchy carried the day: 'It is not only the interest but the duty of every parent to take care that his child shall not contract a scandalous or infamous marriage, and if he cannot do this by paternal authority the laws ought to assist him,' said Lord Barrington. 'I cannot suppose that any gentleman who has ever known what it is to be a father, will be against it,' was the view of the Solicitor-General.[57] One result was a jump in the number of bastards, as Laslett's figures (above, p. 41) show. The Act altered the definition of marriage, for it made clear the interest in publicity, record, legitimacy. Patriarchy's concern was not only with controlling women's sexuality, but also with the smooth transmission of property. Formal marriage suited the needs of the upper class for reasons of security of contract, legitimacy of heirs and protection of the rights of property-owners. Publicly and openly celebrated marriage was difficult to deny or to avoid later. Clandestine marriage to unsuitable partners by their children had posed a real threat to the propertied. To understand this we must see how the various definitions of marriage, and the consequent absence of clear legal form, gave rise to such a threat.

Secret marriages, celebrated privately by a minister before witnesses, had been valid prior to 1753. These clandestine marriages were provable and, so long as neither party was already promised or married to another, were recognised as legal. The publicity and cost of banns or licence were avoided. The history of clandestine marriage is somewhat different from that of marriage promises or spousals. Spousals, or common law marriage, was the traditional form of marriage of the people. In the case of clandestine marriage there seems to have been an awareness on the part of the couple, or one of them, of difficulties of proof. At the same time private rather than public marriage was chosen. So a clandestine, but provable, ceremony before a minister and witnesses was used. Each area of the country had its own customs and the reasons for secrecy varied. Gillis describes how Catholics, dissenters and renegade clergy of the Church performed marriages:

In all, these irregular marriages may have accounted for at least a fifth of all marriages in the first half of the eighteenth century. The ubiquity of the Friar Lawrences and the willingness of the church courts to uphold all manner of vows, especially those made before a priest, meant that all piecemeal attempts at suppression were frustrated. Participants might be disciplined, but their unions were indissoluble.[58]

During the interregnum of the seventeenth century an attempt had been made by the Marriage Act of 1653 to impose on the populace civil marriage before a justice of the peace. The Act appears to have failed in its short lifetime up to the Restoration in 1660. Dissenting sects had their own theories and practices concerning sexual conduct, including a rejection of monogamy and of Church control over marriage. Another legislative attempt to control clandestine marriage made in 1696 also failed. Marrying people privately became a useful source of revenue to some clergy. The Fleet Prison had pre-eminence in the performance of clandestine marriages. An estimated 150,000 to 300,000 marriages took place there in the first half of the eighteenth century. One priest celebrated 36,000 marriages between 1709 and 1740.[59]

There can be no doubt that there was a demand for such services, but why? The suggested answer looks to three factors: cost, privacy and autonomy. Formal marriage involved expenditure not only on licence or banns, but also on entertaining friends. Privacy was sought by those whose marriage would not be socially approved. 'Widows or widowers marrying too soon after the death of a spouse or against the wishes of their family: couples disparate in age, social status, or religion; bigamists and bankrupts'.[60] The desire for autonomy derives from the need, felt by those who wanted to marry in a hurry or without parental consent, to escape the restrictions of the law.

Autonomy was also desired by married women who wished to remain in control of their personal status and finances. The legal effect of marriage, which was a civil death for women, has already been explained. Women apparently believed that clandestine marriage, or even common law marriage, preserved their legal identity, whilst at the same time satisfying the opinion of the community. In the case of some common law marriages the wife retained her place of settlement, name, property and children – all of which she lost in formal marriage.

For women who wished to keep a separate legal identity, common law rites were extremely attractive. Conventional wedding endangered a woman's access to trade, and Mary Vinson, a London chimneysweep with her own business, was well aware of this when she placed an announcement in the newspaper in 1787: 'Many in the same Business have reported I am married again, which is totally false and without Foundation, it being calculated to mislead my Customers.'[61]

And clandestine marriage was, according to some customs, dissoluble.

Another reason that has been suggested for the popularity of clandestine marriage is the preservation of a widow's jointure which would have been lost on formal marriage; servants, soldiers and others bound to celibacy could marry nevertheless.

Church interest in the regulation of marriage by the 1753 Act was a consequence of its loss of control over conjugal and sexual behaviour in the previous century. During the medieval period the ecclesiastical courts supervised morals, and these courts continued to exercise their jurisdiction over matrimonial litigation until 1857. Marriage contracts dominated the litigation of the medieval period as parties attempted to establish the existence of or to gain enforcement of these promises. But during the Civil War the Church lost some of its control.

Hostility to the control by the Church courts of sexual relations was a marked feature of the interregnum. Religious dissenters and Civil War sects did not accept the authority of these courts, which therefore lost their hold over sexual matters and do not seem to have regained it. The dissenters believed that it was for the individual to determine his or her own conduct in accordance with conscience, and this emphasis on individualism changed perceptions of authority. The idea that sexual morality was a private matter was beginning to take hold.

Puritan doctrine insisted on the wife's rights in the family partnership, on marriage for love, on choice for children. By exalting family life and rejecting a double standard of sexual morality the Puritans changed attitudes towards the position of women in society. Nonconformist belief in the spiritual equality of women meant that the religious sanction for patriarchy was removed. If the father's headship of his family is not seen as a matter of religious authority, the whole of society and all its institutions are open to review. Winstanley described his ideal community: 'every man and woman shall have the free liberty to marry whom they love, if they can obtain the love and liking of that party whom they would marry. And neither birth nor portion shall hinder the match, for we are all of one family of mankind.'[62] Hill suggests that Ranters

gave ideological form and coherent expression to practices which had long been common among vagabonds, squatter-cottagers, and the in-between category of migratory craftsmen. The revolution meant the temporary breakdown of the settlement system. There was a whole mobile itinerant population of evicted cottagers, whether peasants or craftsmen, slowly gravitating to the cities. Over such itinerants church courts and J.P.s had little control: de facto marriage and divorce must have been common.[63]

Control over marriage, whether directly or through the medium of the Church, is clearly essential to a state which treats the married couple as a unit. For administrative purposes the modern state, concerned with the distribution of the burdens and benefits of taxes and welfare payments, needs to establish who is married to whom. In the welfare system, in particular, private responsibility for dependants is built into state calculations on distribution. Lord Hardwicke's Act was a response to threats to patriarchy and property and the resulting state control over the formation and dissolution of marriage was an inevitable development. With the growth of ideas about conjugal and parental responsibility for the maintenance of dependants it was necessary to constitute legal relationships. The Poor Law, settlement laws and the new ideology of work and responsibility all played a part in this development. A centralised bureaucratic state could not tolerate the ambiguities of the pre-Hardwicke era. And, as the common law rule on the unity of the spouses became the rule for all, legal definition was necessary. Patriarchy was secured to work with the state in regulating the family. Gillis's view is that Lord

Hardwicke's Act was 'an undisguised triumph of property, patriarchy and male dominance generally'.[64]

Modern lawyers have been quick to condemn the people for marrying informally and the Church for allowing it. Thus Richard Helmholz: 'The Church was right in condemning these clandestine unions, perhaps even in punishing them. They were the source of dispute, uncertainty, wrangling and fraud. They lay open to difficulties of proof and of interpretation not found in marriages duly contracted and celebrated in the parish church.'[65] In this Maitland concurred. This viewpoint is essentially that of the legal mind which looks for clarity, definiteness, finality, a distinction between A and non-A. The untidiness of common law marriage shocks the modern legal mind, but popular custom in the past was established by people, not lawyers.

Popular resistance to the Act was strong. This was not merely a matter of going across the border to Scotland to marry, although this practice was prevalent until 1856 when three weeks' residence in Scotland was introduced as a legal requirement. Local marriage customs, such as jumping the broom, continued. Dissenters and Catholics, who were required to be married under alien church rites, did not conform: this was in accordance with their consciences. There are many examples of practices and customs which survived both in rural areas and in towns. No doubt in some cases the customs continued because of ignorance of the law but many participants were well aware of the significance of the law and had their own reasons for rejecting it. These reasons were not dissimilar to those which accounted for common law marriage prior to 1753: women kept their legal identity, relationships were legitimated quickly or secretly, community respect was retained, transient relationships were legitimated.

Common law marriages after 1753 had no legal validity: however, they had one great advantage. They could be ended by the couple themselves. It is likely that the peasantry and the urban poor regulated their own marriages privately, because there was no divorce. Henry Mayhew found that legal marriage was exceptional among nineteenth-century London costermongers.[66] Forms of wedding such as besom wedding provided for both self-marriage and self-divorce. The couple to be married jumped over a besom broom into the open door of the house in front of witnesses. If divorce was desired the couple jumped backwards over the broom. In some forms of common law marriage the exchange of rings was the contracting of the union. Return of the ring was divorce. This private ordering of divorce was gradually eliminated by state regulation from the mid-nineteenth century.

Legal Regulation of Divorce

Before 1857 divorce was a private matter arranged by the couple themselves, if at all. Legal and religious theory was that marriage was indissoluble, although it was possible for the rich and powerful to be divorced by private Act of Parliament. The termination of marriage was regarded as a matter to be regulated by the couple themselves, or by one of them. Modern scholarship has concentrated on the introduction of public, judicial divorce in 1857 and on the lack of remedies for the poor and for women within that divorce legislation. The movement of what had previously been regarded as a private matter into the public category has hardly been discussed at all. There are a number of possible reasons for this. A private matter is, by definition, difficult to locate and research. Furthermore, scholars have tended to assume that the lack of a judicial remedy meant that couples stayed together. But there is evidence to the contrary.

'Let the husband send her packing' was advocated as the remedy for adultery in the eighteenth century. The practice of walking out on an unsatisfactory spouse and of remarrying without further ado seems to have been fairly common in the unregulated times of the past. Formless marriage has its corollary in formless divorce. The tradition of self-regulation of personal relations affected both marriage and divorce.

Some sought a more public, more explicit termination of their union. 'Will anybody buy her?' said Thomas Hardy's protagonist Michael Henchard, in *The Mayor of Casterbridge*. 'I wish somebody would,' said she firmly. 'Her present owner is not to her liking.'[67] Sale at a fair or a market is the most common form of sale recorded. Usually this was an auction conducted by a cattle dealer. The practice is consonant with a private, self-regulatory tradition; yet it also contains an element of publicity. It is significant that only wives were sold. There is no evidence to suggest that the king's courts accepted contractual termination of marriage, or wife sale. The first recorded instance is of gift rather than sale. A gift was made by Sir John de Camoys, by grant under seal, of his wife to Sir William Payne, '*spontanea voluntate mea*'. On Sir John's death the couple married.

When the wife claimed dower from Sir William's estate it was denied on grounds of adultery.[68] Despite this lack of legal recognition, wife sale flourished as an informal custom in the British Isles generally for a period of about 500 years.

Ecclesiastical prosecutions became evident in the sixteenth and seventeenth centuries. In 1696 Thomas Heath was presented by the churchwardens of Thame to the Church court for living in sin with the wife of George Fuller, 'having bought her of her husband at 2d the pound'.[69] Inn sales were prevalent from about 1730 to 1890. Nearly 400 cases have been discovered, and given that wife sale was private ordering, and that the literate showed little interest in folkways, these were surely not all.

In a divorceless society self-termination of marriage or of cohabitation is hardly surprising. Why did the spouses not merely desert each other without those rites implied in an auction or sale? The most frequently offered explanation is that wife sale legitimated in social terms an adulterous relationship. The author of *The Laws Respecting Women*, published in 1777, stated:

if the man has a mind to authenticate the intended separation by making it a matter of public notoriety, thinking with Petruchio, that his wife is his goods and chattels, he puts a halter around her neck, and thereby leads her to the next market place, and there puts her up to auction as though she was a brood-mare or a milch-cow. A purchaser is generally provided beforehand on these occasions; for it can hardly be supposed that the *delicate* female would submit to public indignity unless she was sure of being purchased when brought to market.[70]

Yet there are examples of sales where there was no purchaser, or where the purchaser was a stranger, or where the purchaser was already married.[71]

The desire for public dissolution of marriage seems to have been motivated by a variety of factors. Awareness of the legal incidents attached to, and the economic consequences of, marriage led some to seek publicity, in the belief that sale was the equivalent of divorce. The *Record* newspaper of Dudley for 26 August 1859 reported a case where the 'husband, in his ignorance thinks – and this repeated three times – she actually has no claim on him.'[72] Publicity, especially where there was a record of the transaction, also protected the new partners from accusations of adultery. Sale was evidence of condonation of adultery by the husband, which was a good defence should he bring suit for damages for criminal conversation against the purchaser. A record also gave security to the wife: Mrs Dunn of Ripon in Yorkshire said in 1881: 'Yes I was married to another man, but he sold me to Dunn for twenty-five shillings and I have it to show in black and white, with a receipt stamp on it, as I did not want people to say I was living in adultery.'[73] Public sale also serves as a *rite de passage* for the parties; the importance of ceremony to validate personal relations seems to be a constant in human society.

Entry of the sale into the market toll book, and the payment of a toll, ensured a record of the transaction. *The Times*, 30 March 1796, records a toll of 4d. One shilling was paid as a toll by Mr Hilton of Lodsworth on the sale of his wife for thirty shillings, according to the Brighton *Herald* of 27 May 1826. Despite the clear statement by Lord Mansfield in *R*. v. *Delaval* that wife sale was 'notoriously and grossly against public decency and good manners,' beliefs in its legality continued.[74] To those involved, publicity, record, ceremony and legitimation of marriage dissolution or formation were important.

Private ordering of divorce was necessary to a society where divorce was unavailable for legal and financial reasons. Yet the form which the institution took reflected the powerlessness of the wives who were sold. Even where there was consent, the nature of the proceedings underlined the subordination of women. In Gayle Rubin's schema of a sex/gender system, the exchange of women as wives was an early form of social exchange between men.[75] Wife sale was another form of such exchange. That women shared in the ideology that enabled such sales to take place in no way detracts from the point. The internalisation by the subordinate of dominant beliefs is well documented.

Not all women were complaisant, and there is evidence of at least one who turned a proposed sale to her advantage. *The Farmers Journal* of 5 May 1810 tells the following tale:

A youngman in Bewcastle, Cumberland, who was not on good terms with his wife, resolved a few days ago to dispose of her by auction. Not being able to find a purchaser in the place where they resided, she persuaded him to proceed to Newcastle for that purpose. Accordingly they set out, and this modern Dalilah laid her plan so well, that immediately on his arrival a pressgang conveyed him on board frigate preparing to get under weigh for a long cruise.[76]

When judicial divorce was finally permitted in 1857 it was on terms that discriminated between women and men and between rich and poor. As a legal means of marriage termination it replaced the private Act of Parliament. Divorce had become public. Parliamentary divorce provides an example of the gradual movement of control of one area of personal relations from private to public. Between 1715 and 1775 one private divorce Act a year, on average, was passed by Parliament. Thereafter, until judicial divorce was introduced, there were on average three a year. These acts were the successful results of petitions brought by husbands for adultery.

Parliament believed that the marriage should only be dissolved if circumstances had arisen such as to make continuance impossible. This required a judgment to be made in public on a private affair. Adultery by a wife was seen as such a circumstance. Most cases were motivated by the desire for a legitimate male heir to whom property could be transmitted and the safeguarding of the family line and succession. For this reason only four women were successful in obtaining divorces, and these were where aggravating circumstances such as incest or bigamy were proved in addition to adultery.

Public ceremony of marriage or divorce regulated and controlled by law is often seen by late-twentieth-century commentators as an unwarranted intrusion by the state into personal relations. Yet the evidence from the private ordering of the past is that self-regulation often means control by the strong. In the private world of the family, marriage and divorce were governed by patriarchy; women, or children, did not have control. Within past cultural contexts expressed by religion, political philosophy or law, this is hardly surprising. It must be recognised however that, whatever the inequalities embedded in a new legal order in which aspects of personal relations were made public, the advent of legal ordering meant the exposure to public comment and criticism of values that had previously remained unexamined or unexpressed.

Separate Spheres and the Cult of Domesticity

The responsibility of the husband and father to support his family inaugurated with the Tudor Poor Law was reiterated in the nineteenth century. It has been pointed out that this was a means of maintaining discipline and the work ethic. It also proclaimed a division of labour between women and men which was symbolically represented in the ideology of separate spheres. Much has been written about the cult of domesticity which accompanied the separation of life into private and public.[77] It is hardly surprising that women of the growing middle class, who were largely confined to the home, should have developed a code of behaviour to rationalise their existence. Its elements were women's proper sphere confined to the home, the idealisation of motherhood, and the moral superiority of women. Nancy Cott has observed that 'within the home women did gain a new recognition and in the process broke the ancient hierarchy that had assigned superiority to men in all spheres of activity. Domesticity, in short, was an alternative to patriarchy, both in intention and in fact. By asserting a companionate role of women, it implicitly denied patriarchy.'[78]

The idea of separate spheres legitimated certain philanthropic and welfare activities of middle-class women which, in conjunction with state supervision, extended the cult of domesticity to the working class. Thus the Poor Law Commissioners of 1843, while admitting that agricultural labour was enjoyed by women who benefited physically from it, nevertheless felt the family should come first:

To a certain extent also the husband is a sufferer from his wife's absence from home. There is not the same order in the cottage, nor the same attention paid to his comforts as when his wife remains at home all day. On returning from her labour she has to look after the children, and her husband has to wait for his supper. He may come home tired and wet; he finds his wife has arrived just before him, and she must give her attention to the children; there is no fire, no supper, no comfort, and he goes to the beer shop.[79]

The elevation of the domestic realm to a place of privacy, serenity, comfort and cleanliness required certain forms of legislative intervention. This was so particularly where a discourse concerning the protection and education of children prevailed. Anna Martin, writing in 1911, traced the way that 'progressive legislation' concerning protection of children, with wider definitions of what constituted neglect and cruelty, placed strain and conflicting claims on mothers. Women with inadequate resources feared the new legislation. Without the necessary material and emotional support to conform to it, mothers were threatened by the cult of domesticity.[80]

The fears expressed by working-class women indicate the dilemma they faced. They were bound to their families by love, but within a particular culture and with certain expectations. Now the values and customs of a different class were to be imposed on them. New duties were defined. Their position at the centre of the home was undermined, yet their obligation to be there was made clear. Educationalists, doctors, social workers gave them instruction and advice. Donzelot argues that mothers welcomed the intervention of these 'tutelary authorities', especially medical professionals. It may be that mothers did find professionals useful in mediating between husband and wife, and that by controlling their husbands they did reduce patriarchal authority. But the evidence is also that they feared prosecution for child neglect, which would have meant imprisonment and separation from their children. Donzelot sees a 'paradoxical result of the liberalisation of the family, of the emergence of children's rights, of the rebalancing of the man–woman relationship: the more these rights are proclaimed, the more the stranglehold of a tutelary authority tightens around the poor family. In this system, family patriarchalism is destroyed only at the cost of a patriarchy of the State.'[81] But it will have been because of the inequality within the family in the relationship of the spouses that women sought an alliance with the welfare agencies, if indeed they did so.

The .doctrine of women's sphere of domesticity opened and reserved to women a certain social power. The social purity movement of the late nineteenth century which emphasised women's moral superiority to men and yet insisted on a single standard of sexual behaviour for both sexes is an example of translation into the political arena of women's domestic beliefs. This social power was based on ideas of special human rights. Domestic matters remained the concern of most women political activists.[82] It is therefore not surprising to find that it is legislation on divorce, child custody and matrimonial property, rather than suffrage, which was enacted in the nineteenth century in response to women's demands for equality.[83]

Child custody and matrimonial property provide illustrations. At common law married women had no rights to the guardianship of their children. In the course of the nineteenth century the patriarchal system which gave complete power to fathers was gradually displaced. Domesticity had changed perceptions of maternal responsibilities and rights. Motherhood was idealised and became a professional role for women. The celebrated case of Caroline Norton, whose husband refused her access to their three children, led to the first breach of paternal control. The Infants Custody Act 1839, known as Talfourd's Act, provided that a judge in equity had discretion to give custody to mothers of children under seven years, provided that adultery had not been proved.[84] During the nineteenth century further changes were made. Judicial divorce having been introduced in 1857, mothers gradually acquired rights of custody on divorce.

It is significant however that divorce was not available to women on equal terms with men.[85] And during marriage the father remained the sole legal guardian of the children. It was only when the marital relationship was at an end through separation or divorce that women could invoke the aid of the law. In 1925 the Infants Custody Act gave married women the right to obtain a court order for custody and maintenance of children without a prior divorce or separation. The government insisted on including a provision that the order should not be enforceable so long as she continued to live with her husband. The Lord Chancellor made clear the opposition to the idea of joint guardianship which the promoters of the Bill had put forward. Objections to equal guardianship by parents were that the 'net result of the Bill would be to substitute a legal for a domestic forum in every household'; 'that to put mothers on an equal footing with fathers in all matters concerning their children would simply produce deadlock'; that although woman 'has almost the same status as man, she has not altogether the same status because it is necessary to preserve the family as a unit and if you have a unit you must have a head.'[86] Parliament's reluctance to intervene during marriage indicates again official support for patriarchy.

The Matrimonial Causes Act 1857 established two major principles concerning marriage. The first was that indissolubility was no longer the essence of the union. The second was that a divorced or judicially separated wife was an independent woman whose future earnings were her own and who could ask for alimony from her former husband. Her former property or earnings did not revert to her. Certain liberals and feminists who believed in companionate marriage argued for equality in matters of property. John Stuart Mill favoured a rule whereby 'whatever would be the husband's or wife's if they were not married, should be under their exclusive control during marriage.'[87] This individualistic approach of separation of the spouses' affairs was realised in the Married Women's Property Acts 1870 to 1882. This property régime of 'to each her own' focused on legal forms of subordination but leaves untouched questions of power and economic distribution within the family. Separate property is a realisation of formal equality but does not affect economic power within the conjugal relationship.

Conclusion

This chapter has argued that the transition from feudal to market society was marked by a gradual change from private arrangement of matters such as marriage and divorce to public constitution of a legal form. Public regulation controlled the formation and dissolution of conjugal relations but the content of that relationship continued to be ordered by patriarchy. State intervention to impose work discipline, to place financial responsibility for his family on the husband and father, to discourage the birth of unsupported children resulted in a new form of family. Patriarchal powers may have been reduced but the husband continued to head the family.

Within the modern bureaucratic state the nuclear family of husband, wife and their children is treated as a unit. The head and public representative of this unit is the husband, whose wife and children are legally constituted his dependants, not only economically but also because they are subject to his orders. Rather than intervene directly to regulate family relations publicly, the state delegates its power and authority to the husband. His role is to control what goes on within the family in private.

PART TWO
Divisions Between the Sexes and the Public/Private Split

There is a correspondence between sexual divisions and the disjunction of public and private. The partition of persons into two categories, female and male, is based on biology and the seemingly natural. Ideas about the natural vary from age to age. Such cultural views become embedded in institutional forms. Law then takes on an appearance of immanency, its provisions are taken to be inevitable and inexorable.

So it is with ideas concerning the divergence of public and private. The boundary between spheres regulated by law and the unregulated shifts over time and in accordance with cultural, economic and legal factors. This has been particularly so in areas of the personal, such as sexual and reproductive conduct.

This part of this book applies the theoretical and historical perspectives developed in Part One to legal doctrine. In what might be termed an exercise in middle-level theorising, the object is to relate ideas concerning individualism, autonomy and privacy to discrete areas of the law. The examples are chosen from those parts of the law in which gender distinctions are most obvious. This is done to illustrate the thesis that although the bisection of persons and their lives may seem natural, it is historically and culturally contingent. This construction of our perception of sexual divisions affects the way in which we live. Law is an active agent in shaping our ideas; it constructs both sexual and personal dichotomies.

When a particular way of seeing is analysed, what was accepted as natural is made strange. Part of that strangeness is the realisation that beneath the accepted order of life lie hidden power relations. Exposing these by opening up the private shows how patriarchy survives in a modified form.

3
Legal Construction of Sex and Gender

'In many things are you and I apart
But there are regions where we coincide,
Where law for one is law for both.'

ANNA WICKHAM

The English legal tradition, as we have seen, is to recognise and build upon sexual differentiation. Laws relating to motherhood, marriage and succession have provided historical examples. In later chapters further examples from both private and public law will follow. An argument against legal recognition of sex differences is that such recognition is largely unnecessary and reinforces existing sexual stratification. Is this true? In order to examine this argument a distinction must be made between physical differences and social distinction.

The Distinction Between Sex and Gender

A new individual arriving into the social world is assigned into a sex category. When a child is born one of the first questions asked is whether the newcomer is female or male. The answer given constitutes the baby's assigned sex; in the social world this affects the individual's future goals, behaviour, identity, personality, emotions, sexuality and gender role. External genitalia are the sign to the parents, and to those present, of the appropriate sexual classification. There is a legal duty to register the birth within forty-two days, and the infant's birth certificate records the assigned sex, which must be declared.[1]

In the vast majority of cases the sex assignation made at birth is correct, but those cases in which an error is made provide an illustration of the centrality of sex category to social structure. Seven variables affecting sex determination have been identified. These are chromosomal sex; gonadal sex; hormonal sex; the internal accessory organs – the uterus in the female and the prostate gland in the male; the external genitals; assigned sex; gender role.[2] Within these criteria there may be considerable variation. For instance, the amount of the hormones oestrogen or testosterone present in the body varies from person to person, and according to such matters as psychological state and monthly cycle. Errors are made when an individual is assigned to the incorrect sex category, or when there is no predominance among the variables indicating one sex or the other.

Sex assignment, whether correct or incorrect, has enormous consequences for human beings. It is not an exaggeration to say that a person's whole life is determined by it. Whilst this might be an argument for careful testing of infants, the more important question is whether such categorisation of humans should be so important in the first place. Stoller argues that there are considerable variations, with one biological male having different hormonal patterns and different degrees of maleness from another.[3] Oakley argues further that at the simple biological level women and men are not two separate groups: rather, each individual takes a place on a continuous scale with no single dividing line between female and male.[4] This is supported by the fact that the embryo human being is sexually undifferentiated initially. Normal sex differentiation, which commences about forty-two days after conception, is determined by the father's sperm. Each ovum contains an X chromosome and the infant's sex depends on whether the fertilising sperm contains an X or a Y chromosome. The XX pattern will develop as a female, the XY pattern as a male.

Since both the female and the male gonads (primary sex glands) originate from an identical primitive gonad, its cortex (outer layer) can develop into an ovary in the female, or its medulla (center) can develop into a testis in the male. During this early stage, at about the fifth or the sixth week, two sets of ducts, Wolff's and Muller's, also appear in the embryo. The former can develop into the fallopian tubes, uterus, and upper vagina in the female. At about nine weeks in the development of the normal male embryo, and slightly later in the female, the appropriate duct continues to develop and the other one retrogresses.[5]

The gonads, and even the external genitalia, are in their origin more similar than is generally realised.

Research at Johns Hopkins Hospital reveals that there are people who are sexually concordant at birth – born with the same kinds of genitals, gonads, chromosomes and hormones – who were differentially labelled female or male. The problems and successes these patients had in conforming to their labels, and the difficulties they faced if the label was changed, have revealed a great deal about what it means to be a man or a woman in the social world.

Money and Tucker give an example of a child who at birth was labelled male and raised as a boy, because he had a rudimentary penis although no testicles. At puberty breasts developed and an exploratory operation revealed ovaries, uterus and vagina, but no male reproductive organs. Notwithstanding this, the patient's belief in himself as a male was unshaken and his description was that 'they'd found some kind of female apparatus in there by mistake.'[6] Gender identity, that is the psychological experience of being female or male in a social world, was so firmly established that the decision was to administer male hormones to develop external male physical characteristics such as a beard. The patient married and was reported to have established a satisfactory physical relationship with his wife. By contrast another case with very similar external organs at birth was labelled and raised as a girl. At puberty male hormones gained ascendancy over the ovarian hormones. Drug therapy was used to suppress the androgenising effect of male hormones and the woman, who had rejected with horror the idea she might be male, married and gave birth to children. These case histories not only show how error can occur in sex assignment, but also how the social construction of gender and the consequent development of gender identity differentiates human beings who are not necessarily biologically differentiated.

Gender is the term used to denote the social meaning of sex categorisation. Sex is determined through physical assessment; gender refers to the social consequences for the individual of that assessment. Gender stereotypes embody society's view of appropriate behaviour for women and men. These take the form of gender roles, reinforced by law, through which individuals conform to their label and to the community's conventions. Gender identity is the psychological experience of being female or male for the individual; it is the sense of oneself as belonging to one gender category.

The Social Consequences of Error in Sex Classification

Things can go wrong in the development of a person's sex indicia.

There may be too few or too many sex chromosomes; the gonads may be of both sexes; hormonal imbalance or erroneous secretion may occur; internal organs may be missing; genitals may not develop; and there may be confusion over assigned sex. Yet studies of gender identity show that, despite the physical similarities of the sexes, once assigned to one sex significant consequences follow for the individual.

Studies of maternal behaviour have revealed that even with newborn babies mothers behave differently according to the sex of the infant. This is the beginning of learning what it means to be classified as female or male. As the child grows up it will gradually become aware of what society expects of it in the way of attitudes, behaviour, manners, activity and modes of relationship to others, despite medical evidence that gender is undifferentiated at birth.[7] It learns the meaning of being a girl or a boy, its gender role, and its sense of gender identity. An illustration of this is found in Money's report of the raising of a genetic male as a female. The case is one of identical male twin brothers, one of whom lost his penis through medical negligence at the age of seven months. As a result of advice received at Johns Hopkins Hospital the parents decided to reassign the child's gender, permit surgical intervention, and to raise the child as a girl. This happened at seventeen months. Money reports that 'by the time the children were four years old there was no mistaking which twin was the girl and which the boy. At five the little girl already preferred dresses to pants, enjoyed wearing her hair ribbons, bracelets and frilly blouses, and loved being her daddy's little sweetheart.'[8] By the age of nine the two identical (genetically male) twins showed two clearly differentiated personalities, with sharply differentiated behaviour structure based on conventional ideas of what is gender appropriate.

Regarding domestic activities, such as work in the kitchen and house traditionally seen as part of the female's role, the mother reported that her daughter copies her in trying to help her in tidying and cleaning up the kitchen, while the boy could not care less about it. She encourages her daughter when she helps her in the housework.[9]

Thus two persons anatomically identical at birth have been placed in separate gender categories and have learned different roles.

The gender-identity gate is open until a child is at least eighteen months and, in some cases, until puberty. Error in assigned sex can be corrected. The law permits a change in the birth certificate, but only in cases of error of fact or substance, through statutory declaration by two qualified informants of the birth. This is unlikely to cover cases of discordances between gender identity and assigned sex, as happens for instance with transsexuals.

Legal Definitions of Sex

Legal classification of women and men as belonging to two different and separate groups follows from biological and social classifications. Biology forms the material base on which an elaborate system of social and legal distinction is built. As has already been shown, medical research no longer justifies the use of biology as support for treating the social or legal categories woman and man as opposite and closed. Nevertheless the law continues to classify human beings as if there were two clear divisions into which everyone falls on an either/ or basis. In general the way in which this occurs is where legislation uses a classificatory scheme based on sex. A criminal, victim, employee, recipient of public benefit, taxpayer may be specified as belonging to one sex category only. The courts are then called upon to define legally what it means to be a woman or a man, within that legislative classification.

Two methods of approaching this judicial task of sex determination have emerged. These are the essentialist approach and the cluster-concept approach. With the essentialist approach the court looks to one essential feature and assigns all individuals biologically to either the female sex or the male sex. This method is familiar to the lawyer who is continuously engaged on the task of classifying events, things, people. It is the method most used in legal reasoning. The apparent opposition of women and men leads, not surprisingly, to the logical approach in which individuals are either A or Z. The cluster-concept method looks to a group of similar features which then suggest that the individual falls into one category. It is the insistence on one essential feature rather than a group of features that distinguishes essentialism from the cluster approach. Examples of the application of both methods in law will be given below, with a critique and a suggested alternative.

The essentialist approach
In the English case *Corbett* v. *Corbett* a couple had married knowing that, whereas both had been classified as male at birth, one had undergone a sex-change operation in an attempt to move into the

female category. The marriage was a failure and the male partner brought an action to have the marriage declared null and void on the ground that both parties were members of the male sex. The court agreed, taking the view that 'sex is clearly an essential determinant of the relationship called marriage because it is and always has been recognised as the union of man and woman. It is the institution on which the family is built, and in which the capacity for natural hetero-sexual intercourse is an essential element.'[10] Sex as a concept seems to have been used here both in the sense of biological category and in the sense of sexual intercourse.

The court went on to distinguish sex as a biological category from gender. Dealing with the argument that law permits recognition of the transsexual as a woman for national insurance purposes and that therefore it was illogical not to do the same for marriage, the court said, 'these submissions, in effect, confuse sex with gender. Marriage is a relationship which depends on sex and not on gender.'[11] Social appearance or gender identity are irrelevant in determining whether a person is male or female; the *Corbett* case makes clear that the legal test, for marriage at least, is biological.

The biological test laid down by Ormrod J. in *Corbett* is the chromosomal, gonadal and genital test. If all three are congruent, they determine a person's sex. Social and psychological matters of gender identity and gender role were considered irrelevant for marriage where sex was established as 'an essential determinant of the nature of the relationship'.

It is possible to criticise this judgment on a number of grounds. At an individualistic level it may result in hardship to persons who belong neither to the male nor to the female category and who therefore cannot marry, as in the Australian case *C. and D.*[12] There the husband was a genuine intersex with an ovary and a fallopian tube internally on the right side, but with nothing internally on the left. He was classified male at birth because of a small penis and testicle on the left side. Having grown up psychologically and socially as a male, in adulthood he sought surgical treatment for correction of the penile deformity. An article in the *Medical Journal of Australia* written soon after the decision to intervene surgically gives an account of the problem faced by the medical and surgical specialists:

in spite of the bisexual gonadal structure, the female chromosomal arrangement, the female internal genitalia and the equivocal results of the hormonal assays, there was no doubt, in view of the assigned male sex, the male psychological orientation in a person of this age and the possibility of converting his external genitals into an acceptable male pattern, that he should continue in the sex in which he has been reared.[13]

Surgery was performed over a period of time to remove the female internal organs and breasts, and to reconstruct the penis into one of normal size and shape. The patient married, and after some years the wife sought a declaration of nullity on the ground that the husband had been unable to consummate the marriage. The Australian court held that the marriage was null because of an absence of consent on the part of the wife, who was the victim of mistaken identity. The explanation was that 'the wife was contemplating immediately prior to marriage and did in fact believe that she was marrying a male. She did not in fact marry a male but a combination of both male and female and notwithstanding that the husband exhibited as a male, he was in fact not, and the wife was mistaken as to the identity of her husband.'[14]

The effect of this decision and of the *Corbett* case is that hermaphrodites cannot marry, and neither can transsexuals who have undergone surgery. A post-operative transsexual is incapable of consummating a marriage as a member of the category assigned at birth, but does not in law belong to the chosen category. On an abstract level these decisions reinforce belief in the categories woman and man as closed categories, rather than as points along a continuum. Yet to Dr Money the question whether an individual is *really* a woman or a man is meaningless: 'All you can say is that this is a person whose sex organs differentiated as a male and whose gender identity differentiated as a female.'[15] And in the case of hermaphrodites one cannot even make this guarded statement. The legal essentialist approach to the definition of sex is not consonant with medical research.

We are dealing with two aspects of the essentialist approach here. Firstly, there is the sense in which biology is taken to be the quintessence of the legal definition of sex. Secondly, there is the notion that certain areas of law operate on sex as a critical element. There is no doubt that Ormrod J.'s approach in *Corbett* is essentialist in the first sense. He said that 'the biological sexual constitution of an individual is fixed at birth (at the latest), and cannot be changed either by natural development of organs of the opposite sex or by medical or surgical means.'[16] Yet the husband in *C. and D.*, a genuine intersex, did not belong to one sex, and there are medical records of similar patients. Even if chromosomes are taken as the *sine qua non* of a sex category, cases of XO and of XXY may cause problems. Furthermore, the objective of the medical profession has been to bring the physical appearance of patients into line with gender identity. In many cases this means confirming individuals in the sex category in which they were socialised as children. But to Ormrod J., 'a person with male chromosomes, male gonads and male genitalia cannot reproduce a person who is naturally capable of performing the essential role of a woman in marriage.'[17]

What is the essential role of a woman in marriage? It cannot be the biological reproduction of children as the inability to procreate does not render a marriage void, and neither does the unwillingness to have children. It is true that marriages which have not been sexually consummated are voidable in English law, but there have been a number of decisions holding that the use of contraceptives does not prevent consummation.[18] Biological reproduction is not essential to marriage. If procreation is not the purpose of marriage, but the law nevertheless requires the parties to belong to different biological categories, then it seems that marriage is not a private matter for the individuals concerned, but a public institution for heterosexual intercourse. It is highly unlikely that the court in *Corbett* was referring to women's social role in marriage, for the distinction between sex and gender had already been established.

This brings us to the second aspect of biological sex as the essence of the law in some areas, as in marriage. In *Corbett*, by distinguishing sex from gender, marriage law from social security law, the court implied that the law can constitute a person differently, depending on whether sex is essential or not. However, as will be shown below, this approach leads to internal incoherence in the law and may create more problems than it solves.

The cluster-concept approach

Critics of the essentialist method as exemplified in the *Corbett* case argue that the chromosome pattern which can never be changed should be ignored and that the genital test should take account of any changes that have occurred through surgery. If the genitals, gender identity and gender role are congruent, the individual should be categorised accordingly – that is, the category should be determined by apparent sex. These criticisms are based not only on compassion to individuals but also on logic. It is said in relation to adultery and rape, two areas of the law where penetration of one sexual organ by another is a necessary element, that no enquiry as to sexual identity is necessary, and that this should be the general approach. The requirement of penetration presupposes an organ capable of penetration possessed by one and an organ capable of being penetrated possessed by the other, and this establishes a sufficient degree of sexual differentiation.[19]

These critics attack the reasoning on sex determination which proceeds on the basis of either A or Z and suggest that the cluster-concept form of reasoning be substituted. In looking to matters such as physical and social appearances, gender identity and gender role, the court would be looking at a cluster of concepts about what constitutes a woman or a man, rather than at one essential determinant. Compassion towards hermaphrodites and transsexuals tends to be the reason for these criticisms. Examples from other jurisdictions such as Germany, France, Switzerland and the United States, where persons are classified according to appearance and chosen gender, are referred to as examples for English law.[20]

The European Commission on Human Rights has held (in *Van Oosterwijck* v. *Belgium*) that it is a violation of private and family life to require the transsexual to carry documents of identity manifestly incompatible with personal appearance. The Commission made the finding that the refusal by a signatory state to the European Declaration on Human Rights to recognise gender identity results in the treatment of the transsexual 'as an ambiguous being, an "appearance", disregarding in particular the effects of a lawful medical treatment aimed at bringing the physical sex and the psychical sex into accord with each other'.[21]

Fair though these criticisms may be, they nevertheless accept that the law should operate on an assumption that the two sexes are distinct entities. Academic writers also accept two categories. 'As a working hypothesis this is not unreasonable, but . . . it does not quite correspond with physiological reality and is therefore likely to break down from time to time.'[22] Concern is expressed because errors may be made, or because the essentialist approach is inhumane, but the premise that certain areas of the law should be organised around sexual differentiation is not queried. The cluster-concept approach may permit sex classification according to personal choice rather than by ascription. In its acknowledgement of gender in establishing apparent sex and rejection of the essentialist presupposition of two fixed and immutable categories it is preferable to essentialism. However, the cluster-concept approach has not been accepted by the courts in any jurisdiction for sex determination in relation to marriage, or other legal areas where sex has been found to be an essential element. The question remains open as to whether courts will look to apparent sex rather than biological sex in future cases.

The decision by the European Commission on Human Rights in the *Van Oosterwijck* case suggests that another way of approaching issues of sex determination might be to classify matters of gender as covered by the right to respect for private and family life. This would presumably leave states to continue to regulate areas where they considered biological sex an essential determinant. In the *Van Oosterwijck* case the right of respect for private life as laid down in article 8 of the European Convention on Human Rights was explained as not just a right to live without publicity, for 'it comprises also to a certain degree the right to establish and to develop relationships with other human beings, especially in the emotional field for the development and fulfilment of one's own personality.'[23] It was also the view of the majority of the Commission that the right to marry under article 12 of the Convention had been violated, as 'domestic law cannot authorise states completely to deprive a person or category of person of the right to marry.'[24]

There are a number of difficulties with the separation of gender into the private sphere whilst the state continues to regulate what it defines as sex in the public sphere. From the internal viewpoint of legal reasoning, inconsistency and incoherence follow. In *Corbett* the court accepted that a person could be in the male category for marriage and in the female category for contract, employment and social security. However, subsequent legal decisions show that confusion has resulted. Other difficulties are that decision-makers use biology as the basis for gender prescription, one following 'naturally' from the other. Although sex and gender may be analytically distinguishable, social practice has been to entwine the two. And the legal construction of sex as public whilst gender was private would merely be a perpetuation of dichotomies which mask inequalities between women and men. Biology or 'nature' has a social meaning when translated into law, which itself operates on the social.

A more fundamental way of approaching sex-based legal classifications and consequent attempts to define sex is to ask whether such classification in law is necessary. The criticism that it is dispensable will be clarified and elaborated by examination of other legal areas where courts have engaged in definition of sex.

Legal Definitions of Sex Applied

Capacity to marry is, in English law, governed by biological sex, as shown in the essentialist reasoning of the *Corbett* case. Other areas in which judicial definitions of sex have been given are sexual crime, employment law, sex-discrimination law and social security law.

Sexual crime

The decision in the *Corbett* case has influenced criminal law despite Ormrod J.'s statement that the 'question then becomes what is meant by the word "woman" in the context of a marriage, for I am not concerned to determine the "legal sex" of the respondent at large.'[25] In *R. v. Tan and Others*[26] the Court of Appeal decided to apply *Corbett* to an area of criminal law where the sex of the defendant determines guilt. Under s.30 of the Sexual Offences Act 1956 it is an offence for a man to live on the earnings of prostitution. One of the accused who had undergone a sex-change operation from male to female appealed against conviction under s.30. This defendant submitted that a person who was philosophically, psychologically or socially a woman should not be convicted of an offence limited to men. The Court of Appeal held that for reasons of common sense, certainty and consistency the precedent set in *Corbett* would be followed. Thus the defendant's biological sex remained male and the criminal law was declared to operate on that.

Other areas of criminal law are affected by this decision. Legislation which is sex-specific deals with crimes such as rape, sexual assault, prostitution, infanticide. There are two questions here. Firstly, is the focus on biological sex rather than gender correct, and secondly, is it necessary for this legislation to be drafted in sex-specific terms?

The outcome of the *Tan* case is curious. A male-to-female transsexual cannot be the victim of rape. Heterosexual soliciting by a female prostitute is not a crime for such a transsexual, who can, however, be convicted of male homosexual soliciting and so face more stringent penalties.[27] A female-to-male transsexual cannot be convicted of unlawful sexual intercourse with a girl under sixteen.[28] Consistency remains elusive.

Employment law

Legislation regulating the hours that women can work in factories and excluding them from mining underground is presented as being for their protection. This is a matter of debate which will be investigated later. These laws do require a decision as to how a woman is constituted at law. In *E. A. White* v. *British Sugar Corporation* a female-to-male transsexual complained of sex discrimination when dismissed by the employer on grounds of deception as to sex. The employer had believed the complainant to be male when the offer of employment was made. Dismissal followed the discovery that the complainant had previously been classified as female. The industrial tribunal which heard the case held that the complainant was a woman. The reasoning was as follows:

The current edition of *The Shorter Oxford English Dictionary* defines males as of or belonging to the sex which begets offspring or performs the fecundating functions. The same dictionary defines female as belonging to the sex which bears offspring. On her own evidence the applicant, whatever her physiological make-up may be, does not have male reproductive organs and there is no evidence that she could not bear children.[29]

The employers required the employee for the particular job of electrician's mate and this included Sunday work. Under the Factories Act 1961 women cannot work on Sundays.[30] Therefore sex determination was necessary and the complainant, having been defined as a woman, was not unjustly dismissed.

Sex-discrimination law

Public policy, as expressed in the Sex Discrimination Act 1975 and the Equal Pay Act 1970, is against discrimination between the sexes. Researchers have shown that attitudes which stereotype woman and man in particular inflexible ways can lead to discrimination. The anti-discrimination legislation has as its goal the elimination of sex discrimination in the public sphere, in areas of education, employment and the provision of goods, services, facilities and premises. It operates on an individualistic level and requires a particular woman to complain of her treatment by comparison with that of a particular or potential man. A person discriminates directly against a woman when 'on the grounds of her sex he treats her less favourably than he treats or would treat a man.'[31] Individual men can also complain of sex discrimination by comparison with women. The legislation does not directly affect behaviour in the private sphere, yet it clearly requires complainants to fall into one of the two categories, female or male.

The complainant in *E. A. White* v. *British Sugar Corporation* relied on the Sex Discrimination Act 1975 in making her complaint to the industrial tribunal. The tribunal held that the complaint of discrimination required a determination of sex. The complainant having been determined legally a woman, despite having the apparent sex of a man, had not been treated less favourably than a man, because a man who held himself out to be a woman would also have been dismissed.[32] It is clear from this case that biological sex on an essentialist test is to be determined in sex-discrimination legislation. It is indeed an irony that in attempting to abrogate sexual stereotypes the means Parliament has chosen is to require all individuals to be classified in an essentialist fashion. The tribunal concluded, 'the laws of this country and the 1975 Act in particular envisage only two sexes, namely male and female.'[33]

One possible solution to the problem of sex-discrimination legislation reinforcing the injustice it attempts to rectify would be for the courts to adopt the cluster-concept approach as the means of defining sex categories. But, as already argued, this involves a continued acceptance of sexual division. Furthermore, such a solution remains individualistic and does not tackle the general issue of legal dichotomy between the sexes. The question remains whether there is any need to differentiate between the sexes.

Social security law

In *Corbett* it was accepted evidence before the court that the male-to-female transsexual had been issued with a social security card as a woman. From this follow such sex-specific rights as widow's pension and retirement at sixty rather than at sixty-five as for men. The court accepted that 'the authorities, if they think fit, can agree with the individual that he shall be treated as a woman for national insurance purposes, as in this case.'[34] Despite this, biological sex has been held by the National Insurance Commissioner to be the test to be applied for retirement.[35] So, whilst carrying a social security card as a woman, the person legally determined as male cannot draw the state retirement pension until sixty-five. This inconsistency shows again the problems of the essentialist approach.

Summary

The criticisms that have been made thus far of sex-based legislative classificatory schemes and of consequent judicial definitions of sex can be summed up in legal terms as leading to internal incoherence and inconsistency, and in social terms as inhumane and leading to sexual stereotyping. The legal aspect has already been dealt with; the social aspect is further elaborated in the following section.

Gender as a Socially and Legally Constructed Category

Studies of stereotypes assume that people make sense of their social world by categorising other individuals according to easily observable characteristics which signal age, gender and race, and by then attributing traits and characteristics on the basis of group membership. Research on gender shows that the male role is consistently specified as containing items such as being aggressive, ambitious, athletic, competitive, dominant, independent, decisive, self-confident. The female role is less consistently described but includes items such as being gentle, understanding, emotional, expressive, liking children.[36] This research can be summarised in the distinction suggested by Parsons and Bales between expressive and instrumental roles. The traits ascribed to women are indicative of emotion and an expressive dimension, whereas those ascribed to men are concerned with action and an instrumental dimension.[37] These conventional notions of femininity and masculinity are the basis of gender identities in Western society.

Cross-cultural research by Mead, which is still accepted today, reveals how variable concepts of gender and of appropriate behaviour for men and women can be. In studies of tribal groups in New Guinea Mead contrasts the child-rearing practices of the Arapesh with those of their neighbours the Mundugumor. The Arapesh treat the baby as a soft, vulnerable object, emphasising the mouth and with it receptivity and passivity. Adults are gentle, men take part in child-rearing, which is long and protected. Hunting consists of setting traps and waiting for animals to fall in. On the Arapesh, Mead concludes: 'It is a society which makes it much more difficult to be a male, especially in all those assertive, creative, productive aspects of life on which the superstructure of a civilisation depends.'[38]

Amongst the Mundugumor, women dislike child-bearing and children. Rough baskets high on the shoulder far from the breast carry the children, who are pushed away as soon as they are the least bit satisfied. Mead's view is that this develops an angry, hostile personality where the sexes are similar. 'Women are masculinised to a point where every feature is a drawback except their highly specific genital sexuality, men to a point where any aspect of their personalities that might hold an echo of the feminine or the maternal is a vulnerability and a liability.'[39] Mead's work clearly proceeds from her own views of masculinity and femininity, but she makes the point about gender as a basis of social organisation, however variable the content of the roles.

Contrasted with the Arapesh and the Mundugumor are the Tchambuli, where women emphasise their own strength and power in the household. In united groups women work together busily and briskly, whilst small boys are ignored and men sit and wait to be cosseted. Adult males in this society are described as 'skittish, wary of each other, interested in art, in the theatre, in a thousand petty bits of insult and gossip'. Men express themselves through hurt feelings, pettishness, their self-decoration. Mead illustrates the effect of this on the gender identities of the young. 'This is the only society in which I have worked where little girls of ten or eleven were more alertly intelligent and more enterprising than little boys. In Tchambuli the minds of small males, teased, pampered, neglected, and isolated, had a fitful fleeting quality, an inability to come to grips with anything.'[40]

Mead concludes that the explanation for three such contrasting patterns of gender roles must lie in cultural conditions.

If those temperamental attitudes which we have traditionally regarded as feminine – such as passivity, responsiveness, and a willingness to cherish children – can so easily be set up as the masculine pattern in one tribe, and in another to be outlawed for the majority of women as well as for the majority of men, we no longer have any basis for regarding such aspects of behaviour as sex-linked .... We are forced to conclude that human nature is almost unbelievably malleable, responding accurately and contrastingly to contrasting cultural conditions.[41]

Feminist theory has built on Mead's work, using it as evidence for the argument that gender behaviour is a social creation. In an influential anthropological discussion Sherry Ortner puts forward the interpretation that the devaluation of women is a feature of all cultures, world wide. Although this takes different forms she flatly asserts that 'everywhere in every known culture women are considered in some degree inferior to men.'[42] Her explanation lies in the process whereby human consciousness created culture in opposition to nature. Culture is an expression of the need to regulate and control 'rather than passively move with and be moved by the givens of natural existence'.[43] Culture is identified as men's creation and their world whereas women's biology and bodies appear to place them closer to nature. Ortner has been criticised for over-generalisation in both questions and answers. Her point that biology and the association of women with nature leads to the embodiment of this view in institutional forms is nevertheless important. Institutions then reproduce the cultural view of women.

Both English and American law contain many examples of how an essentialist approach to biology spills over into gender-role prescriptions. Thus 'a great difference in the mental constitution of the sexes, just as there is in their physical conformation' led to the view that 'much time must or ought to be given by women to the acquisition of a knowledge of household affairs and family duties,' according to Lord Neaves when preventing women from studying medicine in Scotland in 1873.[44] In a decision of 1873,[45] Myra Bradwell, who had passed the examinations necessary for the practice of law in Illinois, could not be admitted to the bar because 'the natural and proper timidity and delicacy which belongs to the female sex evidently unfits it for many of the occupations of civil life. The constitution of the family organisation, which is founded in the divine ordinance, as well as in the nature of things, indicates the domestic sphere as that which properly belongs to the domain and functions of womanhood.'

Crucial to this reasoning was an unquestioned belief of Victorians that men and women belong to different categories and occupy separate spheres. Biology and assumed great physical and mental differences between the sexes were understood to fit men for public life and women for domesticity. In 1907 the Earl of Halsbury opposed a government Bill to remove sex disqualification of women for a seat on local bodies on biological grounds. 'I think they are too hysterical, they are too much disposed to be guided by feeling and not by cold reason, and they are very much disposed to refuse any kind of compromise. I do not think women are safe guides in government; they are very unsafe guides when they argue from sentiment and not from reason.'[46] Biological destiny prescribes social function, as another speaker explained: 'What is to be feared is that if we take away the position which woman has hitherto occupied, which has come to her from no artificial education, but from nature, if we transfer her from domestic into political life ... the homes and happiness of every member of the community will be worsened by the transference.'[47]

Legislation limiting women's hours of work was judicially justified in the United States in 1908 because:

by abundant testimony of the medical fraternity continuance for a long time on her feet at work, repeating this from day to day, tends to injurious effects upon the body, and as healthy mothers are essential to vigorous off-spring, the physical well-being of woman becomes an object of public interest and care in order to preserve the strength and vigor of the race.[48]

This is not just a matter of Victorian and Edwardian beliefs, for modern examples of harmful gender stereotypes judicially applied to confine women to the private sphere can be given. In 1961 a female defendant convicted by an all-male jury of murdering her husband with a baseball bat challenged a Florida state law exempting women from jury service who had not expressed an affirmative desire to serve. The United States Supreme Court found the Florida statute to be based on reasonable classification. In Justice Harlan's view, 'despite the enlightened emancipation of women from restrictions and protections of bygone years, and their entry into many parts of the community life formerly reserved for men, woman is still regarded as the center of the home and family life.'[49] As Albie Sachs points out: 'Because the initial classification between males and·females is a biological one, it is easy for both supporters and opponents of male ascendancy to assert that behavioural differences between men and women are biologically determined as well. It is particularly convenient for the beneficiaries of social inequality to attribute their advantageous social position to an advantageous biological one.'[50]

The argument here is that beliefs about biology are cultural. The focus on biology alone may be mistaken. Approaching issues of sex discrimination in terms of differential treatment has been the feminist tradition. But the justification for legal differentiation is inevitably couched in social or biological terms. So feminist theory, in a sense, emphasises concepts which it queries. A new perspective is suggested by Catharine MacKinnon referring to sex discrimination: 'There is a real question whether it makes sense of the evidence to conceptualise the reality of sex in terms of differences at all – except in the socially constructed sense – which social construction is what the law is attempting to address as the *problem*.'[51]

Eliminating Sex Classification from Law

Are legislative classificatory schemes based on sex really necessary? The argument has already been put forward that sexual differentiation by law leads to sexual stereotyping, is inimical to anti-discrimination goals of public policy, and ignores the problems of those who cannot fit neatly into either of two categories. These classifications are too large. Differences between those within a category are often far greater than differences across the two categories. No characteristic is universal to one sex only. Recognising this leads to a number of possible prescriptions. One is to eliminate sex categorisation from law and to substitute classifications based on matters such as social functions or medical necessity.

Alison Jagger argues that

a sexually egalitarian society is one in which virtually no public recognition is given to the fact that there is a physiological sex difference between persons. This is not to say that the different reproductive functions of each sex should be unacknowledged in such a society nor that there should be no physicians specialising in male and female complaints, etc. But it is to say that, except in this sort of context, the question whether someone is female or male should have no significance.[52]

This position has been described as assimilationist, or integrationist. It can be criticised as representing the absorption of women into the world of men, with an acceptance of the values of *Gesellschaft* for all. Jagger's emphasis on abolishing public recognition of sex differences challenges neither the concept of difference nor the dichotomy between private and public, both of which she seems to accept. 'Democratic government, the law, the judicial system, the nuclear family, the public school, the vocational order – all male-derived ideas and institutions – are not challenged in themselves by this kind of feminism.'[53] But the alteration of legal classification from sex-specific to sex-neutral, whilst it will not affect gender relations in private, may undermine some forms of institutional sex discrimination.

Objections to sex-neutral legal language have come from both anti-feminists and from feminists. Richard Wasserstrom explains that many non-feminists are against assimilation because it:

would involve more profound and fundamental revisions to our institutions and our attitudes than would be the case in respect to race. It is certainly true that on the institutional level we would have to alter radically our practices concerning the family and marriage. If a nonsexist society is a society in which one's sex is no more significant than eye color in our society today, then laws which require the persons who are being married to be of different sexes would clearly be sexist laws.[54]

The Equal Rights Amendment to the Constitution of the United States, which has not been ratified by a sufficient number of states to become law, provides an illustrative example. The basic principle on which the amendment rests is that sex should not be a factor in determining the legal rights of women or of men. This does not deny that law places different benefits or burdens on members of society. But such differentiation may be because of particular abilities or needs, or because of social functions performed, such as being a parent. According to the most authoritative article on the subject, 'under the Equal Rights Amendment the existence of a characteristic or trait to a greater degree in one sex does not justify classification by sex rather than by the particular characteristic or trait. Likewise the law may make different rules for some people than for others on the basis of the activity they are engaged in or the function they perform.'[55]

There are two exceptions to the absolute prohibition of legislative classificatory schemes based on sex under the Equal Rights Amendment. One permits classifications based on 'unique physical characteristics'. This is intended to cover physical abilities such as sperm production, pregnancy, lactation. The second would permit limited forms of remedial measures to take account of past discrimination on grounds of sex, because 'where damage has been done by a violator who acts on the basis of a forbidden characteristic, the enforcing authorities may also be compelled to take the same characteristic into account in order to undo what has been done.'[56]

The Equal Rights Amendment has not been ratified, because of misunderstandings as to its purpose. Opponents argue that it would force unwilling women into the labour market to support their children because both parents would have equal financial responsibility. But functional classification permits the allocation of rights and duties according to whether a parent is engaged in child-rearing at home or in wage-earning in the market.

Some feminist uneasiness about Wasserstrom's description of a non-sexist society centres on his emphasis on social role rather than on biological reproduction. Creating similarities wherever possible is said to be dictated by an ideal of justice. Equality of the sexes requires the suppression of whatever does not conform to some neutral or masculine norm. Elizabeth Wolgast argues that there is asymmetry in parenthood. Men can never be certain of their paternity; therefore mothers are primary parents with primary responsibility. She explains her position thus: 'The biological differences of men and women do not determine what a good society should make of them, but a good society should take them into account and probably must do so. In order to justify ignoring the asymmetries that characterise human reproduction, that form of reproduction would have to be drastically changed.'[57] Wolgast's view is that the real needs of women in private and as mothers must be recognised by law. This can be done, however, through legislation which looks to social activities and functions.

Sex-neutral language is one tool for the reduction of inequality between the sexes. It is not sufficient in itself; without other changes in cultural beliefs, and in legal and social institutions, it may serve to mask continued discrimination. Family law has been changed to functional classification with reciprocal duties being placed on spouses and on parents. This has not prevented the judiciary in family cases from interpreting neutral language, or other discretionary provisions, in the light of their beliefs about gender roles. Thus the 'loving and unselfish wife' is entitled to recognition of her good behaviour by the courts when awarding maintenance.[58] In child-custody cases 'all things being equal, the best place for any small child is with its mother';[59] although 'one must remember that to be a good mother involves not only looking after the children, but making and keeping a home for them with their father . . . in so far as she herself by her conduct broke up that home she is not a good mother.'[60] A household in which there is some woman at home to look after the children is preferable to one where parents are out at work.[61]

Although spouses come neutrally and equally before the divorce court, there is ready prescription of their gender roles.

When a marriage breaks up, there will thenceforth be two households instead of one. The husband will have to go out to work all day and must get some woman to look after the house – either a wife if he remarries or a housekeeper if he does not. He will also have to provide maintenance for the children. The wife will not usually have so much expense. She may go out to work herself, but she will not usually employ a housekeeper. She will do most of the housework herself, perhaps with some help. Or she may marry, in which case her new husband will provide for her.[62]

The object of providing these examples is to show how cultural views are embodied in institutional forms. As Sherry Ortner points out: 'efforts directed solely at changing the social institutions . . .

cannot have far-reaching effects if cultural language and imagery continue to purvey a relatively devalued view of women. But at the same time efforts directed solely at changing cultural assumptions . . . cannot be successful unless the institutional base of the society is changed to support and reinforce the changed cultural view.'[63] Law plays an active part in transmitting cultural views and in constructing social institutions. Functional classification may challenge cultural assumptions but further measures are required. It is the acceptance of a split between private and public spheres, and what happens in private, that provide the conditions for sex discrimination.

4
The Boundary Between Private and Public

'Woman is determined not by her hormones or mysterious instincts, but by the manner in which her body and her relation to the world are modified through the action of others than herself.'

SIMONE DE BEAUVOIR

The division between women and men has its counterpart in the dichotomy between private and public. It has been argued in Chapter 3 that femaleness and maleness represent points along a continuum rather than opposites. Can the disjunction between private and public be subjected to similar analysis? In order to explore the boundary between these hemispheres of life this chapter takes examples from biological and sexual activities which are central both to notions of the private and to relations between women and men.

Boundaries

Human sexuality involves the biological reproduction of the race and also a whole area of behaviour, including personal relations. 'Sexuality as a general overarching category is used to define and delimit a large part of the world in which we exist. The almost perfect congruence between those spheres of existence and what is viewed as the "private sphere" of life is striking.'[1] Writings about the personal life take the notion of privacy as unproblematic but, as has already been noted, putting an area of life into the private bracket is to close down investigation. In this book the stipulated meaning of private is non-regulation, an absence of law; so it is with the boundary between the regulated and the unregulated that we are concerned.

The thesis of this chapter is that the divide beween private and public is contingent on factors such as beliefs about morals and about gender, legal theories about law enforcement, and social and economic conditions generally. Thus an area of conduct labelled private does not necessarily retain that label forever. Although political and legal discourse maintain the idea of a clear dichotomy between the regulated and the unregulated it is my view that it is not possible to sustain the boundary analytically over time. Areas of conduct move back and forth across the divide. This suggests a continuum rather than a division. Nevertheless the distinction has a clear influence on perceptions of the social world and on legislative and judicial policy.

Activities which are unregulated may be either visible or invisible. The best example of visible but unregulated behaviour is that which was previously regulated. For instance if a state prohibits all prostitution by making it a crime and later deregulates certain aspects of that behaviour, the conduct has been acknowledged, but the decision as to how to view it has been changed. This is what happened in English law on prostitution with the Street Offences Act 1959. Invisible activities are more difficult. If no official notice has been taken of them they remain clearly private and uninvestigated.

Official decisions to place activities on the private side of the boundary may stem from a variety of reasons and may be justified in a number of ways. A frequent explanation for the non-intervention of the law is that prohibition or regulation would be unenforceable. Behind this lies a theory about law itself and its limitations. But there may be other unclarified assumptions. Legal non-intervention does not rule out other forms of social control. Theories about the limits of law may contain views about the suitability of other agencies to regulate activities labelled private. The family is often mentioned in this context; but the delegation of authority to patriarchy remains unspecified.

Legal control of biological and sexual activities provides concrete examples to illustrate these theoretical points. Biology and sexuality are crucial to the feminist argument that the personal is political and also to jurisprudential discussion of private behaviour. The feminist viewpoint clashes with that of conventional liberalism by denying the dichotomy between public and private. As Catherine MacKinnon puts it: 'The very place (home, body), relations (sexual), activities (intercourse and reproduction), and feelings (intimacy, selfhood) that feminism finds central to women's subjection form the core of private doctrine.'[2] The following sections deal with contraception, abortion, infanticide and sexuality.

Contraception

The history of attempts at legal control of contraception provides an example of how state interest in preventing discussion of birth control was replaced by legal recognition of individual interest in personal autonomy. Legal control took the form of opposition to the spread of information of the means of contraception. There was no direct prevention of access to medical preparations or devices. Rather the law was used to inhibit the dissemination of knowledge by preventing publication of birth-control methods. In the case of contraception the state wished it to remain invisible.

Examination of methods of contraception reveals two categories: those within the control of women and those within the control of men. Examples of means used by women are the douche, the sponge, the pessary, prolonged nursing and, in the twentieth century, the intra-uterine device and the contraceptive pill. Male methods are the condom or sheath, and coitus interruptus. Abstinence at the time of ovulation, or completely, depends on both.

As technology developed in the nineteenth century with the vulcanisation of rubber in the 1840s for use in pessaries and sheaths, and for douche syringes in the 1870s, knowledge of contraception spread. Earlier in the century Francis Place popularised the sponge in his handbills published in 1823. At that time the medical profession used sponges to adjust the angle of the uterus, but their potential as contraceptives was quickly realised. Place referred in one of his handbills to 'a piece of sponge, about an inch square, being placed in the vagina prior to coition and afterwards withdrawn by means of a double twisted thread, or bobbin attached to it'.[3]

There is evidence of information about the creation of pessaries with materials such as lard and flour going back to Elizabethan times. Folk knowledge and old wives' tales will have been used to pass information orally. But as far as the state was concerned this was invisible. It was publication in a written form that was seen as a threat to state interests. In 1832 *The Fruits of Philosophy*, written by Charles Knowlton, was published in New York, and appeared in England in 1843. It was not until 1876 that an English bookseller was charged with the distribution of obscene literature for having copies for sale in his shop. The book gave simple information about contraception. The bookseller, Henry Cook, was sentenced to two years' imprisonment with hard labour.

Prosecution was brought in 1877 against Charles Watt, the

publisher, who initially entered a plea of not guilty. However, when shown the picture said to be of female syringes, with which Cook had interleaved the books, Watt changed his plea to guilty. This so angered other birth-control reformers that they decided to publish a new edition of Knowlton's work. In 1877 Annie Besant and Charles Bradlaugh were arrested and tried as publishers of an obscene libel.

At the close of the trial the prosecutor addressed the jury thus:

I say that this is a dirty, filthy book, and the test of it is that no human being would allow that book on his table, no decently educated English husband would allow even his wife to have it . . . . The object of it is to enable a person to have sexual intercourse, and not to have that which in the order of providence is the natural result of sexual intercourse.[4]

The jury verdict was that the book was 'calculated to deprave public morals' but they exonerated the defendants from corrupt motives in publishing it. Chief Justice Cockburn treated this as a guilty verdict. Surrender of the book was demanded and refused. Besant and Bradlaugh declared their intention to continue its sale and they were sentenced to six months each, plus a fine. On appeal the sentences were quashed, as the indictment had been defective in lacking particulars of the 'obscene libel'.[5]

The notoriety of the trial created a market for Knowlton's book and for Annie Besant's subsequently written *Law of Population*. The birth rate fell dramatically in the late nineteenth century. There is an argument as to whether this had any connection with the Besant–Bradlaugh trial; it does seem plausible that the halving of the birth rate between 1876 and 1936 was related to the democratisation of knowledge about birth control. Thus the attempt by the law to prevent dissemination of information had in fact the opposite effect. This was true also of the later case in which Marie Stopes was involved, and of attempts to control contraceptive knowledge in the United States.

In 1918 Marie Stopes's book *Married Love*, giving advice on contraception, was published. An attack was made on Stopes, for what she had written and for her work in opening family-planning clinics, by Dr Halliday Sutherland in a book entitled *Birth Control* published in 1922. He accused Stopes of experimenting on the poor, who were her natural victims because of their ignorance and helplessness. The book concluded: 'It is truly amazing that this monstrous campaign of birth control should be tolerated by the Home Secretary. Charles Bradlaugh was condemned to jail for a less serious crime.' The implication was that Stopes had committed a crime analogous to the obscene libel for which Besant and Bradlaugh had been tried. Stopes brought an action for libel.

The all-male jury gave as their verdict that the defendant's words were true in substance, and defamatory of the plaintiff, and not fair comment. They awarded £100 in damages to Stopes. Lord Jeward, the Lord Chief Justice, interpreted this finding as a verdict for the defendant. The Court of Appeal allowed Stopes's appeal from this interpretation of the verdict, on the basis of the jury's finding that the words were not fair comment. The defendant then made a final appeal. The House of Lords by a majority decided that judgment should be entered for the defendant on the ground that there was no evidence to support the jury's negative finding on fair comment.[6]

This interpretation by the judiciary of the jury's verdict confirmed the defendant's view that Stopes's book was obscene. But the effect was publicity and increased sales. This was also true of the prosecutions of the American birth-control pioneer, Margaret Sanger.

In 1873 a federal law was enacted in the United States which became known as the Comstock law after its promoter, who was chief special agent for the New York Society for the Suppression of Vice. Section 211 of the Federal Criminal Code provided a maximum penalty of five years' imprisonment and a fine of $5,000 for anyone who sent through the mails any 'paper, writing, advertisement or representation that any article, instrument, substances, drug, medicine, or thing may, or can be, used or applied, for preventing conception', or any 'description calculated to induce or incite a person to so use or apply any such article, instrument, substance, drug, medicine, or thing'. The legislation classed contraceptive information with pornography. Mr Comstock's methods of enforcement involved writing to suspects as a decoy, pretending to be a woman in search of help.

In 1914 Margaret Sanger launched a monthly sheet entitled *The Woman Rebel* to test the Comstock law. All issues were barred from the mails and Sanger was indicted for nine alleged violations of federal law. The publicity received in various legal battles and for Sanger's vigorous campaigns paved the way for the democratisation of birth-control knowledge. When, in 1929, there was a police raid on the Clinical Research Bureau in New York and medical records of patients seeking help were illegally seized, the outcry from the medical profession and the public helped to change official attitudes. The court case which followed was a *cause célèbre* in which press, public and medical sympathy was with the birth controllers. Subsequently, clinics were founded across the country.[7]

The interest of the state in preventing birth control was an interest in population growth. When the Birkett Committee in 1939 was faced with a proposal that public health authorities should disseminate contraceptive knowledge without discrimination, it rejected the idea. The proposal was opposed on the broad ground that the extension of the use of contraception in the previous fifty years had been accompanied by a sharp and progressive decline in the birth rate. 'A proposal that public money should be spent on a measure which is likely to aggravate this position by making contraception universally available on request, and thereby to affect adversely the continuity of the state, is one we feel we cannot endorse.' Furthermore, 'it would tend to lower the traditional and accepted standards of sexual morality in this country.'[8] Once birth-control methods had moved from being invisible into public knowledge the question arose as to whether the state should regulate access to the means.

In American law this is defined as a question of privacy. In *Griswold* v. *Connecticut*,[9] a state law which prohibited the use of birth-control devices and made it a criminal offence to give information or instruction on their use was held unconstitutional. The statute violated a constitutional right of privacy. It is significant that the area of privacy referred to in the *Griswold* case was that of the couple in planning a family. The later case of *Eisenstadt* v. *Baird* redefined this area of privacy as individual. 'If the right of privacy means anything, it is the right of the individual, married or single, to be free from unwanted governmental intrusion into matters so fundamentally affecting a person as the decision whether to bear or beget a child.'[10] The *Griswold* notion of privacy is an aspect of the common law doctrine of the unity of spouses, and the consequent deliberate policy of non-intervention by the state. In *Eisenstadt* privacy becomes the right of the autonomous individual in the liberal state to make her own personal decisions within a circumscribed area.

The scope of the American constitutional right of privacy still remains unclear but in *Carey* v. *Population Service International* it was explained 'that among the decisions that an individual may make without unjustified government interference are personal decisions relating to marriage, procreation, contraception, family relations, and child rearing and education'.[11] This is clearly in the individualistic mode. The limitations of privacy conceived in this form are that the split between public and private is reified, and the private area is that granted by the state as free from its unwarranted intrusion. As examples of public policy on birth control, abortion and sterilisation from jurisdictions such as Ireland, China, Singapore or India show, the state retains the power to define where the boundaries lie and to move them at will. So it is to the state definition of privacy that the law looks, and not to personal and individual definitions.

The history of contraception shows that it is when the previously invisible becomes public through discussion and publication that the problem is posed for the state of whether to intervene and regulate, and if so, how this should be done. Contraception has now been redefined as a private matter, for the couple as a unit or for the adult individual. There is pressure on the state to regulate access to the means of contraception for girls under sixteen. In English law this is no longer a private matter for the young patient and her doctor, because it has been held by the Court of Appeal that parental consent to contraceptive advice and/or abortion treatment must be obtained for persons under sixteen.[12]

Abortion

Abortion has always been an alternative to contraception. Historical research suggests it was used by women, particularly from the working class, when their methods of birth control failed – and used despite its status as a crime. Legal regulation of abortion represents the intervention of the state to control whether or not a woman bears a child once she becomes pregnant. This intervention is usually justified in terms of the sanctity of life and the protection of the foetus. State control is, in the long view of history, a fairly recent innovation.

Abortion was made illegal in England in 1803. Until then the common law regarded abortion as a matter for the woman and the abortionist, even when the abortion was the result of a physical attack on a pregnant woman. Fitzherbert reports a case of 1348 where a child was killed 'en le ventr sa mer' and the court's opinion was that since the child had no baptismal name, and there were difficulties of proof, there should be no arrest.[13] The explanation given by several legal commentators of the medieval period was that the child was not *in rerum natura*, i.e. not a legal subject, before birth. Dalton explains it thus:

Note also in murder, or other homicide, the party killed must be *in esse, sc. in rerum natura*, for if a man kill an infant in his mothers wombe, by our law this is no felony: neither shall he forfeit anything for such offence: and whether (upon a blow or a hurt given to a woman with a child) the child shall die within her body, or shortly after her deliverie, it maketh no difference.[14]

It is true that the ecclesiastical courts regarded abortion as a spiritual offence and punished it until the mid-seventeenth century. But in common law it was an unregulated matter. Despite the explanation couched in terms of the child's lack of legal personality, the concern of legal scholars was with those cases where the abortion was brought about by a third party against the mother's will. Those cases where the mother procured an abortion were classified as sin rather than as illegal, as a private matter of conscience.

Blackstone took the view that there was a distinction at common law between abortions before and after quickening which occurred at three months. In this he followed Coke's Third Institute and suggested that abortion induced after quickening is 'no murder, but a great misprision'.[15] There is a dispute as to the accuracy of this statement since it quarrels with the theory of lack of legal personality. What is remarkable is the silence, on abortion, of the authorities on the history of English criminal law. Such references as do exist are either confined to ecclesiastical law or, if in criminal law, report no cases where the abortee herself was tried or found guilty. The invisibility of abortion in writings on medieval law can be confirmed from the silence on the fate of the abortee and the abortionist, particularly where the former died as a result of the latter's actions. It was only in 1670 that Hale suggested that the abortionist could be tried for murder if the woman died.[16] The modern discourse concerning the foetus's right to life does not appear in medieval or early modern writings.

The first attempt made by the state to outlaw abortion and bring the hitherto invisible into public law was in 1803. Lord Ellenborough's Act made it a felony, punishable by fourteen years' imprisonment, for any person to administer medicines, drugs or potions with intent to procure a miscarriage. The felony created was limited to the person administering the potions, and there was no offence by the woman taking them, and so the Act was interpreted. This Act and its successor of 1828 distinguished between the case where the woman was quick with child, being over twelve weeks pregnant, and earlier pregnancies. If quickening had occurred the offence was capital; if not, the penalty was imprisonment, transportation or whipping. Despite the fact that the third Act of 1837 made no distinction based on quickening, women continued to believe that abortion within the first trimester was legal. They had their own beliefs and their own morality. Even those women who knew the law did not feel they were acting immorally in obtaining or inducing an abortion. This continued into the twentieth century. The Birkett Committee in 1939 accepted that this was so, and advocated education to convince women of the dangers to their health from abortion.

The 1837 Act abolished the death penalty for procuring by an abortionist. Until 1861 there was no specific legal statement that it was an offence for a woman to obtain her own abortion. Then the Offences Against the Person Act 1861 made it a felony punishable by penal servitude for life for both the woman and the abortionist.

Women's attitudes to abortion, and to birth control generally, were quite different from values expressed in the law and by the medical profession. There is evidence that the glorification of biological destiny and motherhood in official discourse was not shared by all women. Thus a mother of six children wrote to the Malthusian League in 1883, 'my life is spent in weary dread of again becoming a mother'. Another wrote in 1914, 'all that is beautiful in motherhood is very nice if one has plenty to bring up a family on, but what real mother is going to bring a life into the world to be pushed into the drudgery of the world at the earliest possible moment because of the stress on the family exchequer?'[17] Recent scholarly work strongly suggests that faced with the problems of another unwanted pregnancy, working-class women took practical measures to abort. It was not just that they were subversive of the official values expressed in law, religion and medicine, but that they inhabited quite a different world from these, mainly male, worlds. Letters written to the Women's Co-operative Guild show approval of contraception. Abortion was resorted to when necessary. 'There are three who lost their lives and another who already had seven. These all took some kind of drug, and of course did the work they wanted it to do.'[18]

The Birkett Committee reporting in 1939 came to the conclusion that the medical estimate of 16 to 20 per cent of all pregnancies ending in abortion was likely to be correct. Of these, there was evidence to suggest that 40 per cent were criminally induced.[19] Medical opinion, generally, was that couples employing birth-control methods were selfish and undid the efforts of patriotic physicians to build up the population.

Abortion then moved from invisibility to illegality in the nineteenth century. Under common law it was invisible but from 1803 it became illegal under statute. The harshness of the law, the secrecy of abortion, the lack of practicability of enforcement, and perhaps sympathy for some mothers led to a new discourse in the 1920s. Abortion would never again be invisible. The law had brought it into being as a crime and constituted abortee and abortionist as criminals. The idea that emerged was that the medical profession should control abortion by making decisions as to when and how to perform the operation. The Infant Life Protection Act 1929, s.1(1), placed a burden of proof on the prosecution of an abortionist to show 'that the act which caused the death of the child was not done in good faith for the purpose only of preserving the life of the mother'. Dr Bourne, who terminated the seven-week pregnancy of a fourteen-year-old victim of rape, was found not guilty in a prosecution for abortion in 1939. In directing the jury, the court emphasised the provision on good faith.[20]

Reconstituted as a medical matter legal abortions were performed in both the private and the public sectors of medicine. An educated guess is that about 300,000 abortions took place legally in the 1960s. A further 50,000 to 100,000 operations were illegally performed.[21] Because of concern about the danger to health of patients operated upon illegally, the law was changed again in 1967. Control over the abortion decision remained firmly with the medical profession.

The Abortion Act 1967, s.1, requires two medical practitioners to form the opinion in good faith 'that the continuance of the pregnancy would involve the risk to the life of the pregnant woman, or of injury to the physical or mental health of the pregnant woman or any existing children of her family, greater than if the pregnancy were terminated'. There is also a provision permitting abortion where there is a risk of the child being born seriously handicapped. It is said that:

an unintended consequence of the abortion law was the growth of abortion-consciousness. Women who previously had resorted to criminal or quasi-legal abortions, or given birth only to have their child adopted, or reluctantly accepted an unwanted child, were quick to avail themselves of a legal service. For many abortions moved from the realm of a secret to a socially acceptable act.[22]

The secrecy of abortion was a product of the criminal law. Illegal acts tend to be done in secret.

Since the 1967 Act the abortion decision lies with the woman and her doctors. Although not invisible to the law, as in the pre-1803 days, abortion has moved from public prohibition by the criminal law to become a mainly private matter. In the United States the Supreme Court has pronounced that 'the right of personal privacy includes the abortion decision.'[23] English law does not contain any such direct statement. Abortion is still regulated, and that in some sense remains a matter of public concern. Yet the legal delegation of authority to the two doctors who make the decision has been respected by the courts, as illustrated by the case of *Paton* v. *Trustees of B.P.A.S.*

The *Paton* case concerned the application by the husband of a pregnant woman for an injunction to prevent her from having an abortion, because he had not consented. The court refused the injunction on the ground that the wording of the Act 'gives no right to a father to be consulted in respect of the termination of a pregnancy'.[24] If the two doctors have given a certificate, and there is no imputation of lack of good faith, there the matter ends. 'This certificate is clear, and not only would it be a bold and brave judge . . . who would seek to interfere with the discretion of doctors acting under the 1967 Act, but I think he would really be a foolish judge who would try to do any such thing.'[25]

If this case is analysed in terms of the dichotomy between public and private it is clear that it represents a refusal to reimpose public constraints on abortion. For one of the outcomes of giving a husband or father the right of consultation or veto is that there would have to be a forum for resolving disputes. This would place abortion back in the public arena. On appeal to the European Commission on Human Rights the issue of privacy was made more explicit.

In *Paton* v. *United Kingdom*[26] the Commissioners rejected the husband's complaints of violation of the European Convention on Human Rights on two grounds. The first concerned the priority of the protection of the mother's life over that of the foetus at 'the initial stage of pregnancy'. The second was that the mother's right to respect for her private life took precedence over the father's right 'to respect for his private and family life'. Article 8 of the European Convention recognises the right to respect for private and family life, home and correspondence. The necessity of state interference on grounds of national security, public safety, the public economy, prevention of crime or disorder, protection of health or morals, and protection of rights and freedom of others is also recognised. This seems to mean a careful balancing act between competing claims. No absolute right of abortion has been declared, although in an earlier case three

Commissioners stated their view that article 8 could be interpreted to allow such a right of decision to the mother at the early stage. Given traditional views of the article they admitted that such an interpretation would be hard to sustain. But 'the reality behind these traditional views is that the scope of protection of private life has depended on the outlook which has been formed mainly by men, although it may have been shared by women as well.'[27]

The United States Supreme Court has held that legislation in the state of Missouri requiring the written consent of the husband of a married women or of the parents of an unmarried woman under eighteen years for an abortion is unconstitutional. 'Inasmuch as it is the woman who physically bears the child and who is the more directly and immediately affected by the pregnancy, as between the two, the balance weighs in her favor.'[28]

Infanticide

Modern research on infanticide suggests that it is the product of socioeconomic circumstances and, in some cases, of mental disturbance following childbirth. Given the existence of contraceptive technology and the availability of abortion the great majority of children born in Britain today are wanted. It was not so in the past. The history of infanticide as a crime shows how the act of killing an infant was differently defined according to the status of the victim and of the perpetrator of the deed; and also according to theories about moral and criminal responsibility.

Infanticide as a crime does not appear in the law until 1623. It is true that the ecclesiastical courts dealt with infanticide and that the common law courts had jurisdiction over homicide. But the rule that the child must be a legal person before it could be a homicide victim seems to have meant that the common law was not invoked. Proof was required of the child's legal personality; that is, the prosecution had to show the child to have been born alive and to have completely severed its connection with the mother's body at the time of the crime. Presumably the object of this provision was to distinguish still births from cases of homicide, but the result was to place a difficult task on the prosecution where the victim was newborn. Even in the cases of older child victims there is a paucity of cases revealed by research on homicide. Infanticide, which was regarded as within the province of the ecclesiastical courts, does not seem to have been taken seriously there. In a review of cases from the Canterbury ecclesiastical courts, Helmholz concludes that 'medieval men did not regard infanticide with the horror we associate with premeditated homicide.'[29]

For one category of homicide, however, it was otherwise. The Act of 1623 created infanticide as a sex-specific crime committed by the mother of a bastard child in an effort to hide her shame. Concealment of death was the offence rather than the killing of the child. Concealment operated as a presumption of guilt placing the burden of proof on the mother to disprove it. To do so she had to produce a witness to give testimony that the child was born dead. It was in the nature of accusations of infanticide that such a witness would rarely be forthcoming. For many cases involved total secrecy concerning the pregnancy, even from other women with whom sleeping accommodation was shared. There are recorded cases where the birth was a surprise with the child arriving in the privy, sometimes being killed from a fall at the time of birth.

Medieval legal records have yielded up very few cases of infanticide, although in the nineteenth century such cases composed about a fifth of all homicides. Of the medieval cases discovered, in the great majority the mothers are unmarried. Lecky refers to the popular distinction in the middle ages between exposure and other forms of ending a child's life. Exposure seems to have been tacitly accepted: 'It was practised on a gigantic scale with absolute impunity, noticed by writers with most frigid indifference and, at least in the case of destitute parents, considered a very venial offence.'[30] The reasons why married parents might not wish to accept a new child into the family could have been economic or some problem the child had. Their opportunities for disposing of the infant in private through overlaying, accident, sickness or neglect were far greater than those of single women, for whom an admission of pregnancy was a disaster. Research on medieval coroners' rolls has turned up few inquests on small children. It has been suggested that this was due to attitudes regarding such deaths as insignificant. The incidence of infanticide in the medieval period is unknowable and this is true also of subsequent periods until the late nineteenth or early twentieth century.

Public attitudes to infanticide by unmarried mothers were more punitive than those towards married persons who disposed of unwanted children. Yet single women, particularly those who were living-in servants, were vulnerable to seduction and rape. In the eighteenth century half the unmarried women under the age of twenty-six had that occupation. Pregnancy for these women was a catastrophe because their good 'character' was of economic and social value to them. The Poor Laws and their employment made the option of travelling and abandoning the child well-nigh impossible, so concealment and infanticide often followed pregnancy.

Perhaps the following could be regarded as a typical eighteenth-century incident:

In August 1733 at a place north of York a pond dried up and the body of a new-born baby was unexpectedly revealed. A local servant-maid was suspected; she was examined 'and on first search thought innocent' but she unwisely became 'very pert with the women, who thereupon tried another experiment, and found milk in her breast'. She then confessed that the child was hers 'but pretended it was born dead, and that she had laid it by the way-side that it might be the sooner found, but it appeared to the [coroner's] jury that she went from her master's house late one evening, pretending to go to her mother's house, about a mile off, to take a vomit, and by the way bore the child, and went and lay at her mother's that night, and returned to her service early the next morning, without making the least discovery', the woman was committed to York Castle.[31]

The unmarried mother's subjection to shame and abuse, and the economic disaster she faced, must have led to many cases of infanticide.

The more punitive approach to single women can be explained on grounds other than those related to the crime itself. Protection of children does not seem to have been the object of the law, which as Blackstone said, 'savours pretty strongly of severity'.[32] If it is true that the disposal of unwanted children was not seriously regarded, as scholars and records suggest, then it seems likely that the single woman's crime was in becoming pregnant or in evading her punishment. This ties in with the evidence on public attitudes to single pregnancy from the Poor Law records and from statute. The object of the infanticide law was to discourage illegitimacy rather than to punish a crime. In these terms infanticide was a crime committed by women only, as specified in the 1623 statute.

Lord Ellenborough's Act of 1803 repealed the 1623 Act and placed infanticide on the same footing as other crimes of homicide. This change has been interpreted as meaning that infanticide could be committed with impunity:

So infanticide flourished in England. Disraeli was only the most famous of several writers who maintained that it was hardly less prevalent in England than on the banks of the Ganges. Dr. Lankester, one of the coroners for Middlesex, charged that even the police seemed to think no more of finding a dead child than of finding a dead dog or cat.[33]

Throughout the nineteenth century the law seems to have been little enforced in relation to the death of children. There were scandals over burial clubs and baby-farming. The law was seen to be in disarray and acquittals for lack of proof that the child had been born alive were numerous.

The 1803 Act contained a proviso whereby the jury could, in acquitting the mother of a bastard victim of murder, make a finding of concealment of birth which had a maximum two-year sentence. Trial for concealment, which was extended to all mothers by the Offences Against the Person Act 1828, seems to have taken the place of trial for murder. There were 5,000 coroner's inquests a year on children under seven in the mid-nineteenth century, yet only 39 convictions for infanticide between 1849 and 1864. The victims in 34 of these cases were bastards. Trials for concealment grew from 44 in 1834 to 522 between 1857 and 1861. The Offences Against the Person Act 1861, s.60, which governs the law on concealment today, extended the offence to include persons other than the mother. A verdict of concealment is an alternative verdict on a charge of murder; but concealment is also an independent substantive offence. Making concealment a crime can be interpreted as a statement that birth is no longer a private matter.

Concealment verdicts in the nineteenth century came to replace homicide verdicts where the victim was an infant. Evidence to the Commission on Capital Punishment which reported in 1866 was that the law of murder was a hopeless failure in dealing with infanticide. Witnesses agreed that it was virtually impossible to get juries to convict for murder so long as capital punishment was the sentence. 'It is in vain that judges lay down the law and point out the strength of the evidence, as they are bound to do; juries wholly disregard them, and eagerly adopt the wildest suggestions which the ingenuity of counsel can furnish . . . . Juries will not convict whilst infanticide is punished capitally.'[34] Evidence from the judiciary showed their resentment at having to pass a death sentence they knew would not be carried out. This 'solemn mockery' led them to propose a number of reforms which eventually shaped the law.

The Infanticide Act 1922 inaugurated a new approach. It provided for the equation of infanticide with manslaughter 'where a woman by any wilful act or omission causes the death of her newly-born child', but at the time 'she had not fully recovered from the effect of giving birth to such child, and by reason thereof the balance of her mind was then disturbed.' Although the Act was designed to save the judiciary from having to go through the motions of 'solemn mockery', it was also informed by medical theories about women and the effect of childbirth on them. In the nineteenth century a discourse about physiological and psychological differences between women and men emerged. Drawing on this, Fitzjames Stephen Q.C. suggested to the Commission on Capital Punishment that a special statute be enacted to deal with infanticide:

The operation of the criminal law presupposes in the mind of the person who ·is acted upon a normal state of strength, reflective power, and so on, but a woman just after child-birth is so upset, and is in such a hysterical state altogether, that it seems to me you cannot deal with her in the same manner as if she was in a regular and proper state of health.[35]

The shift was from criminalisation to medicalisation of infanticide.

The medical model of infanticide was made stronger by the later Act of 1938. A new Infanticide Act became necessary because of interpretation of the words 'newly-born child' in the 1922 Act. In *R.* v. *O'Donoghue*[36] a mother convicted of the murder of her 35-day-old infant was sentenced to death and duly reprieved. The judge directed the jury that the child was not newly born and said that although there was evidence of insanity there was none of infanticide. The Court of Criminal Appeal upheld this ruling. To deal with this problem the Infanticide Act of 1938, s.1, defined infanticide as a crime committed by the mother of a child under the age of twelve months where 'the balance of her mind was disturbed by reason of her not having fully recovered from the effect of giving birth to the child or by reason of the effect of lactation consequent upon the birth of the child'.

Pregnancy and lactation were regarded by nineteenth-century medical writers as times when women might become mentally unbalanced. The thesis advanced was that biology, and in particular the ovaries and the uterus, rendered women incapable, at least to some degree, of rational thought and behaviour. The medical model of women influenced nineteenth-century debates not only in infanticide but also on participation in activities in the public sphere such as education and politics. Yet the infanticide law which depends entirely on a medical excuse for criminal behaviour has as its motivating force the desire to spare the judiciary from going through the 'solemn mockery' of passing capital sentences which would not be carried out. Medical discourse concerning hysteria, lactational insanity and puerperal psychosis served to mitigate the rigours of the belief in individual responsibility which permeates the criminal law. The danger is that, as happened in the nineteenth century, this discourse can also be used to justify exclusion of and discrimination against women in the public sphere.

Infanticide has remained a sex-specific crime because of the medical model which remains embedded in the law. Sentencing policy in the twentieth century has also moved in the direction of medicalisation. From an imprisonment rate of about 50 per cent in the 1920s, the preferred policy in the 1940s and 1950s was treatment in mental hospitals. From 1960 on a new policy of probation is discernible.

The medical model of infanticide as a crime has come under attack. It has been argued in a number of reports that the principles on which the 1938 Infanticide Act is based are probably no longer relevant. In 1975 the Butler Committee on Mentally Abnormal Offenders recommended that the special provision for the offence be abolished. 'The theory behind the Act was that childbirth produced a hormonal disorder which caused mental illness. But puerperal psychoses are now regarded as no different from others, child-birth being only a precipitating factor .... Mental illness is probably no longer a significant cause of infanticide.'[37] The Criminal Law Revision Committee's Fourteenth Report in 1980 also took the view that the pathological model for the crime of infanticide is unsound. The evidence of the Royal College of Psychiatrists was that 'the medical basis for the present Infanticide Act is not proven, but . . . the balance of mind after birth may be disturbed by reason of the effects of psychological and environmental stress and incidental mental illness as well as true puerperal illness.'[38]

The Butler Committee's view was that infanticide should be subsumed under the general law on diminished responsibility. This reform proposal was not supported by the Criminal Law Revision Committee, which wished to retain a separate law, delete the reference to lactation, and provide a new statutory formula. The proposed statutory language would specify infanticide 'as being committed when, at the time of the act or omission, the balance of the woman's mind was disturbed by reason of the effect of giving birth or the circumstances consequent upon the birth'.[39] This revised form of words represents an acknowledgement that social and economic factors may be precipitating causes of the crime. The report refers to cases which emerged in the 1960s and 1970s, usually labelled 'battered-baby syndrome'. Social environmental stress, poverty, incapacity to cope with the child and failure of bonding were examples given where mental disturbance might be consequent on giving birth but could not be said to arise from the effect of giving birth.

A long view of the history of the crime of infanticide reveals how, as a sex-specific crime, it has been concerned with theories about women. Its initial object was to punish single women for becoming pregnant and for refusing to live with their shame. The crime concerned moral and social behaviour, and the community's fears of mother and child as an economic burden. In the nineteenth century the discourse changed to discover puerperal psychosis and lactational insanity. The recent past has seen a revival of social and economic explanations for the killing of an infant by its mother. These shifts in the content and explanation of this crime mirror the movement of women's biology back and forth as a subject of private and public concern. Infanticide is not now defined as invisible, unregulated or unsuitable for intervention. Yet the medicalisation of the crime and the continued insistence that it is different from other crimes of homicide does relate to the private sphere as the place of women and biology.

Separation of infanticide from other crimes of homicide and its specification as a crime that can only be committed by a woman who has given birth within the previous twelve months is difficult to justify. The victim must be the child to whom the mother gave birth. Killing other children or adults might give rise to the defence of diminished responsibility, but infanticide as charge or jury finding would not apply. Yet if the medical model of the crime is accepted, why should it not cover all homicides by the new mother? This suggests that there is something in the relationship of mother to infant that precipitates the crime; that it is the role of motherhood itself that produces psychosis and that the infant is somehow the cause.

If the socioeconomic model for infanticide is to become dominant it then appears odd that adoptive mothers, and other caretakers such as fathers, cannot be charged with infanticide. The law's tenderness to biological mothers has been justified on grounds of public opinion:

For over 150 years now, at first by the prerogative of mercy to grant reprieve from hanging and since 1922 by changes in the substantive law, women killing their new born babies have been treated differently from others guilty of intentional killings. This difference probably reflects what the public expects of the administration of justice.[40]

It is true that there is sympathy for infanticidal mothers, possibly because of the pain and difficulties associated with childbirth itself. And it seems likely that the location of this biology in the private sphere is part of the explanation.

Sexuality

Questions of regulating sexuality bring into focus the liberal view of a world split between public and private. The dilemma is whether to place practices such as prostitution, incest, sexual intercourse with children and homosexuality on the public or private side of the divide. Since, as has already been shown, the boundary between these two areas of life shifts over time and according to dominant beliefs, the dilemma constantly presents itself. The form of presentation is that of an exercise in line-drawing; the source is the belief that life can be so divided. Once it has been decided where to draw the line the problem does not end. The means of regulation must be incorporated in the law. This latter decision is not merely technical, for the choice of means affects the perception of the dichotomy.

Earlier in this chapter, three aspects of the private were suggested. These were invisibility, non-regulation and non-intervention. In relation to sexuality it is regulation and non-regulation that will be elaborated. Invisibility is of limited use as a concept to help our understanding; for once behaviour becomes visible through discussion, prohibition, regulation, it cannot slip back to invisibility. This point will be investigated further in relation to male homosexuality. Chapter 5 elaborates the policy of non-intervention as applied to family life.

Regulation of sexuality takes various forms. Behaviour unregulated in private may be prohibited, controlled or regulated in public. Much of the discussion on decriminalisation of sexual behaviour fails to specify whether it is boundary-shifting which is being advocated, and if so what form public control of sexual behaviour should take. The notion of public in discussions of sexuality often seems to be equated with prohibition and control and to have territorial connotations. Private is then equated with freedom. But this is not so, as our examples of prostitution, incest, sexual intercourse with children and homosexuality will show.

Prostitution

The regulation of prostitution, since the enactment of the Street Offences Act 1959, depends on the distinction between public and private. According to the Wolfenden Report the criminal law should not concern itself with matters of private morality but should aim 'to protect the citizen from what is offensive or injurious'.[41] This expression of liberal philosophy has come to dominate thinking about control of sexuality. The result was a recasting of legal provisions whereby prostitution itself is not illegal but any public manifestation, such as soliciting, advertising or making agreements with clients, is. Street offences, since 1959, are punished more severely than previously because: 'both loitering and importuning for the purpose of prostitution are so self-evidently public nuisances that the law ought to deal with them, as it deals with other self-evident public nuisances, without calling on individual citizens to show that they were annoyed.'[42] To safeguard citizens from having to prove their annoyance the law uses the notion of the 'common prostitute' as part of the mechanism of control of prostitutes' behaviour in public.

Section 1 of the Street Offences Act 1959 provides that 'it shall be an offence for a common prostitute to loiter or solicit in a street or public place for the purpose of prostitution.' Common prostitution is shown by police evidence that the woman persisted in conduct for which she has previously been cautioned by a constable. The police operate a system, approved by the Home Office, of not charging a woman unless she has been formally cautioned on two occasions and the cautions have been recorded. The law's object is to reduce the visibility of prostitution by getting it out of public places.

The use of the term 'common prostitute' dates back to the Contagious Diseases Acts in force from 1864 to 1886, when state control of prostitution was established in certain military and naval towns. By 1869 there were eighteen such districts in which any woman could be arrested on suspicion of being a common prostitute. Unless she could prove otherwise to the police, or in court, she was registered a common prostitute and had to submit to fortnightly medical examinations. Refusal to be examined meant imprisonment. If found to be suffering from venereal disease she would be interned in a lock hospital for up to nine months.

The object of the measures was to protect military men from disease, but the legislation contained assumptions about male and female sexuality which continue to inform law-making today. Sex was considered essential for the fighting men of the empire and no effort was directed at preventing them from visiting prostitutes. But the women were criminalised and controlled. A social identity, which had not previously existed, the prostitute, was constructed. What had been for many poor women a transitional stage in their working lives became, through criminalisation, the only means of livelihood. Prostitutes as sexually active women were separated from virtuous and passive models of femininity.

Josephine Butler led the successful campaign against the Acts, which were seen as a threat to all women. Feminist repealers stressed the double standard implied in the legislation, which punished the women but not their clients. This double standard, so prevalent in Victorian beliefs and morality, remains part of prostitution law. The middle-class women who belonged to the Ladies' National Association, the repeal organisation, had quite different views of morality from those enshrined in the law of today. They subscribed to an ideology of separate spheres for women and men that stressed women's purity, moral supremacy and domestic virtue. They were indignant when confronted by a prostitute who adhered to her way of life. Their public discourse was a condemnation of male sexual licence and it was proposed that the standards of domestic purity and fidelity replace the double standard.

In their criticism of the double standard reformers were confronted not only with differential standards for female and male behaviour, but also with Victorian hypocrisy in which public pronouncements were not matched with private behaviour. The separation, in bourgeois ideology, of private and public morality was complex. On the one hand family, home and domesticity constituted the private place in which those female virtues of chastity and moral purity were upheld and respected. On the other hand the private sphere was that of male sexual licence, as Walter's *Secret Life* makes clear. In the public sphere politicians laid down high standards of public morality; the public was also the place of prostitution, vice on the streets, crime. The resolution of this was to be the imposition of those private, domestic, womanly values on all, in both private and public, through the moral purity movement. Later liberal reforms which imply that private behaviour is personal and no concern of the law, but that what is done in public is what matters, are the direct antithesis of the moral purity reforms.

The double standard that remains in the law on prostitution today is the failure to deal with men seeking sexual services who importune women in public. Section 32 of the Sexual Offences Act 1956 provides that it 'is an offence for a man persistently to solicit or importune in a public place for immoral purposes'. It has been held that, in the case of homosexual soliciting, it is for the jury to decide whether the conduct involved immoral purposes.[43] However, in *Crook* v. *Edmondson*[44] it appears to have been held that immoral purposes are not involved where a man importunes a female prostitute. A new offence committed by 'a man persistently accosting a woman or women for sexual purposes in a street or public place in such circumstances as are likely to cause annoyance to the woman or annoyance to the public' has been proposed.[45] If enacted, this would deal with the complaint that the double standard is discriminatory, but otherwise it merely reinforces the idea that it is public behaviour that is offensive and to be prohibited.

There are reasons why the law no longer wishes to enter the sphere of private morality. Problems of efficacy and enforcement come high on the list. The Wolfenden Report makes clear its belief that strict law enforcement in the public sphere will be more efficacious if the law ceases to be the guardian of private morality. This utilitarian view was in line with John Stuart Mill's argument in *On Liberty* that the only justification for legal intervention in private life was to prevent harm to others. Yet the privatisation of prostitution did not lead to a diminution of control, as indeed the Wolfenden Committee foresaw.

Prostitution has been largely driven off the streets by increasing fines and imprisonment. The disadvantage is the increased opportunities for exploitation of prostitutes by middlemen who organise commercial agencies and call-girl rackets. The object of the legislation was not to abolish prostitution. 'We do not think that the law ought to try to do so; nor do we think that if it tried it could by itself succeed.'[46] The pragmatic approach has been for the law to enable 'the ordinary citizen to go about his business without the constant affront to his sense of decency which the presence of these women affords.'[47]

Incest

The Victorian era saw increased legislative activity in regulating behaviour that had previously been invisible to the law. Despite this, there was a reluctance to enter the domain of the family. Parliamentary resistance to the criminalisation of incest is an example. The first incest Bill was introduced in 1899 and it was only after hesitations that the Punishment of Incest Act was passed by Parliament in 1908. Parliament was reluctant to discuss a taboo subject, did not wish to admit that all was not well with the Victorian family, and was against intervention in the home. Even Lord Shaftesbury, the pioneer of legislation limiting children's work, saw parental abuse of children as beyond the law. He wrote in 1871 that such evils 'are of so private, internal and domestic a character as to be beyond the reach of legislation'.[48]

The Act criminalised sexual intercourse between persons related by consanguinity, that is, grandparent and grandchild, parent and child, brother and sister, half-brother and half-sister. Pressure groups such as the National Society for the Prevention of Cruelty to Children and the National Vigilance Association regarded the enactment of prohibition on incest as a victory. The latter group was central to the social purity movement. Social reformers anxious to intervene within the family for the protection of children clashed with politicians reluctant to do so, prior to the enactment of the prohibition. Lord Halsbury, the Lord Chancellor, in the Parliamentary debate on the 1903 Bill declared that the legislation was 'calculated to do an infinite amount of mischief'. He was against disclosures of incestuous conduct in open court and in the press, as this would produce 'a crop of similar offences at other Assizes'.[49] Through his amendment the Act of 1908 specified that all proceedings were to be held *in camera*. The debate showed the reluctance of members to legislate on 'that d—d morality' and one member argued that 'up to the present time these offences against morality had never been made a crime. The House, therefore, should hesitate before making a sweeping addition to the criminal law.'[50]

Sexual intercourse, and incest, with a girl under sixteen was already a crime under the Criminal Law Amendment Act 1885, as were also male homosexual acts. Therefore the enactment of the Incest Act would seem to have been directed in legal terms at heterosexual intercourse between members of the family over sixteen. A possible explanation is the eugenic argument concerning defects in any children born of such a union. But it also represented a victory for the social purity movement which secured the legislation as a symbolic statement of the moral values of social purity, and as a manifestation of its political strength. At the same time the successful passing of the Act represented a statement that intervention in the family would take place where socially necessary.

The law is now found in sections 10 and 11 of the Sexual Offences Act 1956. Many cases of incest are bound to remain secret. Research data reveal that about 300 cases a year come to the notice of the police and in about 80 per cent of these a prosecution is brought. Most convictions in 1973 were for incest with a daughter under sixteen.[51] The Criminal Law Revision Committee is considering limiting the offence to cases where a daughter or one of the parties is below a specified age, such as eighteen or twenty-one.[52]

Age of consent

'The social purity movement can be defined as an attempt on the part of a disparate collection of reformers to change social attitudes about sex. For most purity reformers, the achievement of a single standard of sexual morality for men and women was a prime goal. The single standard was conceived of as a high one – men were to conform to the standards of chastity Victorian society enjoined on women.'[53] The outcome of one campaign was public acceptance that young girls were in need of protection from sexual exploitation. The Criminal Law Amendment Act 1885 raised the age of consent to sexual intercourse for girls from thirteen to sixteen. It was a felony to have sexual intercourse with a girl under thirteen, and a misdemeanour in the case of a girl under sixteen. Consent by the girl involved was no defence to a charge under the Act.

Legislation on age of consent reflects a difference in the perception of female and male sexuality. For heterosexual intercourse it applies only to girls, who are seen to need protection, either because of ignorance or because of foolishness. The present law is contained in sections 5 and 6 of the Sexual Offences Act 1956. Unlawful sexual intercourse with a girl under thirteen is punishable with a maximum of life imprisonment, whereas that with a girl under sixteen carries a maximum of two years' imprisonment. A review of the legislation published in 1981 came to the conclusion that for girls the law should remain as it is.

What is the case for differentiating young girls from young boys with regard to protection from early sexual intercourse? The age for consensual homosexual acts between males in private is twenty-one, so it could be said that the idea of protection applies there also. The Policy Advisory Committee on Sexual Offences has recommended that the minimum age for lawful homosexual relations between males should be reduced to eighteen.[54] The rhetoric in both cases is that of protecting those who are physically or psychologically immature from premature sexual experience. Yet the suggestion that boys under sixteen or eighteen should be protected from heterosexual intercourse was rejected by the committee. One obvious difference between girls and boys is that girls may become pregnant if they engage in sexual intercourse. The Lane Committee found that problems arising from pregnancies in girls under sixteen were greatly increased because they often denied their pregnancies even to themselves. Three out of four of these pregnancies end in abortion. But whether a girl under sixteen years old gives birth or has an abortion, such early pregnancy is physically harmful.

Male homosexuality

In 1533 an Act was passed making sodomy a felony 'forasmuch as there is not yet sufficient and condign punishment appointed and limited by the due course of the laws of this realm'.[55] Prior to that the ecclesiastical courts had jurisdiction over sodomy. However, the above wording of the 1533 Statute suggests that there was little or no enforcement of the Church law. According to Blackstone, 'the infamous crime against nature, committed either with man or beast', was treated in indictments as a crime not fit to be named.[56] The no-name crime was punishable by death until 1861. Other forms of homosexual activity were either ignored or subsumed under the general law of assault. This remains so with lesbianism today.

The Offences Against the Person Act 1861, sections 61 and 62, made committing or attempting to commit buggery offences punishable with maximum sentences of life imprisonment and ten years' imprisonment respectively. This was followed in 1885 by the Criminal Law Amendment Act which by s.11 provided that it was a misdemeanour for a male person, in private or in public, to commit or be party to an act of gross indecency with another male. This not only marked homosexual activities as a crime but also characterised the homosexual person as a criminal. Previously 'the law was directed against a series of sexual acts, not a particular type of person, although in practice most people prosecuted under the buggery laws were probably prosecuted for homosexual behaviour (sodomy).'[57] The homosexual as a person, a social category, emerged from the social and legal discussion of the crime. Debates on sexuality and on social purity in the nineteenth century led not only to greater regulation of extra-marital sexuality, but also to a public discourse which increased knowledge and awareness.

The Act of 1885 was followed by the Vagrancy Act 1898 and the Criminal Law Amendment Act 1912, and increased regulation required discussion and definition. As with legal attempts to prevent the dissemination of knowledge about contraception, the effects were contradictory. There was a growing awareness of homosexuality which contructed homosexuality as an identity. As Michel Foucault explains it:

There is no question that the appearance in nineteenth century psychiatry, jurisprudence, and literature of a whole series of discourses on the species and sub-species of homosexuality, inversion, pederasty, and 'psychic herma-phrodism' made possible a strong advance of social controls into this area of 'perversity'; but it also made possible the formation of a 'reverse' discourse: homosexuality began to speak on its own behalf, to demand that its legitimacy or 'naturality' be acknowledged, often in the same vocabulary, using the same categories by which it was radically disqualified.[58]

Thus from being invisible in pre-Tudor law homosexuality moved from regulated act to criminal identity.

The law of 1885 covered private and public acts of gross indecency, and the modern law, contained in sections 12 and 13 of the Sexual Offences Act 1956, maintained control over private acts. Following on the Wolfenden Committee's elaboration of a distinction between law and morals the Sexual Offences Act 1967 decriminalised homosexual acts in private between consenting males over the age of twenty-one in England and Wales. As with prostitution, the reform was motivated by pragmatic considerations of law enforcement. The Criminal Justice (Scotland) Act 1980 formally brought Scottish law into line with that of England and Wales. But in Northern Ireland the relevant provisions remain the 1861 Act, the 1885 Act and the common law. In *Dudgeon* v. *United Kingdom* the European Court of Human Rights held that Northern Irish law breaches the right to respect for private life contained in Article 8 of the European Convention on Human Rights, insofar as it prohibits homosexual acts committed in private between consenting males over the age of twenty-one. The court justified as necessary to a democratic society some degree of regulation of male homosexual conduct but defined 'necessary' as implying the existence of a 'pressing social need'. Since the *Dudgeon* case concerned 'a most intimate aspect of private life' there must exist serious reasons before interference by public authorities can be legitimate. No such pressing social need was shown by the United Kingdom government for differentiating Northern Ireland from the rest of the United Kingdom.[59]

5
The Private Relationship of Marriage

'Far from being the basis of the good society, the family, with all its narrow privacy and tawdry secrets, is the source of all our discontents.'

SIR EDMUND LEACH

Privacy, in relation to personal and family life, has been given a stipulated meaning of non-regulation by law. Social policy supports such privacy. The belief that law, when it intrudes in the area of personal relations, is a destructive force is clearly a belief about law. But it also contains assumptions about personal and family life. Home is thought to be a private place, a refuge from society, where relationships can flourish untrammelled by public interference. Yet it is conventional to suggest that the intimacy of the nuclear family has overloaded it, leading to breakdown. Denied community in the public sphere, demands for emotional support at home lead to suffocation and breakdown, but a return to the public world reveals its impersonality and sterility. This picture is only partially painted. For although it acknowledges that what goes on in society affects the private sphere, it does not colour in the conflicts generated by the disjunction between intimacy and inequality, sharing and power, which arise from the very forces which create the need for refuge and privacy in the first place. I refer to the division of labour between spouses or partners, which makes their relationship one of unequal dependence.

The division of labour referred to here is a system of responsibility whereby the mother is usually the primary parent caring for children, whilst the father undertakes wage-earning in the market-place. Despite all the changes that have taken place both in families and in the labour market in the past twenty years, this pattern remains unchanged. It affects women's participation in the labour market, the wages they earn, the kind of work they undertake, the hours they can work, both actual and potential, and their future benefits in social security and pensions. All this has been well documented.[1] But less emphasis has been placed on the values which animate the private sphere as compared to society at large.

Do the values of community (*Gemeinschaft*) continue to inspire family relations or have the values of society (*Gesellschaft*) penetrated the private sphere? Individualism, competition, self-interest mark society; in private, persons are expected to be altruistic. Given the impersonality of the world of *Gesellschaft* it is not surprising to find the statement that 'in the face of the Market, all that is "human" about people must crowd into the sphere of private life, and attach itself, as best it can, to the personal and biological activities which remain there.'[2]

What goes on in private relationships? Without law, how does that black box we call marriage regulate itself? In popular credence men act in accordance with self-interest, women in accordance with self-sacrifice. An examination of family law, where beliefs in privacy maintain both patriarchy and societal institutions, illustrates this point. The family is not private. It may provide a 'haven in a heartless world'[3] but it is that external world which has brought it into being and which constitutes it. Examination in this chapter of six areas of conjugal relations unregulated by law confirms this. The six areas are contracts, finances, property, sexual relations, violence and conduct.

Contracts or Agreements Between Spouses

Promises and contracts between spouses will not be enforced by the courts unless sealed and witnessed. The rationale for this refusal by the law to intervene in marriage is that such agreements lack 'the intention to create legal relations'. Atkin L.J., as already discussed, regarded such promises as belonging to the private domain. According to his fellow judge, Duke L.J.:

The proposition that mutual promises made in the ordinary domestic relationship of husband and wife of necessity give cause for action on a contract seems to me to go to the very root of the relationship and to be a possible fruitful source of dissension and quarrelling. I cannot see that any benefit would result from it to either of the parties, but on the other hand it would lead to unlimited litigation in a relationship which should be obviously as far as possible protected from possibilities of that kind.[4]

Managerial considerations also concerned the court, as Atkin L.J. explained:

All I can say is that the small courts of this country would have to be multiplied one hundredfold if these arrangements were held to result in legal obligations . . . . Their promises are not sealed with seals and sealing wax. The consideration that really obtains for them is that natural love and affection which counts for so little in these cold courts.[5]

Natural love and affection are judged unsuitable for legal regulation and there is a fear that legal intervention would cause dissension, and perhaps break up a marriage. Using the law implies a lack of trust; love and trust go hand in hand. Thus law can only operate in the impersonal public sphere where individuals secure their agreements through contract. The values implicit in personal relationships are perceived as antithetical to law. This judicial view is comprehensible in terms of the dichotomy between private and public. Unrecognised however is the effect it has of legitimating inequality. The practical effect of the ruling is that agreements about financial support do not have to be honoured, unless made under seal.

Finances

But there is more regulation in marriage than in cohabitation! (So far) (at least not arises automatically on dissolution)

Despite the prevalence of a division of labour in which one spouse, usually the husband, supports the family through earnings in the market-place, whilst the other spouse, usually the wife, accepts primary responsibility for the children and household, family finances are unregulated by law. The only legislation to deal directly with the allocation of money within the household is s.1 of the Married Women's Property Act 1964 which provides that any saving from a housekeeping allowance given by the husband to the wife belong equally to both. Quite apart from its enshrining of gender roles (wives are assumed, probably correctly, to be housekeepers), the legislation implies that housekeeping money is for expenses; it is not personal earnings. Nevertheless, the ideology of sharing propounded in this rule could, if contained in other legal principles, provide a fair basis for marriage. But there are no other legal rules except a mutual duty of maintenance. The enforceability of the duty of support is doubtful so long as the couple live together.[6] The non-earner has no right to part of the earner's wages. Despite a family wage structure in the national economy there is no obligation in English law on the primary earner to share his earnings with the other spouse. This is usually explained in terms of the ideology of privacy and, pragmatically, by the assumption that persons living in the same household do share. Yet there is evidence to show that 'the economic relationship between husband and wife is a very unequal one and that a man's earnings are not necessarily put at his family's disposal.'[7]

In the past women generally organised the domestic economy. Tilly and Scott report that the pattern in early modern England was for the family economy to be managed by wives.[8] So long as the household mode of production continued, parents and children contributed their labour and shared in its fruit. As the real value of wages rose in the last decade of the nineteenth century, and as the notion of a family wage was gradually accepted by employers and the state, there was a decline in women's wage-earning activities. Increasingly men were the primary or sole wage-earners. There was a gradual shift in control of the allocation of money coming into the household from women to men.

A study of pawnbroking in Edwardian England shows how the market economy diminished the housewife's traditional role as household manager. For as cash purchase was substituted for home manufacture she was totally dependent on what her husband was able, or wished, to give her. It was a woman's management of the family budget that led her into the pawn shop. Thus, although this control might appear as a source of power, in fact it was often more a source of anxiety and self-deprivation. 'Whatever the quality of the marriage a wife's personal standard of living was an elastic one, continually eroded by the demands of family life.'[9] Because husbands had little to do with the day-to-day running of family finances, and because wives' ability to manage reflected on a husband's reputation, they were usually kept in ignorance of pledging and credit. This caused some anxiety to the 1870 Select Committee on Pawnbrokers.[10] But it was the secrecy about income and its segregation from household expenditure that led to the secrecy about pawning. Melanie Tebbutt concludes that 'the financial control exerted by the male breadwinner was a crucial factor in domestic power relationships, and even in situations where women were able to organise their own credit or commercial transactions, their activities were similarly circumscribed.'[11]

There has been a significant return by married women to the labour market, both periodically during wartime, and as a continuous trend since the mid-1950s, often as part-time workers. But it is also clear that reproductive activity in giving birth to and socialising children means that most women will spend part of their lives as houseworkers, working in the home for subsistence. Women's earnings remain consistently lower than men's. These may be crucial factors in the shift that has taken place from female to male control of household finances. Today, with the weekly supermarket visit where the husband pays by cheque, there may be little or no control of money by the wife.

If it is being suggested that houseworkers perform their duties for subsistence what evidence is there that in the absence of legal regulation they actually receive it? In their English study published in 1972 Todd and Jones found that 5 per cent of husbands gave their whole pay packet to their wives, 76 per cent of wives hoped to be kept informed of money matters by their husbands, and 19 per cent of wives knew nothing about family finances.[12] There is evidence that women are more likely to underestimate than to overestimate their husbands' earnings, and a study made in 1974 revealed that only 49 per cent of wives knew precisely what their husbands earned.[13] Four main ways in which family finances are managed have been identified. These are: 'tipping up', in which the whole wage packet is handed over to the wife who then returns a fixed amount to the wage-earner for personal spending; the allowance system, in which the wife receives a fixed amount for housekeeping but may not be kept informed about earnings and outgoings; the pooling system, where both spouses contribute from their earnings to the household finances; and the separate finances system, in which the partners keep their own money but agree on the allocation of financial respon-sibilities.[14]

Where the income going into a household is low and most of it is used for subsistence, the likelihood of sharing is greatest, although there is still evidence of greater consumption by the wage-earner. Shortage of money generally means that its management is regarded as a chore rather than a source of power for the manager. In families living on welfare benefits the wife usually handles management. Where the wife is earning it is common for the husband's income to be spent on necessaries such as housing, furniture, heating and large consumer items such as a car, whilst the wife's earnings may be spent on food, clothes, holidays, and other items considered as luxuries. Hilary Land refers to a 'general finding which seems to apply to all income groups . . . that wives are more likely to be responsible for making frequent purchases (daily or weekly) and husbands for less frequent payments (monthly or quarterly)'.[15] If the income is such as to permit choices to be made, 'the decision-making power lies with the one who brings in the sole or major income.'[16] The husband is more likely to pay the mortgage or to buy consumer durables. This gives him a great advantage if a dispute arises over marital property. For the judiciary does not look to evidence of national patterns of allocation of money within the household. Rather strict rules of property are applied. This will be considered further below, but the point here is that an ideology of community is neither lived in fact nor laid down in principle. The particular division of labour prevalent in marriages today puts women at a disadvantage in the labour market with the result that men have substantially greater economic power both in the market and in the home.

Property

There is no concept of community of property of married couples in English law. An ideology of equality suggests that the spouses should share equally their material possessions, yet despite discussion of the problems of matrimonial property since the mid-1950s there has been a constant rejection of the one solution that would enable that ideology to be lived. A number of explanations can be given for the rejection of community of property. The arguments can be identified as pragmatic, individualistic and technical. The pragmatic argument holds that in the ongoing marriage, so long as there is no dispute, there is no need to determine ownership. This misses the point that law is not just about dispute resolution. It also represents symbolic-ally the values of society. In fact the majority of married couples do believe that ownership or tenancy of the matrimonial home should be equally shared.[17] Another variant on the pragmatic theme is the argument that it is occupation of the matrimonial home that needs to be protected for the non-owner or non-tenant. This has been achieved through legislation and case-law.[18] Again this variation of the pragmatic argument misses the point about symbolism. It is also doubtful whether it is good law.[19]

The individualistic argument relies on the reforms achieved by the Married Women's Property Acts 1870 to 1882. It is said that the structure of separate property set up by the Acts, as a reaction to the common law rules on unity of the spouses, is a statement of equality, in that individuals have autonomy over their own property and their own affairs. A debate has taken place in the United States as to whether equality is best achieved through sharing principles or separate property. Susan Prager sees 'a fundamental choice for marital property policy: whether individualistic or sharing principles should be given predominant status in determining the property rights of married people'.[20] She argues that sharing theories of property law should prevail in marrriage-type relationships. Mary Ann Glendon questions whether compulsory sharing is desirable now that there is a widespread expectation that marriage will last only so long as it provides personal fulfilment. She points to 'an eternal tension in matrimonial law, in social attitudes, and in every marriage between the community of life that marriage involves and the separate, autonomous existence of the individuals who are associated in this community of life'.[21] It seems that a régime of separate property may be in tune with the needs of professional dual career couples. They are not, however, the majority. The individualistic argument ignores the division of labour in marriage and its operation as a joint enterprise. As Otto Kahn-Freund pointed out, the rule of separation of property in England, which was designed to realise the principle of equality of the sexes in matters of property, failed in its purpose. He concluded that 'to treat as equal that which is unequal may . . . be a very odious form of discrimination.'[22]

Technical arguments against the introduction of a community of property régime into English law point to examples in the civil law system of continental Europe. Here there are problems of management for the partners, expenses of administration for the state, and complexities of structure. By comparison, it is said, the English system of separate property during marriage has the virtue of simplicity. But empirical evidence of the cost of running community-property systems by comparison with the cost of adjudicating matrimonial property disputes in Britain is lacking. Current English and Scots law is complex and unsatisfactory in technical terms. This is why there has been a long series of reform proposals.[23]

When the Divorce Reform Act 1969, which introduced a 'no-fault divorce' element into English law, was debated in Parliament in 1968, criticism was directed at the lack of financial provision for 'innocent' divorced spouses. One response was a Bill concerning matrimonial property, introduced in late 1968 by Edward Bishop. The Bill proposed a system of deferred community of gains, with equal division of property on the termination of the marriage. Full community of property during marriage was rejected because of problems of management. But even this partial reform, which would have required consent of both spouses before the disposal of matrimonial assets, was too radical for the legal establishment and much of the legal community. For instance an editorial in *The Times*, agreeing with the government's opposition to the Bishop property Bill, said: 'It picks up the promising idea of community of matrimonial property but leaves the legislature with too little, and the courts with far too much, of the work of translating the idea into a system of law.'[24] Despite government opposition Bishop's Bill passed a second reading, but he was persuaded to withdraw it on a promise of a Law Commission Bill to replace it. The outcome was the Matrimonial Proceedings and Property Act 1970, later consolidated with the Divorce Reform Act 1969 in the Matrimonial Causes Act 1973.

The provisions of the Matrimonial Causes Act dealing with property apply only on divorce. They do not affect the ownership of property during marriage and any claims by or disputes between the couple are still resolved under s.17 of the Married Women's Property Act 1882 and the subsequent case-law. This will be shown to be out of touch with the way in which many, if not most, marriages are lived. It is ironic that one objection to the Bishop Bill should have been the work-load on the courts, because the discretionary provisions of the Matrimonial Causes Act have caused an expansion in the family law jurisdiction of the County and High Courts, and of the Court of Appeal, unparalleled in other legal sectors.

Other common law jurisdictions are moving to a community system. In the United States a Uniform Marital Property Act which implements sharing principles during marriage is being drafted. The reasons for this are explained thus:

Unless a present shared interest exists in both spouses' earnings, wives (especially full-time homemakers) may be severely restricted during marriage in their access to credit. Even more dramatic are the consequences for unpropertied women in common law or deferred community states who disagree with their husbands about family finances or predecease their spouses. These wives have no assets subject to their control during marriage or subject to testate or intestate disposition on their deaths, a poor contrast to the position of married women in community property states, who are ordinarily entitled to equal control of the community during marriage and to disposition of one-half of the family's marital assets at death. However carefully protected wives are in non-community property states as widows or at divorce, they are relatively impoverished in other contexts.[25]

The English research done by Todd and Jones in 1971 revealed that 52 per cent of married couples were owner-occupiers, 45 per cent were tenants and 3 per cent lived otherwise. Among owner-occupiers 52 per cent owned the home in joint names, 42 per cent owned it in the husband's name and 5 per cent owned it in the wife's name. Fourteen per cent of renters had the tenancy in joint names, 82 per cent rented in the husband's name, and 3 per cent rented in the wife's name.[26] Despite this, however, most of those who owned their home in one name only thought of it as common property. The survey as a whole showed that the great majority of spouses interviewed felt that the matrimonial home and its contents should be jointly owned by both, regardless of who paid for it, and regardless of whether both worked or not.

The assets that constitute matrimonial property are not just the owner-occupied home. They may include tenancy of the home, furniture, consumer durables, a car, pension rights, savings, a job. The evidence available suggests that the majority of couples believe that their assets belong to them equally and jointly, although specific items such as washing machine or car, where used exclusively by one, are seen as belonging to that one.

Research done in Scotland by Manners and Rauta ten years later suggests that the majority of married couples think of their savings, houses, furniture and other property as being jointly owned by both of them. In other words, the ideology of marriage is of a partnership in which there is equal sharing of matrimonial property. Present Scots law does not conform to the beliefs of these couples. Proposals for reform, whilst having the laudable aim of remedying the defects and injustices of the current law, do not approach the matter as one of principle. Rather it is hoped to deal with the defects through piecemeal legislation.[27]

Realising the goal of equality through a reform of matrimonial property law is not easy. There is genuine disagreement as to how this can best be done. Yet it is significant that in continental European jurisdictions such as France, which has a system of deferred community of property, there is a reasonable level of satisfaction with the present law. Other common law jurisdictions such as the various states of the United States and the Australian states are moving to systems of community of property. New Zealand has already done so (Matrimonial Property Act, 1976), although the property concept is confined to the home and chattels.[28]

Aside from issues of ideology of marriage, there are practical problems with the present English law governing marital property. On the bankruptcy of one spouse, the couple may lose all their assets unless the other spouse can prove ownership. Bankruptcy provides a good example of the disjunction between the spouses' view of their marriage and the law's view. Todd and Jones found that the majority of spouses regarded family assets and property as belonging equally to both. If we look at the legal and equitable rules governing matrimonial property, the picture is quite different. Ownership of the home, or of items of property, if determined during marriage, e.g. on bankruptcy, will be subject to the following rules:

1. At common law the property or item belongs to the spouse in whose name it is registered, or who purchased it.
2. Equity can intervene to impose a trust.
3. Equity will look to the intention of the parties, express or implied.
4. Implied intention can be deduced from contributions directly referable to the acquisition of the property or item.

The common law rules completely ignore the division of labour in which access to income may be confined to one spouse. But equity, despite its role in mitigating the rigours of the common law, does little better. It has already been suggested that patterns of expenditure and control of money within marriage are dictated by the more powerful spouse, and that wage-earning and power go in tandem. Further, research shows that the primary wage-earner will usually pay the major household bills of housing, heating, water, etc. A construction, which may be contrary to the spouses' perception of their marriage, is put on this conduct by the courts.

Indirect contributions to the purchase of the home, for instance where the husband makes the mortgage payments but is relieved of other household expenditure by his wife's earnings, have been suggested to be sufficient to give the wife an equitable interest.[29] So where family finances are managed by the pooling system where both partners contribute from their earnings to the household expenses, equity will give the non-owner spouse an interest.[30] But in the *Kowalczuk* case, where the wife did contribute financially, the Court of Appeal's view was that these payments were not directly referable to the purchase of the home. Therefore the wife had no equitable interest in the property, i.e. there was no trust in her favour. The registrar, who first heard the case, described the wife thus:

She has certainly lived frugally. She makes her own clothes. She is in no way extravagant. She utilised her wages towards the upkeep of the home and latterly she worked extremely long hours in a restaurant . . . . She saved and bought a car which she took with her . . . . She says that she paid some of the mortgage instalments . . . . There is no doubt that both utilised their resources for their joint living and benefit . . . . I feel myself that both in respect of the home and upkeep, the occasional mortgage payments, some of the electricity bills, tiles and fittings, some of the articles and the food came from her, the applicant's, earnings.[31]

It is probable that, if there had been a common pool from which the mortgage, rates and other household expenses were paid, this woman would have been an equitable owner of the matrimonial home.

The disjunction between how people live and organise their households and relationships, and the construction placed on this by the law, can be further seen from the *Kokosinski* case:

From 1947 until 1950 the wife had always used her wages towards the maintenance of the house which she and the husband had set up together. He had undoubtedly contributed by buying specific items, but her wages had consistently been used towards the household maintenance. From 1950 onwards . . . her income has been used, virtually in its entirety, towards the maintenance of the household.[32]

Notwithstanding these financial arrangements the wife was not an owner of the home. Had her husband, who was the legal owner, gone bankrupt, it is unlikely that she could have established any claim.

In a case where the wife was the owner of the property, received a housekeeping allowance from the husband, earned an equivalent amount herself and spent most of this on mortgage repayments, the husband's housekeeping contribution was sufficient to give him a half share in the house.[33] This recognition of a joint venture was fair. But, in general, couples do not organise their household finances with the complexities of marital property law in mind. It is not only financial management that the law looks to; it looks also to what the couple intended at the time of the purchase of the home. This, again, is an artificial process whereby the court reconstructs and interprets what was in the parties' minds at some time in the past.

In *Cowcher* the wife provided one-third of the price at the time of purchase. The rest of the purchase price was obtained by various means, and the house was placed in the husband's name. Because Bagnall J. was unable to find any common intention at that time to share equally in the property he awarded two-thirds of the value of sale to the husband, who really had done very little to deserve it. He reasoned thus:

neither contemplated that in future the wife would go out to work to supplement the family income, or receive money from any source other than the husband, or do anything other than carry out the normal duties of a wife and mother . . . . I am wholly unable to draw from [the facts] an inference that the parties in 1962 [date of purchase] intended to contribute equally to the purchase of the house . . . . I am of the opinion that . . . the then contemplation of the parties that in future the husband alone was to be the source of the family income . . . [is] conclusive against any such inference.[34]

Therefore, the work of the wife in looking after the husband and the home, and in bringing up four children, was ignored, because in the public world it has no economic value and is therefore accorded no recognition. The only factor taken into account is the actual money she contributed. Had she known of the *ex post facto* construction the law would place on her actions, no doubt she would have behaved differently. Decisions made on the allocation of money within the household have unforeseen consequences in the world of law.

A fairer view is that a causal connection must be shown between the contribution of the non-owner and the discharge of financial obligations by the owner. Only if it can be shown that the non-owner's contributions were necessary to the owner's fulfilment of obligations such as mortgage payments, rates, etc., will the non-owner be given a share, as Lord Denning has explained: 'It is sufficient if the contributions made by the wife are such as to relieve the husband from expenditure which he would otherwise have had to bear. By so doing the wife helps him indirectly with the mortgage instalments because he has more money in his pocket with which to pay them'.[35] So, depending on the judge's view, indirect contributions may be sufficient. But no one has yet recognised that shopping, food preparation, cooking, cleaning, washing, ironing and looking after children 'relieves the husband from expenditure'. In other words the cash nexus remains paramount along with the commercial values of the public world, whilst the private existence of mother and housewife is invisible to the law.

On the termination of marriage through death or divorce quite a different set of legal rules apply. These are concerned with need, rather than with property rights or intention.

Sexual Relations

The most private aspect of the conjugal relationship is seen as the partners' sexual life. Marriage is defined by law as a relationship between biological male and female. Sexual consummation of the marriage is required if it is not to be voidable (Matrimonial Causes Act, s.12). The best example of the privacy of sexual relations is the assumption that these are best left to the couple to sort out for themselves, whether by consent or force. A major result of this is that marital rape, unlike other rapes, is not a crime.

The origin of the marital-rape exemption is usually attributed to Sir Matthew Hale, writing in the seventeenth century. In his *History of Pleas of the Crown* he explained it thus: 'But the husband cannot be guilty of rape committed by himself upon his lawful wife, for by their mutual matrimonial consent and contract, the wife hath given up herself in this kind unto her husband which she cannot retract.'[36] In *R. v. Clarence* Baron Pollock pronounced of a wife that: 'She has no right or power to refuse her consent.'[37] It has been argued that neither this case nor Hale's writing establish the exemption; it was only established in 1954 with acknowledgement of the possibility of conviction for assault.[38]

There is considerable evidence of unwilling participation in sexual activities by wives, from the law reports and from researchers on wife abuse.[39] Examination of the criminal law presumption of consent granted through marriage which cannot be revoked reveals that no matter how serious the wife's injuries, conviction for rape is not possible. It is true that in matrimonial law a wife may refuse unreasonable demands,[40] or refuse a husband who has venereal disease.[41] But as Bromley states, 'the courts are demanding different standards of sexual participation from husbands and wives. The wife is expected to submit to her husband's demands even though she is inhibited by invincible fears; a husband on the other hand cannot be expected to conquer his innate disinclination and engage in a . . . kind of disciplined act to keep his wife happy.'[42] But even if a wife on marriage has consented to sexual intercourse, does she consent to the assault and injuries which accompany it?

The theory of consent to sexual intercourse, so long as the marriage lasts, runs counter to any idea of the marriage partners as equals. What it implies is that there is a hierarchy of dominance and submission in marriage. Justifications can be couched in ideas of property of husband in the wife as chattel, or in terms of the unity of the spouses as one flesh. Neither of these ideas is consonant with sharing marriage.

Why is it that an act which if committed by a stranger would be rape is not so classified if committed by the husband? The leading criminal law textbook suggests that the immunity rule may be justified on public policy grounds: 'if the wife is adamant in her refusal, the husband must choose between letting his wife's will prevail, thus wrecking the marriage, and acting without her consent. It would be intolerable if he were to be conditioned in his course of action by the threat of criminal proceedings.'[43] But it is not clear why the wife's action will wreck the marriage, whilst the husband's will not.

The Criminal Law Revision Committee's *Working Paper on Sexual Offences* (1980) adopted the generally accepted opinion that a husband who forces his wife to have sexual intercourse in marriage does not commit rape. Furthermore this common law rule has been incorporated into s.1 of the Sexual Offences (Amendment) Act 1976 which limits the crime to 'unlawful sexual intercourse'. A majority of the committee favoured a change in the law, partly because 'the present rule denies married women something to which all other women are entitled'[44] – that something being, presumably, the protection of the law. However, because of various misgivings which will be analysed below, the committee suggested that the consent of the Director of Public Prosecutions be obtained for prosecutions for marital rape.

An examination of these misgivings gives a good insight into the continued belief in the privacy of the marital relationship. The committee's view was that divorce or a non-molestation order are remedies available to a wife who does not wish to have sexual intercourse with her husband (divorce for behaviour such that the petitioner cannot reasonably be expected to live with the respondent is obtainable under the Matrimonial Causes Act 1973, s.1; non-molestation orders may be granted under the Domestic Violence and Matrimonial Proceedings Act 1976, s.1, or under the Domestic Proceedings and Magistrates' Courts Act 1978, sections 16 to 18). The committee saw matters of sexual conduct in marriage as best handled by the family courts. They felt that the threat of improperly motivated charges against husbands would be avoided by reference to the Director of Public Prosecutions.

Some members of the committee expressed doubt about changing the law at all. These doubts were expressed in terms of increasing the likelihood of breakdown of marriage and decreasing the possibility of reconciliation, with adverse effects on all family members. The argument on privacy from intrusion by the police was expressed thus:

The type of questions which investigating police officers would have to ask would be likely to be greatly resented by husbands and their families. The family ties would be severed and the wife with children would have to cope with her emotional, social and financial problems as best she could; and possibly the children might resent what she had done to their father. Nearly all breakdowns of marriage cause problems. A breakdown brought about by a wife who had sought the protection of the criminal law of rape would be particularly painful.[45]

The majority dealt with this objection by saying that, since prosecution for assault is possible under the decision in *Miller*, the police are already faced with the task of making 'distasteful enquiries into the details of married life'. And furthermore:

The fact is that the police are reluctant to bring criminal charges in these circumstances, since they think that such matters are better left to the remedies provided by the family court. There is no reason to suppose, therefore, that an abandonment of Hale's rule would result in a great intrusion of the criminal law into family matters.[46]

This reluctance of the police to prosecute or even become involved was severely criticised by the Select Committee on Violence in Marriage.[47] It is somewhat odd therefore to find the Criminal Law Revision Committee using such an argument as reassurance. Perhaps the reason lies in the next paragraph, where the committee states that 'there are technical as well as social reasons for acknowledging the simple principle that a wife is as much entitled to withhold consent to sexual intercourse as anyone else.'[48] Should one add the words 'so long as family privacy is not invaded'? Nevertheless the principled approach, however hedged about by reference to the Director of Public Prosecutions, is to be welcomed. Even if the enforcement of the principle gives rise to difficulties of proof, or police reluctance to investigate, the statement of the principle is important as a symbol of equality of spouses and of the mutual respect they owe one another.

The Canadian Criminal Code, s.246.8, provides that a husband or a wife may be charged with offences of sexual assault (s.246.1, 2) or of aggravated sexual assault (s.246.3), thus making no distinction between married persons and other persons or between the sexes. The principle that sexual assault is wrong is of general application. Furthermore under s.246.4 no corroboration is required for conviction. There is no offence of rape under Canadian law; it has been replaced by the offence of sexual assault.

There have been a variety of approaches to the marital-rape exemption in the United States. New Jersey and Oregon have abolished the rule completely. Other states look to such matters as the amount of force used, whether the parties live apart, whether there has been a petition for divorce or separation, whether there has been a court order for separation.

Canadian law points the way for the future. It recognises that individuals have autonomy over their own bodies. At present the message in English law is that wives are at the disposal of their husbands. Even the restricted reform proposed by the Criminal Law Revision Committee will alter that message. The statement of principle that all women, married or not, decide for themselves whether or not to consent to intercourse is of symbolic significance. It may be that the clash of this statement with police beliefs in privacy of domestic life will result in non-enforcement. But to those who acknowledge that law contains symbolic statements the change will be important. It will also represent a movement from treating the spouses as one flesh to recognising the autonomy of each.

Violence

The view that a husband could confine and even chastise his wife was not obsolete until the late nineteenth century. In *R. v. Jackson* (1891) the Court of Appeal established that a wife could not be imprisoned by her husband in order to enforce his rights of cohabitation.[49] A later court commented that 'from the date of their decision the shackles of servitude fell from the limbs of married women and they were free to come and go at their own will.'[50] But this freedom and the denial of the husband's legal power to administer corporal punishment did not mean that the courts would intervene to protect a wife. Until 1876 English law contained no provisions directly concerned with violence in marriage, which was largely invisible. In order to get a restraining injunction divorce proceedings were necessary. The view that what happened within a marriage was private to the spouses was enunciated by the Association of Chief Police Officers in their evidence to the Select Committee on Violence in Marriage:

It is important to keep wife battering in its correct perspective and realise that this loose term is applied to incidents ranging from a very minor domestic fracas where no police action is really justified, to the more serious incidents of assaults occasioning grievous bodily harm and unlawful woundings.

While such problems take up considerable police time during, say, 12 months, in the majority of cases the role of the police is a negative one. We are, after all, dealing with persons 'bound in marriage', and it is important for a host of reasons to maintain the unity of the spouses. Precipitate action by the police could aggravate the position to such an extent as to create a worse situation than the one they were summoned to deal with. The 'lesser of two evils' principle is often a good guideline in these situations.[51]

The police view, then, was that intervention might aggravate the situation, and that 'every effort *should be made to re-unite the family*.' But why should this be so? If privacy of the family prevents intervention, why should it not also prevent treatment and therapy? The idea of preserving family unity is an aspect of the privacy of the family.

The House of Lords has decided that a spouse who has been injured by the other spouse cannot be compelled to give evidence against him.[52] The defendant had injured a woman who became his wife two days before the trial. Her injuries were severe, but at the trial she was treated as a compellable witness because of her unwillingness to give evidence. The defendant was convicted. On appeal a majority in the House of Lords accepted that at common law the wife was a competent witness in cases of personal violence. Although the majority admitted that competence at common law would normally mean compellability it was held that a wife was an exception. Lord Wilberforce explained: 'a wife is in principle not a competent witness on a criminal charge against her husband. This is because of the identity of interest between husband and wife and because to allow her to give evidence would give rise to discord and to perjury and would be, to ordinary people, repugnant.'[53] Lord Salmon's view was that it was 'altogether inconsistent with the common law's attitude towards marriage that it should compel such a wife to give evidence against her husband and thereby probably destroy the marriage',[54] and that although the law offered protection to the wife she could choose whether to accept it. Lord Dilhorne spoke of his repugnance to a wife being compelled 'to testify against her husband on a charge involving violence, no matter how trivial and no matter the consequences to her and to her family'.[55] In a dissenting opinion Lord Edmund Davies gave the facts of the assault. The defendant had called his victim from a public house where she was with her mother.

Shortly thereafter she fell back through the door 'screaming and covered with blood'. On examination in hospital her injuries were found to be two stab wounds in the chest, penetrating the lung on each side, and a nine-centimetre cut to the left forearm. His Lordship's view was that the wife, a competent witness, was compellable. The essence of his opinion was that 'such incidents ought not to be regarded as having no importance extending beyond the domestic hearth. Their investigation and, where sufficiently weighty, their prosecution is a duty which the agencies of law enforcement cannot dutifully neglect.'[56]

An examination of the reasons given by the majority and their refutation in the dissenting opinion does much to reveal the beliefs which undergird the judiciary's view of the law's non-function in relation to marriage. The majority relied on *Coke* where husband and wife are said to be one flesh and that to allow the wife to give evidence 'might be a cause of implacable discord and dissension'.[57] Bentham had earlier called this 'the grimgribber, nonsensical reason'[58] for the rule, and Wigmore described it as 'the merest anachronism, in legal theory, and an indefensible obstruction to truth in practice'.[59] There was reliance also on Gilbert's view that to allow the wife to give evidence would 'destroy the very legal policy of marriage . . . that the interest should be but one'.[60] It seems that the interest concerned is that of the more powerful.

Is the preservation of marriage a function of the criminal law? Lord Salmon said in the *Hoskyn* case that the 'rule seems to me to underline the supreme importance attached by the common law to the special status of marriage and to the unity supposed to exist between husband and wife'.[61] But Lord Edmund Davies agreed with the trial judge that a court dealing with personal violence is investigating crime and not merely 'a domestic dispute'. There is an interest on the part of the state and members of the public that evidence of the crime should be available to the court.[62] In effect, this argument is based on an idea of a public concern with the defendant's actions rather than these being confined to the private or domestic domain. The other point made in dissent was that, given a public interest, the case should not depend on the victim's willingness or reluctance to testify: 'Reluctance may spring from a variety of reasons and does not by any means necessarily denote that domestic harmony has been restored. A wife who has once been subjected to a "carve-up" may well have more reasons than one for being an unwilling witness against her husband.'[63] But even for the spirited dissenter there is a clear distinction between a public interest in crime prevention and matters confined to the private domestic hearth. As one writer concludes: 'while *Hoskyn* perhaps gives the illusion of giving freedom of choice to the married woman, in reality it constitutes a backward step reaffirming her position in the family and stressing the need to preserve that family no matter what the cost to her.'[64]

Ideas of the undesirability of public involvement in private argument were expressed in the Home Office Memorandum of Evidence to the Select Committee on Violence in Marriage:

It can perhaps be argued that the Government (or the police) cannot have the same responsibility for the day-to-day behaviour of members of a household within their own walls. Some disagreement may be inevitable within a family. Even a degree of minor violence may be normal in some homes. It can perhaps be argued that the point at which the state should intervene in family violence should be higher than that which is expected in the case of violence between strangers or even that the State has no particular responsibility for compensating those who suffer violence in circumstances which are largely (in the case of adult members of a family) under their own control.[65]

Behaviour

Common law does not lay down any code of behaviour for the spouses. It is true that decisions on consortium do give some guidance as to the law's expectations of conduct in marriage. So too do divorce cases, but this *ex post facto* judgement comes on termination of, rather than during, marriage. The idea of consortium is that the spouses shall live together, providing one another with support, services, sex and privacy. A leading family law textbook explains it thus: 'Consortium, then, connotes as far as possible the sharing of a common home and a common domestic life. It is difficult to go beyond this and to define with more precision the duties which the spouses owe to each other: that is, after all, a matter of common knowledge rather than a subject for legal analysis.'[66] The essence of this view is that external conditions, particularly the economic factor of financial support, will determine decision-making in marriage.

In many families the husband's duties will be largely conditioned by the fact that he is the breadwinner: the wife will then usually be primarily responsible for the running of the home, a duty which may take the form of supervising domestic staff or of doing the household 'chores' herself, such as cooking, cleaning, mending and looking after children.[67]

If this is the pattern of the marriage (and in the majority of marriages 'the husband is usually the wage-earner and has to live near his work', according to Lord Denning), it is therefore 'a proposition of ordinary good sense' that the husband can choose the place of residence. Lord Denning qualified this proposition as follows:

> The decision where the home should be is a decision which affects both the parties and their children. It is their duty to decide it by agreement, by give and take, and not by the imposition of the will of one over that of the other. Each is entitled to an equal voice in the ordering of the affairs which are their common concern. Neither has a casting vote, though to be sure they should try so to arrange their affairs that they spend their time together as a family and not apart.[68]

But if one spouse is unreasonable and this produces a separation, the unreasonable spouse is in desertion, and the other spouse can obtain a divorce after two years.

Enforcement of consortium rights is problematic, yet it is only from that case-law that the legal principles, such as they are, can be derived. It has already been shown that financial support is only enforced on breakdown of marriage, although a possible interpretation of the Domestic Proceedings and Magistrates Courts Act 1978 could alter that. There are no legal rules or guidance on household services, although empirical research shows very clear patterns. Enforcement is only attempted through divorce or judicial separation. Sexual conduct is unregulated, although on divorce the courts may have to pronounce on matters such as the quality and quantity of sexual relations.[69]

The privacy of the marital relationship, which the foregoing illustrates, can be confirmed through judicial decisions on marital confidences. The law will protect the relationship by granting an injunction to prevent disclosure of information about 'private life, personal affairs and private conduct, communicated to the defendant in confidence during the subsistence of the marriage'. Ungoed-Thomas J. said:

> There could hardly be anything more intimate or confidential than is involved in that relationship, or than in the mutual trust and confidences which are shared between husband and wife. The confidential nature of the relationship is of its very essence and so obviously and necessarily implicit in it that there is no need for it to be expressed.[70]

So it is on a mixture of common knowledge, good sense and matters so implicit that they do not need to be expressed that the judiciary believes that marriages should be conducted.

Once a marital matter moves into the public sphere it is no longer protected by the law on marital confidences. If a marital matter becomes public through the behaviour of the spouses and through gossip, then, having left the private realm, it is unprotected. On divorce, what was hitherto private is made public in court. It is as if, the marriage being over, it is no longer private, although confidences will still be protected.

Divorce

On divorce the courts explain to the couple the judicial view of marriage, so it is to an analysis of these views that we now turn. Since the Divorce Reform Act 1969 (now consolidated in the Matrimonial Causes Act 1973) there has been only one ground for divorce, and that is breakdown of marriage. Breakdown is evidenced in one of five possible ways: adultery by the respondent, and the petitioner finds it intolerable to live with the respondent; behaviour such that the other spouse cannot reasonably be expected to continue living with the respondent; separation for two years and consent of both spouses to the divorce; separation for five years; desertion for two years by the respondent. In deciding whether the facts show unreasonable behaviour, in particular, the judiciary are forced to indicate their view of appropriate behaviour in marriage. Yet the case-law shows a consistent upholding of the view that each marriage is peculiar to itself and that no general principles or rules can be derived:

a violent petitioner may reasonably be expected to live with a violent respondent; a petitioner who is addicted to drink can reasonably be expected to live with a respondent similarly addicted; a taciturn and morose spouse can reasonably be expected to live with a taciturn and morose partner; a flirtatious husband can reasonably be expected to live with a wife who is equally susceptible to the attractions of the other sex; and if each is equally bad, at any rate in similar respects, each can reasonably be expected to live with the other.[71]

Standard textbooks on family law contain lists of items which in one case or another have been considered sufficient for the grant of a divorce on grounds of behaviour. These range from alcoholism, assault, boorishness, bigamy, constant criticism, criminal conviction, depression, drunkenness and false charges to nagging, neglect, obscene language, physical violence, sexual perversion, sterilisation and venereal disease. What these examples show and the practice of the courts confirms is that each case is judged according to the particular spouses in that particular marriage. The test is: 'Can this petitioner, with his or her character and personality, with his or her faults and other attributes, good and bad, and having regard to his or her behaviour during the marriage, reasonably be expected to live with this respondent?'[72] From this it is clear that no general principles or guidance could, or are intended to, emerge.

Despite a lack of guidance on behaviour in marriage, the law does contain implicit ideological views of the relationship of spouses, which is expressed on divorce. The 'loving and unselfish wife' is entitled to recognition of her good behaviour by the court in awarding maintenance. This has been internalised by the legal profession: 'The wife put in an answer, some part of which is in what has become the standard cliché in these cases, alleging that she was a "loyal, faithful and good wife". Just why these three adjectives have crept into the standard form of pleading, I do not know.'[73]

These views are most clearly expressed when the court comes to decide on the financial consequences of divorce. Faced with a list of items from the Matrimonial Proceedings and Property Act 1970 (now consolidated in the Matrimonial Causes Act 1973) to which the court must look in deciding division of capital assets, including housing, and also in deciding maintenance, the court has discretion. The items range from the primacy of the welfare of the children to the ages of the parties, the length of the marriage, their income and earning capacities, their financial needs and their contribution to the family from paid or unpaid work.[73a]

The first major case was decided by Lord Denning, who laid down that the starting point for dividing the property acquired during marriage was to give one-third to the wife. His view was that it would be 'tempting' to divide the property equally 'if the wife afterwards went her own way'. But if she also wanted maintenance for herself and the children then one-third was fair. He justified this by his reference to gender roles, which has already been quoted. In his view the professional husband needs a woman to look after his house – either a wife or a housekeeper – which involves expense. The divorced woman may work, but can do her own housework, or can look for another husband to support her.[74]

Divorce court registrars whose function is to deal with issues of maintenance, property and custody of and access to children have also indicated that they bring certain assumptions about the sexes to their work. Registrars have wide discretion in the exercise of their powers and, consciously or unconsciously, they use it to favour the party in a conflict with whom they identify and of whom they approve: 'My own view is that I think some weight should go in favour of the good wife and I would be likely to order a bad wife less. The local community, which still retains strong traces of its religious upbringing, would respect this view.'[75] Another registrar clearly operated on the 'just deserts' theory of justice: 'Must one treat all wives in the same way unless they are nymphomaniac or of the worst order – are they to be treated like a faithful wife of 20 years standing who has been nastily and shabbily treated by her husband?'[76]

In such cases it is a private-law obligation of property sharing and maintenance on divorce with which the courts are concerned. Public-law support of those without adequate resources of their own is clearly taken into account by registrars also. In that context the man stigmatised as a 'bad husband' is often the one who cannot support two relationships, both with an ex-partner and a present partner. 'His bread is buttered on the side of the woman he is sleeping with,' said one registrar.[77]

The courts have a firm idea of how a 'good wife' behaves. In *Trippas* Lord Denning said: 'she did what a good wife does do. She gave moral support to her husband by looking after the home. If he was depressed or in difficulty, she would encourage him to keep going.'[78] Scarman L.J. said: 'for over 25 years of marriage she maintained his home; she brought up his children, and she provided . . . the general and moral support to a man sometimes hard pressed by business worries that a good wife does.'[79] The wife in *H*. v. *H*. was described thus by the then President of the Family Division of the High Court:

Her case is that she has contributed to the welfare of the family, including looking after the home and caring for the family: see section 25(f) of the Matrimonial Causes Act 1973; that in the 15 years of marriage she bore the four children, was a wife and mother, and in the early days, washed, ironed, cooked for and looked after a paying guest; that with the husband she decorated a flat they had early in the marriage and part of a house they had in 1963; that she cleaned the stairs and bathroom of a tenanted house the husband owns; and that she gardened and supervised decoration and workmen.

She now says that share should be one-third of the house. If the concept of earning is to be applied to a domestic situation, then it should be applied with all its normal consequences. One is that if the job is left unfinished you do not earn as much. A builder agrees to build four houses. He goes off to a job which he prefers to do, leaving them in various stages of completion . . . . Is there any difference between four houses and four children? I think not.[80]

In *Kokosinski* Wood J. described the wife as follows:

This wife has given the best years of her life to this husband. She has been faithful, loving and hardworking. She has helped him to build what is in every sense a family business. She has managed his home and been a mother to and helped him bring up a son of whom they are both justly proud. I believe that she has earned for herself some part of the family business.[81]

There are a number of other cases in which the judiciary has indicated that there is some norm of behaviour to which a female partner will conform. Thus 'she did much more than many wives would do';[82] 'much more than most women would do'.[83] In these cases 'doing much more' gave the woman in question an equitable share in the home. What is of interest here, however, is the implied normal behaviour for women in marriage-type relations – which is clearly quite different from what is expected of men. As Mary McIntosh observes, 'ultimately the very construction of men and women as separate and opposed categories takes place within, and in terms of, the family.'[84]

The private nature of marriage does not endure after breakdown of the relationship. Judgement is passed on conduct, whether explicitly or implicitly, despite the theory of no-fault divorce. Questions of financial consequences of divorce, although defined as private law, inevitably raise issues of public law, through either social security or taxation. If the future custody of children is in dispute between parents, then questions of work roles adopted during the marriage, future plans concerning employment and marriage, and place of residence arise. Although the custody issue is defined as one in private law, the supervisory powers of the state and legislative powers to take the children into the care of the state mean that public law enters in.

Private Regulation of Marriage

Thus far the argument is that the marriage relationship is unregulated by law. This begs the question as to how marriages are organised, how decisions are made. Attempting to answer this question shows its naivety. Analyses of marriage have been made in terms of power, the division of labour, patriarchy, and constraints imposed by wider society. A review of the literature confirms the private nature of marriage, and it is precisely this privacy that creates the conditions in which inequality flourishes. In a society in which the values of the public world such as competition, individualism and acquisitiveness dominate private lives, and where status is measured by earnings, it is not surprising that those outside the public world with little or no access to money should lack power.

Studies from the 1950s on, starting with Elizabeth Bott's *Family and Social Network*, accept a division of labour in marriage but nevertheless argue that marriages are becoming more equal. Bott distinguished two types of conjugal-role relationship, 'segregated' and 'joint'. In the *segregated* case, 'husband and wife have a clear differentiation of tasks and a considerable number of separate interests and activities'. In the *joint* case, 'husband and wife carry out many activities together with a minimum of task differentiation and separation of interest. They not only plan their family together but also exchange many household tasks and spend much of their leisure time together.' Bott was not concerned with a division of labour; rather she takes this for granted and notes that 'in all families there was a basic division of labour by which the husband was primarily responsible for supporting the family financially and the wife was primarily responsible for housework and child care.'[85] Her interest is in the variations in relationships within this generalisation.

Young and Willmott also accept a traditional division of labour and, in Bott's terms, their study shows a move from segregated role relationship to joint conjugal relationship. They also suggest a gradual assimilation of working-class to middle-class styles of marriage. To the authors there is 'a new kind of companionship between men and women, reflecting the rise in the status of the young wife and children which is one of the great transformations of our time'. Other research does not support this and the thesis has been criticised as highly contentious. It does, however, represent the authors' views of progress towards a more egalitarian family, with a blurring of traditional roles. At the same time it confirms that the sexual division of labour, although not as rigid as in the past, is still in place.[86]

Jan and Ray Pahl's study of managers and their wives shows how the division of labour endures amongst a sector of the middle class. In interviews the wives revealed their personal definitions of their identities as being bound up with their performance of the role of housewife and mother. These women, although lacking any clear sense of social identity, viewed their primary role as domestic. But they felt constrained by their helpmeet role and did not see themselves as autonomous individuals. The Pahls concluded that although the spouses had a perception of marital equality they were constrained by the husband's work role and this gave him the final voice in major decisions:

Many wives are in an ambiguous position, in that the relationship which is most salient to them is one in which they are the less powerful partner, and one in which their roles as wives are dependent on and determined by their husbands. Yet the husbands too are in the position of having their most salient role under the control of others; the competitive nature of their work situation means that they, and so indirectly their wives, must accept such constraints as frequent mobility and a commitment to work of most of their time and energy.[87]

Commenting on these and other studies, Harris suggests that the 'evidence warrants the claim that the traditional division of labour had become less rigid, not that it was in the process of being abolished, or that marital relationships were becoming more *equal*'.[88] His view is that geographical mobility distanced spouses from their kin and that home-centredness became a more pronounced pattern, thus privatising the family. Harris concludes:

Inequalities in domestic activities and decision making have to be understood as the resultants of the persistence of the closed domesticated nuclear family, characterised by intense emotional relationships which have become normatively expected, which entails a division of social life into public and private spheres associated with men and women respectively.[89]

Edgell in his study of middle-class couples published in 1980 finds that power is rooted in the sexual division of labour. In the marriages of his sample, decision-making on matters of money and place of home was not egalitarian but husband-dominated. Even wives with careers of their own who strongly objected to moving elsewhere for the husband's job reasons acquiesced because 'it was good for him' or other self-sacrificing sentiments. His study provides abundant evidence of the survival of patriarchy. 'The research couples legitimated their patriarchal attitudes and practices with reference to custom, biology and sometimes the greater knowledge and involvement of the husband in the more "important" areas of family life.'[90] Edgell concludes that it is the husband's permanent, full-time employment outside the home that determines and legitimates his power. Even if the wife is participating in income-producing economic activity, the tendency for her to be mainly responsible for home and children means that she accommodates the husband, who in turn accommodates to the occupational system. 'Once this pattern of sex role differentiation has been established and is widely supported ideologically, the socio-economic dependence of married women on their husbands is virtually assured.'[91] The couples in the research accepted this: 'neither husbands nor wives apparently felt the need to pay lip service to egalitarian ideas, but boldly asserted their respective domination and subordination.'[92]

What this research makes clear is that structures outside the family fundamentally affect what happens in private. One sphere is not, and cannot be, insulated from the other. As Harris explains: 'while the exclusion of women from the public sphere does not cause, but logically entails, their confinement in the domestic sphere, this confinement has consequences for the behaviour of males in the domestic sphere which, in turn, affects their behaviour in the public sphere.'[93]

Family law textbooks often pose the question whether the law defines marriage as a contract or as an institution. The purpose is to suggest that a contract would be negotiable by the spouses whereas an institution is unchangeable by personal preference. Diana Leonard argues the institutional view, finding that the state supports 'a particular, exploitative relationship between men and women in which the wife provides . . . her labour for life – with limited rights to quit, and herself as an instrument of production, supposedly in exchange for protection, assured upkeep and some rights to children'.[94] To Leonard marriage leaves little negotiation open to the wife, whose relationship to her husband is that of employee to gaffer, the wife deferring to domination. She explains the absence of terms thus: 'the lack of specification reflects the totality of the relationship – of the husband's appropriation of his wife's labour, time and body – . . . it is a relationship of *personal* dependency. The couple work out together what the husband wants her to do.'[95]

Lenore Weitzman argues the contractual view. In a comprehensive review of legal regulation of marriage in the United States she provides considerable evidence of an unwritten contract between spouses whose terms are dictated by the state. This contract is not negotiable, and the argument tends to support the institutional view of marriage. A single model of marriage is imposed on all, which is an unconstitutional invasion of marital privacy, which discriminates on the basis of gender by assigning one set of rights and obligations to husbands and another to wives, denying the diversity and hetero-geneity of pluralist society. Traditional marriage was a hierarchical institution in American society, and although 'the more onerous aspects of patriarchal authority over married women have gradually been removed, vestiges of the traditional system remain firmly entrenched in modern family law'.[96] Weitzman's answer is to regulate marriage by private contract. This will be investigated in Chapter 8.

From Weitzman's work it appears that the terms of marriage are more specific in American law than in English law. But in both countries the boundaries of negotiation in marriage are set by the economic system, and the labour market in particular, as well as by the state. English law leaves it to the couple to sort themselves out in private; but dominance within personal relations is determined by structures external to the family. Gender ideologies and identities ensure that the resulting inequality is accepted as natural and inevitable. 'We are up against something very profound, very stubborn, something we cannot rout out simply by rearranging a few tasks and roles in the social system, or even by reordering the whole economic structure.'[97] The law's role in this is active, despite its absence from the personal. For it constructs gender ideologies and identities for the private as well as public structures which determine the relationship between the sexes. It is to this we turn in Chapter 6.

But the necessary consent to the contract exists. May be more relevant to regard it as a standard form contract which, like the commercial type, is subject to legal regulation when certain consequences result.

6
Public Law from the Private Perspective

'Private faces in public places
are wiser and nicer
Than public faces in private places.'

W. H. AUDEN

Individualism as a theory of society presupposes men who are born free and equal.[1] Steven Lukes has argued that notions of autonomy, privacy and self-development are central to the concept of liberty. 'A person is free in so far as his actions are his own, that is, in so far as they result from decisions and choices which he makes as a free agent, rather than as a result of external or internal forces independent of his will.'[2] An essential component of the ideal of liberty requires some 'minimum "private" area, free from "public" interference' which is essential to the 'inner domain, integral to the self or personality'.[3] The third aspect is the power of self-development. Autonomy, then, rather than interrelation with others, marks individualism.

The theory of society which individualism represents sees society as the product of contracts and associations into which free individuals enter for their own advantage. Economic individualism assumes that it is up to the market participants to strive and use their talents. Each man in pursuing self-advancement is autonomous, and makes personal choices for private ambition. In this analysis it is up to women, as free, equal, autonomous beings, to pursue their own self-interest. In private law it must be largely assumed that women are individuals who make provision for their own economic security. This is why there is no enforced sharing of earnings or community of property. The contradiction is that public law makes no such assumption.

The liberal account of man as a rational choice-maker posits that he enters the public sphere for his own ends. This implies that he has a private aspect apart from his participation in *res publicae*. As Benn and Gaus point out, the idea that all citizens have a dual aspect has not been realised historically in relation to women, who were 'restricted to the domestic realm – the sphere of private, particular interests. Indeed, to the extent that families have not been organic wholes but rather aggregations dominated by a particular will – which was Rousseau's paradigm of a private group – women have been deprived of even domestic common life. In a significant sense, then, women have been private persons, par excellence.'[4]

In his *Social Contract* Rousseau distinguishes a 'people', 'nation' or 'organism' from an 'aggregation' or group of individuals.

No matter how many separate individuals a single person might enslave, they would amount to nothing but a master and his slaves, not at all to a people and its ruler; it would be, perhaps, an aggregation but not an association; it has no public good and no body politic. Even if he should enslave half the world, he remains only a particular individual, his interest, always something apart from the interest of the others, is never anything except a private interest.[5]

An aggregation is a collection of particular private persons, whereas an organic unity is marked by generality of interest which pertains to the whole.

The description of an aggregation dominated by a particular will could be applied to the family. It is the antithesis of individualism as the political theory which explains liberal Western society, and which is called upon by politicians and decision-makers to legitimate the status quo. Yet the state has not treated married women as individuals before public law, whether they are economically active or not. Despite some gradual reform, the household is still regarded in public policy as headed by the husband, with wives as dependants. The family is regarded as a unit and not as a group of autonomous individuals. Married women, then, in public law remain private persons, part of an aggregation we may term the patriarchal family, headed by the husband and father. Yet in private law they are treated as economic individuals. To justify and explain this assertion about public law, examples follow from laws covering social security, taxation and pensions.

Taxation

In 1799 income tax was first introduced by William Pitt to finance war. A married woman's income was to be 'stated and accounted for by her husband'. An Act passed in 1806 to tax 'profits arising from property, professions, trades, and offices' laid down the rule that the income of a married woman living with her husband 'shall be deemed the profits of the husband' (c.65). This rule still applies today in s.37 of the Income and Corporation Taxes Act 1970, which states:

A woman's income chargeable to income tax shall . . . [for any year] during which she is a married woman living with her husband be deemed for income tax purposes to be his income and not to be her income.

The origins of the rule are understandable. It springs from the common law position that husband and wife are a unity legally represented by the husband. But as we saw in Chapter 2 the reforms resulting from the Married Women's Property Acts 1870 to 1882 enabled a married woman to have her own income and separate property as an individual.

Why then should the married couple continue to be taxed as a single unit? And, so long as the couple is treated as a unit, why is it the husband who is legally responsible for the unit's tax affairs? The Royal Commission on Income Tax, which examined the rules on taxation of husband and wife in 1920, explained:

The aggregation for Income Tax purposes of the income of husband and wife is not dependent upon any medieval conception of the subordination of women . . . . The incomes are aggregated because the law of taxable capacity is, in fact, found to depend on the amount of the income that accrues to the married pair, and not upon the way in which that income happens fortuitously to be owned by the members of that union. It is beyond question that in the immense majority of cases where the wife has separate means she contributes to the common purse, either by the actual merger of her income with her husband's, or by bearing expenses which in less fortunate households would fall upon the husband.[6]

This language suggests that the married couple are assumed by Parliament to share equally the income that enters the household. As we saw in Chapter 5 this may be an unwarranted assumption and it is certainly not the basis for judicial allocation of property between married persons. Nevertheless, if implemented elsewhere in relation to the affairs of married couples, the theory would reflect an attractive ideology. Unfortunately, not only is the theory not applied elsewhere, but it is not applied in taxation. The treatment of the married couple as a unit headed by the husband has a deleterious effect on efforts to improve women's position, according to the Equal Opportunities Commission (G.B.):

The aim of seeking to improve women's position in relation to pay will be continually thwarted if the pay that they take home is eaten into by a discriminatory taxation system. Secondly, the principles underlying the current tax law play an important part in reinforcing the second class status of women in other respects and the concept of the male breadwinner who must alone bear all responsibilities for spouse and family.[7]

Aggregation of the income of a married couple means that their incomes are added together and tax is charged, subject to allowances, on the total as if it were the income of one person, and only one set of rate bands is available against the joint income. The principle of aggregation was defended by the Royal Commission on the Taxation of Profits and Income (the Radcliffe Commission) in 1954 as follows:

We see in the existing rule nothing that embodies an outmoded or unworthy conception of the relations of man and woman in marriage . . . . It does appear to us . . . that marriage creates a social unit that is not truly analagous with other associations involving some measure of joint living expenses and that to tax the incomes of two married people living together as if each income were equivalent to the income of a single individual would give a less satisfactory distribution than that which results from the present rule.[8]

It is true that either member of the marriage unit has had, since 1914, the option to apply for separate assessment. This permits the individual to handle his or her tax affairs separately, but does not reduce the total amount of tax payable. Their tax is worked out as a unit but then apportioned individually by the Inland Revenue. The Green Paper, *The Taxation of Husband and Wife*, explained:

The advantage of separate assessment is that it secures for the wife the right to handle her affairs independently, and releases her husband from the responsibility for paying the tax due on his wife's income. It secures for the wife greater privacy.[9]

A further reform to enable the couple to be taxed as two single individuals was introduced in 1971 and is known as the wife's earning election. This is of advantage to a couple earning a sufficient amount as a unit to be taxed at a high rate. The wife's earning election reduces the total tax bill. Although the wife is treated as a single person with respect to her earnings, any investment income she has continues to belong to her husband for tax purposes and he is responsible for the payment of tax on it. Additionally he remains responsible for completing income tax returns for the total income of both spouses. Thus this is not an escape from the theory of marital unity.

To take advantage of the wife's earning election the couple must jointly agree to make the option, which involves forsaking any claim to the married man's tax allowance. That allowance, which was the object of attack and review in the 1970s, was first introduced in 1918. It gives a married man an allowance higher than that given to a single person 'in recognition of the special legal and moral obligations he has to support his wife'.[10] The married allowance is 1.56 times the single allowance but it does not preclude an additional allowance to be set against income earned by the wife. This wife's earned income allowance is the same as that for a single person.

The principle of aggregation means that, regardless of whether the couple receive the married man's allowance or the wife's earned income allowance, or whether they have opted for separate assessment or the wife's earning election, tax reliefs and allowances have to be claimed by and given to the husband even where the expenditure giving rise to the allowance (e.g. mortgage repayments) is incurred by the wife.

It is clear, then, that as far as tax is concerned the state regards marriage as an economic unit. This marriage is not a unit of two equal partners, but is represented and headed by the husband. As the Meade Committee observed:

The idea that a woman on marriage becomes a dependant of her husband, who is then responsible for her welfare and for that of the family, accounts for much of the present treatment of the tax unit. This notion of the dependency of the woman on the man does in fact correspond with reality in many of the older married couples, where the wife, having from the start of the marriage stayed at home to bring up the children, has only a limited possibility of supporting herself at a later date by her own earnings. On the other hand, the notion is becoming less and less compatible with modern attitudes to the relationship between men and women, and in fact it corresponds less and less closely with reality when an increasing number of married women work in paid occupations.[11]

Dissatisfaction with the tax structure gave rise, in 1980, to a Green Paper which outlines the possibilities of reform. The main criteria by which the tax system is to be judged are stated to be fairness, simplicity, sex equality and privacy. Criticisms of the present system are summarised as stemming from social changes which have resulted in greater participation by married women in the labour force since 1960. Financial independence for much of their married life means that many women are critical of the assumptions contained in legislation on income taxation.

The Green Paper identifies two major strands of criticism. One points to discrimination within the marriage unit where the married man's allowance and tax reliefs give the husband preferential tax treatment. The other criticism points to the privileging of some family units over others. Discrimination within the family arises from the aggregation rule which as a matter of principle treats the wife as an appendage of her husband. The practical effects were experienced by those women who wrote to the Inland Revenue only to find that letters and rebates were addressed to their husbands. Administrative procedures have been modified and the Revenue now deals with married women directly. But the principle means that the couple remain a unit headed by the husband.

Preferential tax treatment for husbands through the married man's allowance and other tax reliefs means that where both spouses earn the same amount the husband has a larger take-home pay. This is contrary to the ideology of equality contained in the Equal Pay Act 1970. If the wife has no income she has no claim to a share of the married allowance which, in a sense, is for her.

Criticism of discrimination between family units compares one-breadwinner marriages with couples where both partners are employed. The latter are able to enjoy total tax allowances 2½ times those of a single person. The married man's tax allowance may be an unnecessary privilege for two-earner couples. However, a second strand of criticism identifies the married man's allowance as the source of the problem. Here the argument is that where there are no home responsibilities in caring for dependent or invalid family members, both partners could work and that it is wrong, in principle, for the tax system to subsidise the full-time homemaker.

An interesting aspect of the Green Paper is its comments on privacy. The unitary approach to taxation of married couples means that wives have to reveal to their husbands their earned and unearned income, whereas husbands making the tax return have no such obligation to their wives. This situation is reflected in the following complaint received by the Equal Opportunities Commission:

I have had a Post Office Investment account since 1971 and have saved my own money, and never told my husband, because I wanted to feel I could help my family, i.e. my daughter setting up home, and feel independent. When I withdrew the whole amount, the interest was calculated and [the information] sent to the tax office.

They immediately wrote to my husband, and told him he had omitted something from his return and he was very cross – told them he had declared everything. Eventually they wrote and told him about my interest. *I was not consulted* by the tax office. This has absolutely upset my marriage of many years. Cannot a woman have a little cash to call her own, without upsetting a marriage and causing a lot of misery?[12]

The desire to 'have a little cash to call her own' is a response of the wife to the particular type of marriage structure in which a breadwinner husband's legal responsibility is confined to maintenance; he is under no obligation to share his income or assets with his wife. As the Green Paper puts it:

Some wives object to having to tell their husbands about any savings and investments which they have. They see it as a breach of their personal privacy, perhaps the more so because there is no obligation on the husband to give corresponding information to his wife.[13]

It is not surprising that the public response to the opening up of this issue was to favour individualism. Faced with the existing structure and the criticisms of it as unfair and discriminatory, most respondents opted for individual autonomy. The case for individualism has also been made on grounds of economic efficiency. It is argued that 'the individual basis is unambiguously superior to family unit taxation on the grounds of allocative efficiency and individual equity' and that the present system 'has no compelling advantages in terms of either economic efficiency or administrative ease'.[14] The problem with the individualist approach is that it takes no account of the non-earner spouse. If each person is to have a simple tax allowance to set against earnings this leaves the non-earner without resources. One solution is to press the logic of the family wage to its conclusion and to attribute half the spousal income to each partner. No serious consideration has been given to this.

The Green Paper makes out a strong case for partial transferability of the non-earner's allowance to the earning partner. The proposed proportion reflects exactly the addition received under the current married man's allowance. This approach assumes income-sharing between the partners, but as we saw in Chapter 5 'there is a considerable amount of evidence to suggest that such sharing of income cannot be taken for granted.'[15] Partial transfer of the non-earner's tax allowance is different from an attribution to her of half the earner's income. Objections to transferability have centred on the non-earner who has been described as 'an unjustified financial burden on the community'.[16] The argument is that the needs of those who cannot work because of caring responsibilities should be given priority, and that the proposal is merely a reintroduction of the married man's allowance in a new guise.

The Green Paper brings out the crucial fact that married women's participation in the labour market is conditioned by the presence of children or infirm persons in the household. 'It is noteworthy that in 1978 only 28 per cent of mothers whose youngest child was under 5 worked at all, compared with 67 per cent of mothers whose children were all over 5.'[17] Of an estimated 1,355,000 economically inactive wives without dependent children, 270,000 live in households containing an elderly or disabled person. A powerful case has been made for the redistribution of the married man's tax allowance to households with children.[18] This would mean that a subsidy to married status would be removed and replaced by increased aid to families with children. The objective of making the individual the basis of the tax system would be accomplished. Yet there would be recognition that households with children do not contain aggregates of self-sufficient monads but interdependent members of a small community.

Social Security

The issue of whether the individual or the household should be the unit for the administration of benefits arises in social security policy. For a variety of reasons the state has always based social security legislation on the assumption that the married couple's needs can be aggregated. This presumed unity, which implies that the couple share material needs and satisfactions, stems from the common law doctrine of the unity of marriage, from the Beveridge Report and from the financial cost of individualism.

The merging of the legal personalities of both spouses into that of the husband under common law gave rise to a corresponding duty on the husband to maintain his wife. This was not reciprocal, as it arose from the husband's control of his wife's property. Both spouses have been under a legal obligation to maintain each other since 1971 (Matrimonial Proceedings and Property Act 1970, now consolidated in Matrimonial Causes Act 1973, s.27). This reciprocity was reinforced by the Domestic Proceedings and Magistrates' Courts Act 1978, s.1. Despite this change, the husband's maintenance duty, which has never been enforceable so long as the spouses cohabit, continues to be used by policy-makers and government officials as a justification for treating the couple as one. In social security, because of international treaty obligations, there is a movement towards equal treatment of spouses. However, Beveridge's view that 'on marriage a woman gains a legal right to maintenance by her husband as first line of defence against risks which fall directly on the solitary woman'[19] still remains official.

The Beveridge Report provided the basis for the welfare state. Despite the fact that the report was written in 1942, when women were participating in the war effort by working in unprecedented numbers in factories and on farms, Beveridge foresaw a society in which 'the great majority of married women [are] occupied on work which is vital though unpaid, without which the nation could not continue.'[20] Beveridge believed that most married women would not be gainfully employed, a belief which history shows to have been short-sighted, both prospectively and retrospectively. Also unforeseen was the escalation in divorce, leading to a breakdown-of-marriage rate which is nearing one in three.

Beveridge's assumption that most married women would confine themselves to unpaid work led to three consequences. The first was that the couple were a unit consisting of a breadwinner husband and a dependent wife. Married women were insured through their husbands as wives or widows. The second was that, if they did engage in paid work, wives could elect to pay reduced national insurance contributions: 'it should be open to any married woman to undertake it as an exempt person, paying no contribution of her own and acquiring no claim to benefit in unemployment or sickness.'[21] The third was that even if the married woman 'prefers to contribute and to requalify for unemployment and disability benefit she may do so, but will receive benefits at a reduced rate'.[22]

Thus the married woman had the option either to be insured through her husband as a dependant or to pay a full contribution but to receive less than a single person. The couple as a unit and the roles of breadwinner and dependant became fixed. The idea of treating husband and wife as individuals or the possibility that a wife might need to provide benefits for her children or husband were not even considered. Changes have taken place, which will be detailed below, but Beveridge's structure continues to give shape to the system.

The issue of finance is probably the major reason why the British social security system does not treat persons as individuals. Two single benefits would cost more than the present relationship of single to married benefit which is 1:1.6. The unmarried couple living together are also not treated as individuals by social security law. This is because of the fundamental principle contained in the 'cohabitation rule' that the cohabiting must not be treated more favourably than the married.

The political decision to treat the couple as a unit for social security purposes does not necessarily have to be accompanied by the state's choice of the husband as head of the unit. In this respect social security law has begun to move away from taxation law. Because of Directives from the European Economic Community there has been gradual progress towards equality of the sexes for market reasons. Article 119 of the EEC Treaty provides: 'Each Member State shall during the first stage ensure and subsequently maintain the application of the principle that men and women should receive equal pay for equal work.' Community studies showed that further measures were necessary and in 1975 a Directive was issued on equal pay. This Directive 75/117 concerned the approximation of the laws of Member States on the application of the principle of equal pay and was intended to make the principle more effective.

It might be argued that the principle of equal pay established in Article 119 should be interpreted to cover other benefits arising from employment, including social security. But two more Directives, on equal opportunity and on social security, were considered necessary. The United Kingdom, in anticipation of entry into Europe, took action through domestic legislation. The Equal Pay Act 1970, which came into force in 1975, and the Sex Discrimination Act 1975 were the result. Taxation and social security laws were deliberately excluded from the ambit of the Sex Discrimination Act by s.51, and are not covered by the Equal Pay Act. Therefore it was clear that if there was to be an impetus to 'the task of achieving equal treatment and equal opportunities for men and women in society, and particularly in employment',[23] it would have to come from Europe.

Community interest in equal treatment does not necessarily stem from a belief in human rights. Free movement of workers within the Community is an essential part of the EEC Treaty under Articles 48–51. This is facilitated by certain universal principles in social security laws. Equal pay for equal work ensures that unfair competition is not engaged in by countries underpaying women as cheap labour. Harmonisation of social security laws ensures that products sold within the market are not competitively priced at the expense of individual workers' health and welfare. Since a major part of each national social security system is financed by employers' contributions, unfair competition could be engaged in by employing large numbers of women, for whom the employers' contribution is lower. As the then Commissioner for Social Affairs said in 1980: 'The Fathers of the Treaty were certainly not devotees before their time of women's emancipation. This Article [119] was adopted purely and simply out of the fear that if women workers were underpaid, national industries would suffer a negative effect as regards their competitive position.'[24] Thus market considerations have forced this change.

Directive 76/207, which deals with equal opportunity, covers employment, vocational training, promotion and conditions of work. Directive 79/7 deals specifically with equality of treatment in social security laws. The effect of the latter Directive has been to force the United Kingdom to modify its model of marriage as a relationship of dependence by a wife on a breadwinner husband. The extent to which this has occurred and to which the state has accepted equality will now be considered.

Equal Treatment

The principle of equal treatment of the sexes in social security law has been implemented in United Kingdom legislation. However, the household continues to be treated as a unit for benefit purposes and the needs and resources of members are aggregated. So far as the national insurance scheme is concerned, married women no longer have the option to pay reduced contributions and rely on their husbands. By the end of 1984, when all the reforms have taken effect, employed married women will be able to insure themselves and their spouses and children against unemployment, sickness, maternity, old age and invalidity (Social Security Act 1980, sched. 1). Exclusions contained in Article 7 of Directive 79/7 have enabled the Member State to maintain sex discrimination in relation to certain long-term benefits relating to disablement and invalidity, where differential qualifications for dependency are still applied according to gender.

As a result of the changes it is now recognised that women may be breadwinners and this has been extended to the income-maintenance schemes known as family income supplement and supplementary benefit. Family income supplement is a benefit paid to low-income families with a child where the claimant is in full-time work. The Family Income Supplements Act 1970 specifically precluded a married woman from being the claimant even where she was the breadwinner who supported the family. The Department of Social Security's own figures showed 'that in 1975 about 600,000 women were the sole primary earners of a couple where the husband was under pension age.'[25] This has been amended to enable women to claim the benefit from November 1983 (Social Security Act 1980).

Supplementary benefit is paid to claimants in order to bring their income up to the minimum considered necessary to meet their needs and those of their dependants. Traditionally the claimant was designated the household head, which meant the man in a married or cohabiting relationship. There were objections to this as stereotyping both partners and as ignoring the fact that women's earnings make an essential contribution to the incomes of many households. It was recognised by the Supplementary Benefits Commission in 1976 that 'in more and more families both men and women are combining the role of wage-earner with a share of their joint domestic responsibilities,' and that a gender-neutral system was desirable, 'leaving people as free as possible to make their own arrangements in whatever way suits them best.'[26] The Directive gave impetus to this and regulations have been issued which prescribe circumstances under which the claimant is designated by law (S.I. 1983/1004). These regulations are in line with *Social Assistance*, the review of supplementary benefits published in 1978 by the Department of Health and Social Security.[27]

Social Assistance considered three possible methods of bringing about equal treatment of women and men in supplementary benefits law. The first was 'free choice', in which a couple would decide which partner should claim. The second was 'main breadwinner', under which the partner who had earned more than 50 per cent of the family income during a specified period would be the claimant. The third was that of 'nominated breadwinner', which enabled either partner who had been in full-time work for a specified period prior to the claim to choose to be the claimant. This last option has been the basis of the regulations. It is important to note that at no time did the Department consider giving a married woman the possibility of claiming in her own right as an autonomous individual. The household or the couple remains the unit for social security purposes, and the assumption still remains that one person in the couple is supporting the other, who is economically dependent.

The regulations lay down the aggregation rule whereby only one partner can be the claimant. The identification of the claimant is a matter of applying the regulations to determine which partner was in full-time work or in contact with employment in the previous six months. Where both or neither satisfy the conditions they can make a joint decision in writing as to who is the claimant. However, since the claimant must make a declaration of availability for work, persons pregnant or with small children to look after are disqualified. Behind the equal-treatment regulations the previous gender-based quali-fications continue for many couples. Until the social security system dismantles the household or couple unit, it cannot be said to be based on individuals.

The Directive on Equal Treatment in Social Security (79/7) does not affect the limitation of survivors' benefits to widows only, the differential pension age for women and men or benefits for long-term pensioners. The invalid care allowance, which is paid to persons engaged in full-time care of a disabled relative, has not been extended to married women. Both widows' benefits and the invalid care allowance illustrate the problem. Under the social security system there are a variety of benefits and allowances for the widow, depending on her age and whether she has children at home. There is no dependency test for eligibility for these benefits. Rather they are regarded as earned by the national insurance contributions of the deceased husband. But a widower, dependent though he may have been, is not entitled to equal treatment, despite his deceased wife's contributions. On the other hand, a married or cohabiting woman who gives up paid work to care for an invalid does not get invalid care allowance as her husband is expected to support her. Thus the ideology of the united spouses headed by the husband with a dependent wife continues to hold sway, despite the reforms made to comply with international obligation.

The merging of the identity of the spouses for social security purposes means that benefits for the dependant are mediated through the insured. This system does ensure that both the breadwinner and the dependant are provided for – so long as the marriage lasts. The widow is also given special recognition. Divorce, however, an accident that is likely to occur to one in three marriages, leaves the economically dependent spouse with no insurance record in a parlous state. Individual insurance for all adults would be one answer to this.

Pensions

Making provision for old age through state or occupational pension schemes can only be done by wage-earners, through contribution from their earnings. If each spouse has an individual insurance record, each will have an individual pension. A problem arises when one spouse has an insufficient or no record and is dependent on the other to provide for old age. The usual case is the housewife. There are, however, an estimated 600,000 marriages where the wife is the sole earner and the husband is under pension age.[28] Since marriage is regarded as a unit which provides benefits for both spouses under social security law, it would be reasonable to conclude that the contributions of either spouse could provide for the unit's future; this does not always follow.

The male breadwinner who supports a dependent wife is the model for social security legislation relating to the marriage unit. This means that the state pension scheme recognises that provision will have to be made for the dependent wife on retirement or death of the male breadwinner. The retired female breadwinner cannot provide the same pension rights for her husband or widower. The EEC Directive on Equal Treatment in Social Security does not apply to survivors' benefits, such as widowers' benefits (Art. 3.2). Under Article 7 Member States were permitted to exclude equality of treatment of dependent spouses in relation to old-age pension, and the United Kingdom government has done so. These discriminations are likely to be eliminated in the future, and it is already possible for a widower to rely on his wife's contributions in order to obtain a retirement pension (Social Security (Pensions) Act 1975, ss.8 and 16). The extent to which marriage is treated as a unit does vary according to whether its public representative is wife or husband.

The determination of the pension age of state benefit was also excluded by the United Kingdom government under Article 7. The Economic and Social Committee of the Community has recognised that 'the compulsory earlier retirement for women in some sectors in some Member States constitutes a real source of major discrimination against women.'[29] Earlier retirement from a shorter working life means a smaller pension, as does failure to achieve equal pay. Men are discriminated against in that many public concessions in travel, medical and dental care relate to having reached pensionable age.

Occupational pension schemes are not covered by the social security Directive (79/7, Art. 3.3). A report published by the Occupational Pensions Board in 1976 suggested that equality of treatment of men and women on an individual basis should be the goal of legislation on pensions. This is the position adopted by the Commission of the European Community. The suggestion that benefits for each sex group as a class should be compared was rejected. This suggestion would have taken account of differential retirement ages and mortality rates, and would have resulted in lower benefits for women.[30] The individualism under discussion here is the individual comparison of particular men and women to ensure equality of treatment. This does not prevent recognition of their membership of family communities in which they have economic responsibilities. As far as these responsibilities are concerned the Occupational Pensions Board took the view that there should be no distinction on grounds of sex. This is desirable but if the issue of individualism versus community membership is reassessed as a question of family commitment, a major problem remains.

Part-time employees are largely excluded from occupational pension schemes. In Great Britain in 1970 a total of 49.8 per cent of full-time employees were members of occupational pension schemes, but only 5.6 per cent of part-time workers were. Fourteen per cent of male part-time workers had such membership but only 4.5 per cent of women part-time workers had.[31] Between 1951 and 1971 the number of married women part-time workers increased by 296 per cent, and the Department of Employment attributes this to mothers re-entering the labour force.[32] It has already been stressed that family commitments determine women's participation in paid employment. 'By 1971, the birth of the first child, rather than marriage, had become the most usual reason for a woman to give up paid work. In 1921 it had been the other way around. The care of children was not only the main reason for giving up paid employment; it was also the main reason for not seeking work.'[33] The Central Statistics Office reports that in a sample taken of mothers in Britain for 1980–2, 73 per cent of married mothers and 77 per cent of lone mothers were not in paid employment, where their children were under five. Of mothers of children over nine years, 30 per cent of the married and 41 per cent of the unmarried were economically inactive.[34] If individualism is taken to refer to the pursuit of self-sufficiency by the isolated monad then who is to care for the young, the infirm, the elderly and those in need?

Is Marriage an Economic Unit or an Aggregate of Two Individuals?

'Unintentionally, modern welfare states have come close to realising a dream of the French Revolution: the citizen stands in direct relation to the state, without intermediaries.'[35] Thus Professor Glendon sums up what she believes is the inevitable direction of Western family life towards individualism. Yet, as we have seen, the trend is not uniform. In marriage law the treatment of the couple as a private unit remains unchanged. In public law there has been some acknowledgement of individualism but the policy of treating marriage as an economic unit continues. Where Professor Glendon is right is in identifying the post-war rise in divorces as a major challenge to the unity of marriage.

Housewifery is a high-risk occupation. Because during her marriage the housewife is merged with her husband in the private marriage unit, her public persona may be hidden unless she enters the world of paid employment. The majority of women do earn wages for a portion of their married lives. The Green Paper on Taxation estimated that in 1979 about 6.5 million married women were economically active, whilst about 4.5 million were inactive. However, when the economically inactive group was further examined it was clear that over 3 million had dependent children to care for. This meant that the remaining inactive women, of whom over a million were aged between forty-five and fifty-nine, only totalled 1.350 million. About 270,000 of these lived in households containing an elderly or disabled person. Women over sixty were excluded from these estimates.

Since the economically dependent wife is insured through her husband's social security and pension contributions it might be argued that her needs are provided for. It is true that if the breadwinner dies the social security provision for widows is adequate. But what of the risk of divorce? With one in three marriages estimated to end in divorce it is a relatively high risk. If the person caring for spouse, children and home is involved in the accident of divorce she emerges into the public world as an uninsured individual. About half of all divorces take place in Britain in the first ten years of marriage. Two-thirds of the children of divorced parents are under eleven.[36]

The assumption of the role of housewife on marriage by the majority of women cannot be ignored. Over 90 per cent of women in Britain marry and in 95 per cent of marriages the husband is the chief economic support of the family.[37] Married women do take paid employment, as shown above, but there is a clear pattern of part-time work, shorter hours and lower earnings in work done by women by comparison with men. One accepted explanation for the pattern is that duties in the home interfere with women's full participation in work; and the evidence is that, even where both spouses work, women retain prime responsibility for home and children. Withdrawal from the labour market in order to raise children, or working part-time, has serious consequences. The loss of training, work experience, insurance and pensions record leaves the housewife without economic protection. For instance in 1977 about one in five female part-time employees were defined as 'non-employed' for social security purposes. They were not insured persons. By 1981 this had increased to one-half.[38]

In the course of marriage, housework and childcare by a partner are unpaid. This is not to say that the work has no material value. There are legal procedures in tort for valuation of household services on death or disablement. The contribution made to the family by work in the home is one of the factors taken into account by the divorce court in considering financial and property allocation. But this recognition only comes when the private becomes public. To suggest that household services be valued and quantified during marriage is to import commercial values into the private world. Yet the work is unpaid precisely because it is performed in private. It is only when the work becomes a public issue that an attempt is made to value or quantify it.

Quantifying the value of household services is seen not only as the intrusion of commercialism where it is out of place, but also as meaningless: 'Domestic labour is unproductive in the economic sense.'[39] The very fact that housework is performed privately poses a problem. 'There are no public rules dictating what the housewife should do, or how and when she should do it.'[40] Yet in tort cases the courts have found it possible to make an estimation of the value of particular houseworkers to their families. Whether the housewife's services are valued by calculating the cost of employing a replacement, or by calculating the opportunity cost of the housewife's time in an alternative use in the market, the courts do put a price on those services. But this reference to the values of the market-place is made only at time of crisis in the household due to injury or death.

The unease of the courts in this exercise of public valuation of private services can be illustrated by consideration of the policy on remarriage. In dealing with a claim by a husband for the loss of his wife under the Fatal Accidents Act 1976 the likelihood of his remarriage is taken into account, and may reduce his compensation for his loss. The remarriage reduction suggests an assumption that a later wife will accept the role of the deceased including care of existing children, and that these services will be unpaid, whereas until marriage they will be paid. The remarriage prospects of widows are no longer considered by courts under similar circumstances. This is because it was considered distasteful for courts to have to make estimates about a widow's prospects as this required judgements about sexual attractiveness (Law Reform Act 1971, s.51). This double standard has judicial sympathy:

I think that generally speaking a widower has a greater chance of remarriage than a widow for the simple reason that if a widower is desirous of seeking another partner to assist him in the rest of his life he can go out and search. He can put himself into circulation. He can create circumstances that will enable him to pass a diplomatic message to those of the opposite sex whom he meets that he is indeed anxious for remarriage. A widow, of course, is not in the same position, and if she is a lady, of course, she will not want to go out and forage, looking for a man.[41]

If the policy is to compensate for financial loss of breadwinner or housewife, remarriage of widow or widower seems equally germane. If the policy is that of compensation for loss of an individual rather than of an economic part of the marriage unit, remarriage should be ignored. The tension between treating the family as an economic unit and maximising the autonomy of the individual is obvious here.

So long as housework is performed within marriage it is unpaid. When it emerges into the public world a value is attributed to it. Cohabitants have no right of action under the Fatal Accidents Act 1976, so any housework performed in that relationship remains private, although the children can act. If housework performed in the course of a relationship of marriage or quasi-marriage were classified as work there would be many practical consequences. Housewives would be insured persons under the state insurance scheme. (At present the only recognition is that where a contributor is 'precluded from regular employment by responsibilities at home' up to twenty years may be credited for retirement pension, widow's pension and widowed mother's allowance. The contributor must, however, have been in 'regular employment', in addition, for a minimum of twenty years – Social Security Pensions Act 1975, s.19(3).) Accidents in the home would be treated like accidents at work. The housewife would be regarded as an individual worker, rather than as the dependant of a breadwinner. The one-in-three risk of divorce would be insured against.

State policy is largely directed towards marriage and the nuclear family as a single economic unit. There are some exceptions which are the product of piecemeal change. The outlines of the structure remain in place. The message to those within is changing, however. Dependence on marriage for economic security is risky. The argument is now about 'who is to bear the cost of the deadly combination of child care, marriage and serial polygamy practised by persons of modest means'.[42]

There are a variety of legal models for risk-distribution on marriage and divorce. An individualist model suggests that dependence should be avoided and the individual should insure herself. An accident model of divorce suggests that either the negligence/fault approach should be used for compensation or that (as has already happened) a no-fault/no-liability model be introduced. An employment-contract model suggests redundancy payments. A welfare model suggests need. But the thesis here is that the crux of the problem is the movement from private dependant to public individual on divorce.

Women's Work

An individualist answer to the problems of married women's dependency is to suggest entry into the labour market. A job, a wage, a social security record, a pension, all the attributes of an individual in market society, will be acquired, it is thought, through labour-market participation. This is a solution approved by marxists and most feminists also. But analysis of existing gender roles and consequent identities which are internalised by women leads to the conclusion that this is only a partial solution. If we consider the clash of values between the private and the public, the difference between giving and sharing on one side and calculating and competing on the other, we see the dilemma for those who are socialised into self-sacrifice other than self-interest. Furthermore there are genuine material problems for the primary parent of young children in adapting to the demands of the labour market for full-time committed workers unhampered by the needs of the private. This is why married women's labour-market participation shows a pattern of outwork and part-time work.

The outworker or homeworker is a private worker. The term is given to 'someone working in or from the home for an employer or contractor who supplies the work and is responsible for marketing and selling the results'.[43] Since the term homeworker may be confused with that applied to the unwaged doing domestic labour, for purposes of clarity the term outworker will be used. There are similarities between the isolation of the outworker and the domestic labourer but the former is waged whereas the latter is not.[44]

A survey done in 1981 estimates that people working at home or from home as a base are about 3 per cent of the labour force. If construction, transport/haulage and family workers are added, the estimated figure is 4 per cent, although some guesstimates put it as high as 7 per cent.[45] Not all these workers are women. Although outworking is traditionally associated with manual work, particularly sewing, it now includes clerical work, market research and computer-related work such as systems analysis. What is striking however is that although married women only made up 26 per cent of the labour force overall in England and Wales in 1981, they formed 38 per cent of outworkers. And it seems that male outworkers predominantly use their home as a base from which to work (71 per cent), whereas women form the great majority of those doing the outwork at home (71 per cent). In other words male outworkers are likely to be doing the transport, construction, clerical and professional jobs whereas female workers are likely to be doing manufacturing work, typing, paid childminding.[46]

Although these figures belie the traditional image of the outworker as a woman at a sewing machine, this worker has been a cause for parliamentary concern:

many homeworkers are poorly paid; work in unpleasant conditions; and enjoy no security of employment. To some extent, these are features of the homeworkers' weak bargaining position: homeworkers are generally not unionised and so tend not to be covered by collective agreements; they are relatively isolated from other workers, especially if caring for children or elderly or disabled relatives.[47]

Outwork performed at home fits in with the demands of the family, whether young, ill or old. Persons working at home must be distinguished from those who work from home. The 1981 survey suggests that although outworking now encompasses white-collar and service work, which has overtaken traditional manufacturing work as the predominant type of home-based work, motives, perception and conditions are very different according to the work performed. Manufacturing outworkers are likely to work for one employer, to regard themselves as employees, to be women, and to be largely unprotected by and invisible to the law.[48] Their motives for outwork are that it is home-centred. The work is similar or identical to that performed in factories. Self-employed outworkers are more likely to work from home but outside the home, for two or more clients or employers, and are more likely to be male. They may have high earnings, make provision for social security and pensions, and choose to work from home because it gives them freedom of manoeuvre and negotiation.

Manufacturing homeworkers are excluded from wages-council protection, and 'because there are no adequate records, little is known of the industries in which these workers are engaged, or of the conditions in which they work.'[49] For social security purposes these workers are treated as self-employed, but recent court decisions have raised doubts as to whether this is so for purposes of unfair dismissal and redundancy payments. To be covered by the Employment Protection Act outworkers must have a contract of service and must have been continuously employed for 52 weeks to claim unfair dismissal and for 104 weeks to claim redundancy payments.

Cases holding that a contract of service exists give some insight into conditions of outworkers. In *Airfix Footwear Ltd* v. *Cope* the employers provided the machinery and the objects to be manufactured, gave directions as to performance, and kept the outworkers supplied with work and production targets. The Employment Appeals Tribunal held that there was an 'overall' or 'umbrella' contract obliging the employers to continue to provide and pay for work, and the employees to continue to accept and perform the work provided. This was because 'the respondents decided the thing to be done, the manner of performance, the means of performance, and in reality the time and place of performance'.[50] In other words, the conditions of work were very close to those in the factory. This was so also in *Nethermere (St Neots) Ltd* v. *Taverna and Another*.[51] The employers manufactured boys' trousers and employed about seventy people in their factory. In addition they used outworkers in whose homes were installed machines provided by the company. From the wages of the factory employees were deducted taxes and social security payments; this was not so with the outworkers. There was a daily delivery of garments to the outworkers who worked between four and seven hours a day. A dispute arose over lack of holiday pay, the work was discontinued by the company, and the two applicants complained of unfair dismissal. The Employment Appeal Tribunal found that a contract of service existed.

These cases are of interest partly because they reveal the vulnerability and relative weakness of outworkers. The intervention of the law to protect them is to be welcomed, although the hurdle of proving continuous work for the periods of 52 or 104 weeks required by the law is difficult to overcome. This is because many employers do not keep the workers supplied, or because family responsibilities interfere.[52] Outworkers are not unionised and there is evidence of trade-union agreements which require that they be dispensed with as soon as any short-time occurs in the factory.

Women's work is still shaped around the family. Work part-time, or at home, is essentially supportive work both in financial terms of the main earner and in domestic labour terms, in that it enables the combination of two roles. Where married women are economically active they are more likely to work part-time than full-time. In 1981 in 25 per cent of marriages the wife worked full-time and in 32 per cent of marriages the wife worked part-time. Four per cent were unemployed and 39 per cent were economically inactive.[53] Part-time work has the advantage of providing some financial support to the family whilst at the same time putting the family first. However, there are dangers that the part-timer will not qualify for a social security record or a pension. If a worker is employed for less than sixteen hours a week, or has wages below a minimum level, no social security payment is made by employer or employee. This may be an attraction for employers in using part-timers. The point has already been made that in 1976 about one in five female part-time employees were defined as non-employed for social security purposes. By 1981 this had increased to one-half.[54] So these women remain their husbands' dependants within the national insurance system. Despite their economic activity they are not classed as individuals.

Conclusion

The criticism that is levelled against marriage and the family as an economic unit is directed against a particular form of family structure. It does not necessarily follow that the answer is to treat the individual as the unit to be administered. Many of the criticisms of the current marriage form relate to its structure of male breadwinner and female dependant, which is seen as neither just nor corresponding to reality. It is not obvious that a switch in public law to individualism in the administration of persons will necessarily bring about justice. Although current state policy of treating the husband and father as public representative of the family reinforces the deference accorded to the breadwinner, both as earner and as man, the woman's role as primary parent, allied to the subordination of her individual interest to the family, means that for a period of her life, both in reality and in law, she will be a dependant. She will lead her existence in private and not in the public market-place of labour. If she is married, she will encounter the state and its officials only through her husband as mediator.

The contradiction involved here is that the state imposes communality and sharing of the burdens and benefits of taxation and social security in public law, thus denying the individualism of the spouses. Yet in private law, individualism with its central values of privacy and autonomy provides the justification for state refusal to intervene to impose a form of community. Compare the sharing implied by the notions of family wage and widows' pension with the individualism of no rights to a share of earnings or occupational pension, and no pension for widowers. Patriarchy is legitimated and reinforced in both private and public. As Roberto Unger rightly points out,

familial relationships are abandoned to the exploitation of power advantages within the family under the guise of respect for the integrity of the family group. In liberal society, the law of communal solidarity is repeatedly imposed upon public life in the name of the law of the jungle and the law of the jungle upon private life in the name of the law of communal solidarity.[55]

The private woman stands in opposition to the general movement towards individualism that has occurred in Western democracies over the past two centuries. Family values are ancient and the denial of individualism may be the attraction for many mothers and families, even for those who are required to subordinate their personal self-interest. It is sad that we seem to be forced to choose between the competitiveness and egoism of the modern industrial world, and the values of love, trust and interrelatedness of family and the personal life.

PART THREE
Crossing the Divide: Reformist Possibilities

The analysis contained in the two preceding parts is designed to expose law's contingency on cultural and other factors. Yet law is relatively autonomous and therefore possibilities of changing it do exist. That is what the final part of this book considers. Chapter 7 examines reforms which deal with the market-place and which are premised on individualism. Chapter 8 is concerned with various strategies to change family relations through law. The conclusion is that reforms which do not confront the division between private and public will fail, for within each proposed reform are the seeds of conflict.

7
Reforming the Public: Why Can't a Woman Be More Like a Man?

'The woman who lives for others . . . and you can tell the others by their hunted expressions.'

C. S. LEWIS

Analysis in previous chapters has exposed the dichotomy between men and women, between public and private, between market and family, between individualism and community. The suggestion is that, although boundaries may shift, these dichotomies nevertheless continue. Maintaining a divide does not mean complete separation of public and private. This chapter continues the argument that what happens in one sphere influences the other and that consequently it is an illusion to think that complete separation can occur. This is illustrated by reforms which have taken place in response to women's demands for equality.

The ideology of equality which nineteenth-century women relied on in their struggle against discriminatory laws and practices which denied them access to education and employment was formal equality. Freedom from legal restriction and equal access to law and the vote were the goals. The interaction between private and public and the consequent restraints on freedom were ignored. Hidden behind the rhetoric of equality were issues of whether to recognise in the public sphere needs which arise out of the private. This continues today. The conflict reformers face between the values of individualism in the market-place and community in the family has been managed hitherto through reliance on language of freedom of contract and formal equality.

This chapter examines reform strategies designed to affect the public arena; reforms which have been presented as ensuring equality. Chapter 8 will consider the reform of the private.

The Demand for Equality

In locating the origin of an idea it is not easy to be precise. Ideas about equality of men and women, or of all men, can be identified as coming from a number of sources. Classical political thought as exemplified by Plato and Aristotle accepted as natural male dominance and female subordination. In his *Politics* Aristotle claimed that the good life is possible only through participation in the *polis*. Men, but not slaves, women or children, are intended to live in a *polis* where the highest good is attained. Those in the *polis* are dominant but 'there must necessarily be a union of the naturally ruling element with the element which is naturally ruled, for the preservation of both.'[1] Women's non-participation in the *polis* meant that they were to be ruled. Their place was in the household, which was not part of public life.

Participation in public life was confined to freemen and was essential to the possession of moral goodness in its full and perfect form. The 'naturally ruled' needed only to possess moral goodness to the extent their situation required. As Elshtain explains: 'Aristotle's women were *idiots* in the Greek sense of the word, persons who either could not or did not participate in the polis or the "good" of public life.'[2] As private persons women lived out their lives in the realm which supported and made necessary political life. Their lives were deemed inferior in essence, intent and purpose to those lives which participated in *res publicae*.

Subordination and non-participation in political life were closely connected in Aristotle's schema. Nineteenth-century suffrage reformers agreed with his analysis. Acquisition of the right to vote was seen as a badge of adulthood and equality with other adults. Although the suffrage campaign was the major rallying point for women's demands for equality one of the earliest denunciations of women's inequality concentrated on education. In 1790 Mary Wollstonecraft answered Edmund Burke's dismissal of the ideas of the French revolution with a spirited defence of egalitarianism entitled *A Vindication of the Rights of Men*. Two years later she followed this with her similarly titled book on women. Equality is not the basic premise from which the second volume starts. It is with certain pragmatic arguments about the unsuitability of uneducated women to be mothers and the consequent evils for society if women concentrate on being toys for men. Wollstonecraft argues that if women are educated for dependence and submission there are dangers of tyranny by the husband when alive, and later of insecurity for the widow and fatherless children. The book does not directly advocate equal access for women into the public world of work and state. Marriage, children and the domestic world are accepted as the province of women and the argument is directed at improving women's performance of their role in this sphere. Wollstonecraft's belief in education for women and the co-education of children was the cornerstone of her philosophy. It is not surprising that she did not directly challenge the exclusion of women from participation in public affairs, for many men were also excluded at the end of the eighteenth century. She does occasionally reveal another vision:

A wild wish has just flown from my heart to my head, and I will not stifle it, though it may excite a horse-laugh. I do earnestly wish to see the distinction of sex confounded in society, unless where love animates the behaviour. For this distinction is, I am firmly persuaded, the foundation of the weakness of character ascribed to women.[3]

Wollstonecraft's vision of a society in which there is no distinction between the sexes, except in love, has not been realised.

New ideas were brought into Parliament with the Reform Act 1832, which broadened the group of male electors. The new Members held bourgeois beliefs; they believed in the family as the foundation of society, in the partnership of spouses and in the role of legislation in engineering social reform. A new composition of Parliament enabled the passing of legislation on judicial divorce, married women's property and, eventually, women's access to professional and higher education, and the vote.

One of the major nineteenth-century exponents of liberal ideas on the equality of the sexes was John Stuart Mill. *The Subjection of Women*, published in 1869, opens with the statement that the legal subordination of women to men is wrong in principle and ought to be replaced with perfect equality. This equality was formal in that Mill argued that individuals should choose their own destinies and that status-regulated society was a relic of the past. Mill detailed the instances of the wife's slavery in marriage, particularly under common law, in relation to property, sexual intercourse, children and physical force.

In arguing for equality in marriage Mill favoured a property rule whereby 'whatever would be the husband's or wife's if they were not married, should be under their exclusive control during marriage.'[4] This individualistic approach of separation of the spouses' affairs sums up the problems of the liberal position. For Mill accepted a division of labour between the sexes and separate spheres. His object was to make women equal to men by the removal of juridical obstacles. He did not recognise that the maintenance of separate spheres would constitute a major problem. His notion of equality was limited to the lifting of *de jure* barriers to women's participation in the public sphere.

The liberal belief in formal equality leaves untouched issues of power and privilege. Yet in its time it provided an ideal around which reformers and feminists could coalesce. Mill's focus was on law reform. 'The disabilities, therefore, to which women are subject from the mere fact of their birth, are the solitary examples of the kind in modern legislation.'[5] Remove these disabilities and educated women voters could compete equally with men in the market. This definition of equality as equality of opportunity, with tangible goals of repealing legislation which treated women differently from men, provided targets for campaigns. Disparate groups which did not agree in their philosophies could come together in efforts to change the law.

The claim of women to be treated equally with men seems, in retrospect, to be obviously just. Once the idea of a fundamental principle of equality has arrived we wonder how the opponents justified their case. A fundamental principle does not, however, necessarily give direction as to its realisation. It is easy to assent to a principle that there should be no legal restrictions on women's competition with men in the market-place. But whether such formal equality creates material equality remains a matter for disagreement and debate. Protective legislation provides a good example of the complexities of the issues.

Protective Legislation: A Problem?

Legislation providing for differential treatment of women and men in factories, and that prohibiting work by women underground in mines, is called 'protective'. Under the Factories Act 1961, s.86, women's factory hours of work must not exceed nine a day, nor exceed forty-eight a week; the period of employment must not exceed eleven hours a day, nor begin earlier than seven o'clock in the morning, nor end later than eight o'clock in the evening, nor, on Saturday, later than one o'clock in the afternoon; no continuous period of work shall exceed four and a half hours without an interval of half an hour, or, if there is a rest period of not less than ten minutes, then the period can be increased to five hours. Under s.89 Sunday and night work are prohibited and overtime is restricted. Exemptions are possible for individual factories, or, by ministerial regulation, for entire industries. Under the Mines Act, women cannot be coalminers underground.

From the 1960s discussion of separate classification of the sexes has proceeded on the assumption that this leads to discrimination against women. Protective legislation has posed a problem. Do the dictates of the principle of equality require that such legislation be repealed? This has been a disputed issue and it gives a clue to major problems which underlie it. The enactment of protective legislation in the nineteenth century was a victory for reformers interested in the welfare of women and children. Engels's description of conditions amongst the working class in the mid-nineteenth century includes several laments for the destruction of the family by the employment of women:

That the general mortality among young children must be increased by the employment of the mothers is self evident, and is placed beyond all doubt by notorious facts . . . . The employment of the wife dissolves the family utterly and of necessity, and this dissolution, in our present society, which is based upon the family, brings the most demoralising consequences for parents as well as children.[6]

Lord Shaftesbury's Mines Regulation Act 1842 and Ten Hours Act 1844 restricting the work of children and women in factories and mines was approved by Engels.

Protective legislation was undoubtedly influenced by the bourgeois ideal of the family incorporating separate spheres. It overlooked the fact that the home was a place of work for lacemakers, straw-plaiters, glove-makers, nail-makers, frame-work knitters and domestic workers. Women dressmakers and milliners also worked very long hours. Because nineteenth-century reports concentrated on factories, women workers there came in for public scrutiny; but the charges that were made of long hours – destruction of home life, ignorance of domestic economy, moral degradation – could have been made against the conditions of working-class women generally. Protective legislation was only directed at that group of women workers who had been the subject of investigation. Yet the desire to protect these women was informed by the belief that their primary duty was to their families.

Some writers have suggested that it was in the interests of working men to remove women as competitors in mine or factory and to restore them to the home. In a detailed study of the Mines Regulation Act 1842 Jane Humphries has found no evidence to support this.[7] No doubt additional services or comforts in the home were appreciated but these could only be the result of an acceptance by employers of a family wage to support wife and children. The mid-nineteenth-century evidence is that manufacturers opposed any form of regulation of work for women or children, or indeed for anyone. It is true that the early twentieth century saw the domestic ideal made possible for most families with the rise in the male wage. To Ivy Pinchbeck the assumption that men's wages should be paid on a family basis prepared the way for the 'conception that in the rearing of children and in home-making, the married woman makes an adequate economic contribution'.[8]

Marxist historians explain the emergence of the idea of the family wage in terms of the reproduction of a working class fit to carry out its task. It seems that the state and bourgeois philanthropists on the one hand, and the emergent Chartist and trade-union movement on the other, shared an interest in limiting hours of work, protecting women and children, and introducing compulsory education. The family wage, whether or not it raised the value of labour power, was a powerful support to the liberal philosophy of separate spheres. It assisted the withdrawal of women from the labour market in the early twentieth century, and combined with the theory of the unity of the spouses it has informed state policy towards the family. Resulting from this new family form embodying the cult of domesticity we find that the 1910 census recorded only 10 per cent of married women with paid employment, a decrease from the 25 per cent recorded in 1851. However, the census may not be entirely reliable in that it does not record women's economic activities which were an extension of their domestic role, such as taking in washing or boarders, or child-minding.

Protective legislation, then, was imbued with beliefs about the primacy of women's domestic role, couched in the language of paternalism. This was made clear in *Muller* v. *Oregon* where judicial approval for limiting days, times and hours women could work was based on arguments about motherhood, duties to the family, lack of physical strength and separate classification.[9] Examination of motherhood gives a clue to one source of conflict for equality proponents.

Motherhood: A Source of Discrimination?

In the 1960s evidence of women's lack of participation in the public world of education and employment was widely accepted. Since *de jure* obstacles to participation had been largely removed, the suggestion that *de facto* discrimination by employers and others be made illegal gained credence. The result was the passing of the Equal Pay Act 1970 and the Sex Discrimination Act 1975. Both Acts were designed to enforce equality of opportunity by prohibiting discrimination against women in relation to wages, provision of goods and services, education and employment. The belief was that if the market was forced to accept women on equal terms with men then women would also participate in equal numbers. It is at this point that protective legislation becomes a problem and also illustrates the tension between home and work.

'Our legal structure will continue to support and command inferior status for women so long as it permits *any* differentiation in legal treatment on the basis of sex.'[10] Three reasons are offered for this: many women do not fit the female stereotype on which differential treatment is predicated; all aspects of separate treatment are interrelated, creating discriminatory patterns from one area to another; a dual system of rights and responsibilities in which different values govern each group results in domination and subordination. If this is true, the repeal of protective legislation would seem to be the answer. If, on the other hand, women's biological role in reproducing children is the rationale of protection, the legislation is serving children's needs. Under current policy women's ability to give birth, their social role as mothers and the health of future generations are seen as requiring state control of women's hours of employment. But it is children who are being protected and for their sake women's freedom is being restricted.

Anti-discrimination legislation contained in the Equal Pay Act 1970 and the Sex Discrimination Act 1975 promotes equal access and rewards for women and men in the public world of the market-place. Education, employment, goods, services and credit terms are to be available to women on the same terms as men. The goal is equal opportunity for both sexes to share in the benefits and burdens of competition in the market. Equality of opportunity in liberal philosophy presupposes persons who start out equal. But 'the more the wife/mother devotes herself to the supporting, nurturing and socialising functions of the family the more she disables herself in market terms.'[11] Thus many women do not get an equal start with their male competitors. Furthermore state legal rules in public law fields such as taxation, pensions and social security were deliberately omitted from the anti-discrimination legislation, leaving the state as possibly the most discriminatory public body of all.[12] And, of course, the Acts do not affect the domestic world.

Equality of opportunity might be considered a minimal goal for the laws on equality of the sexes. At present the reality of legislative provision does not attain that minimum. To do so, further measures would be necessary. Ensuring that all women get an equal start with men would require legislation which takes account of private domestic roles. To some extent, as will be shown later, the concept of indirect discrimination has the potential to do this. Other measures that have been suggested include greater involvement of men in the home, alteration of work patterns for all workers to take account of domestic responsibilities, and rights of parental leave for childcare created by legislation.[13]

There are alternative conceptions of equality other than just opening up opportunities. So long as equality remains a formal notion, like the Ritz hotel which is open to all, structural obstacles will prevent those for whom opportunities are opened from taking advantage of them. Another way of approaching sex equality is to look at the distribution of burdens and benefits in the society under consideration. From the results of this survey a conclusion can be reached as to the success or otherwise of legislative measures. A result-oriented approach tries to go beyond the formality of equality of opportunity. Both measures of equality however are confined in academic discussion to the public sphere. So unless equality of results is allied to changes in the private sphere it is only a half measure.

Even where the goal of equality of opportunity has been spelled out in anti-discrimination legislation it comes up against contradictions in state policy towards women because biology is thought to necessitate the protection of women as workers, whereas the market demands participants devoid of the personal. Protective legislation in market and individualistic terms seems to be contrary to the spirit of anti-discrimination.

In the past the justification for protective legislation covered women's unsuitability for market participation because of their 'natural and proper timidity and delicacy';[14] the threat posed to men by women's employment, a 'condition which unsexes the man';[15] the moral corruption of women through working alongside men; the proper roles of the sexes; the threat to the health and welfare of the children. This latter argument, which is still used, illustrates the conflict that exists for individual women between the demands of family and independent paid employment. In abstract terms this conflict can again be described as between the values of self-sacrifice and those of individualism.

The justification for protective legislation based on the needs of children does not result in the limitation of the effects of legislation to parents only. Rather, statutory restrictions apply to all women regardless of their age or reproductive status. In *Page* v. *Freight Hire Ltd*[16] a woman aged twenty-three brought an action against her employers for discrimination under the Sex Discrimination Act 1975 because she was prohibited from carrying out her job as a lorry driver under circumstances in which a man would have been allowed to work. The load which the lorry would have carried was DMF, a chemical which had risks for men and women, but particularly of female sterility and for a foetus inside a pregnant woman. The lorry driver was willing to accept the risks of working with the chemical and indemnify her employers against liability, but was prohibited from doing so. The Employment Appeals Tribunal held that there was a statutory duty on the employers to ensure the health, safety and welfare of their employees and that therefore there was no discrimination under the Act. A distinction between the interests of any potential foetus and those of the lorry driver is not made in the judgment. Yet this is a crucial distinction, particularly in an individualist society.

The case illustrates the contradictions contained in legislative policy. If, in the interests of a free market in employment, women are to be encouraged to compete as individuals, protective legislation is an artificial restraint. If the state, acting as *parens patriae* to infants, born and unborn, wishes to restrict women's competition for the sake of their children, then this should be made plain. Is it possible to promote a free labour market which all persons enter devoid of personal aspects concerning their reproductive capacities and their family responsibilities? At present all women are assumed to carry with them their personal baggage, and no men are. The classification is not only over-inclusive, but also wrong.

On an individual level the lorry driver had made her position clear. She was divorced and had decided to be childless. She knew the dangers and wished to accept the risks. The Appeals Tribunal said: 'We accept that the individual's wishes may be a factor to be looked at, although, in our judgement, where the risk is to the woman, of sterility, or to the foetus, whether actually in existence or likely to come into existence in the future, these wishes cannot be a conclusive factor.'[17] Thus there was no freedom of choice for this individual because of her sex, and the employer's judgement of her welfare was substituted for her own. This 'for her own good' argument was rightly characterised by the United States Supreme Court as ' "romantic paternalism" which, in practical effect, put women not on a pedestal, but in a cage'.[18]

The conflict, then, is between freedom of contract for women employees and state paternalism which judges what is in their best interests. In liberal philosophy individuals are independent islands with their own interests, wants, needs, motives, etc. State authority is derived from free consent of these persons whose freedom to pursue their own ends is protected in return. For Locke, man in the state of nature is 'free . . . absolute lord of his own person and possessions, equal to the greatest and subject to nobody'. The social contract is made in order to create a society with others for 'the mutual preservation of their lives, liberties and estates, which I call by the general name, property'.[19] As Macpherson points out, the 'core of Locke's individualism is the assertion that every man is naturally the sole proprietor of his own person and capacities – the absolute proprietor in that he owes nothing to society for them – and especially the absolute proprietor of his capacity to labour'.[20] If we compare this description of individualism with state paternalism as embodied in protective legislation, it is clear that women are not treated as full individuals. The contradiction is self-evident.

In his essay *On Liberty* Mill lays down that 'the only purpose for which power can be rightfully exercised over any member of a civilised community, against his will, is to prevent harm to others.'[21] Mill's definition of the boundaries between public control and the private sphere includes an express rejection of paternalism, with an exception for children; and a weak paternalism for those who are to be protected from harming themselves because their decisions are impaired through lack of knowledge, lack of control or undue influence. In terms of freedom of contract women, controlled by protective legislation, are not free. They carry with them into the market-place their responsibilities for children and their specialised gender role. It is true that employers can ask for an exemption from the legislation, and that many do, but the necessity of doing so means that a refusal to employ women is permitted under the Sex Discrimination Act. This is because job working hours longer or other than those permitted under the Factories Act 1961 constitute a genuine occupational qualification for which sex discrimination is permitted. In *E. A. White* v. *British Sugar Corporation Ltd* the Industrial Tribunal held that sex was a genuine occupational qualification for a job which entailed Sunday work and that therefore a biologically female employee was not discriminated against when dismissed since 'the job requires a man because of legal restrictions on the employment of women.'[22] The state is being paternalistic in claiming to know better than women where their interests lie and in depriving them of freedom of contract. The evidence is that women factory workers wish to be free to negotiate their own hours of employment without the constraints of protective legislation.[23] The 'for your own good' form of argument denies women's capacity to make their own choices.

It might be objected that the state does have a legitimate role as protector of children, unborn or born. Their welfare demands the control of potential or actual mothers, whose interests cannot be completely separated from those of their offspring. This is why legislation provides maternity rights for women in employment. Yet the state as protector of babies and mothers only does a limited job. To receive protection against unfair dismissal for pregnancy there is a two-year qualifying period. For the right to return to work, for paid maternity leave and for paid time off work, the pregnant woman must have been in the continuous employment of one employer for a minimum of two years. Mothers who fall outside the scope of these statutory rights have no claims against their employers.[24] Nor does anti-discrimination legislation provide a solution. The approach taken by the courts has been to deny the applicability of sex discrimination law.

Faced with the question whether the dismissal of a woman on grounds of pregnancy constitutes sex discrimination the courts have retreated into an individualistic comparison of the complainant and a hypothetical man. In *Reaney* v. *Kanda Jean Products Ltd* the Industrial Tribunal decided that since a man could not become pregnant it was impossible to compare the applicant to a man. Direct discrimination under the Sex Discrimination Act involves 'an act or treatment which in the case of a woman is less favourable than that which is or may be accorded to a man'. The Act requires comparison of persons of different sex, but the relevant circumstances in one case must be the same or not materially different from those in the other.

In so far as the applicant complains that she is the victim of discrimination by comparison with the case of any other (hypothetical) man, the respective circumstances in each case are very materially different for obvious reasons . . . . It is physically impossible for a man in the instant case to receive preferential treatment for the reason that his case and that of the applicant is incomparable.[25]

In *Turley* v. *Allders Stores Ltd* the Employment Appeals Tribunal took a similar approach, stating that the Sex Discrimination Act requires a woman to be compared with a man.

Suppose that to dismiss her for pregnancy is to dismiss her on the ground of her sex. In order to see if she has been treated less favourably than a man the sense of the section is that you must compare like with like, and you cannot. When she is pregnant a woman is no longer just a woman. She is a woman, as the Authorised Version of the Bible accurately puts it, with child, and there is no masculine equivalent.[26]

There are a number of possible responses to these two cases, both of which found that discrimination on grounds of pregnancy is not direct discrimination on grounds of sex. A very general response is to suggest that since anti-discrimination legislation is concerned to increase market competition between atoms it is hardly surprising to find that the mechanisms by which the legislation operates involve comparison of individual women and men. This explanation is consonant with the argument of this chapter. The narrow approach of tribunal or court fits this picture, as a woman with child no longer conforms to the market requirement for monads divested of biology and the personal.

Another possible response is to suggest legislative amendment which includes in the definition of discrimination 'less favourable treatment on grounds of a characteristic that appertains to one sex only'. This reform would attempt to force the market to meet women's special role in the reproduction of human beings. A third response is to reconsider the interpretation of the statutory words by the court. This raises the question whether dismissal on grounds of pregnancy might be indirect discrimination.

Faced with a complaint of discrimination on grounds of sex a court or tribunal can consider whether the issue is one of direct or indirect discrimination. Direct discrimination, as already explained, requires the comparison of the complainant with an actual or hypothetical man.[27] Indirect discrimination is defined by s.1(1)(b) of the Sex Discrimination Act as occurring when an apparently neutral condition is imposed on both sexes, but where the proportion of one sex who can comply is considerably smaller than the proportion of the other. The requirement must be to the detriment of the person who cannot comply and the person imposing the requirements must be unable to justify it.

Indirect discrimination as a concept switches the focus of attention away from individual comparisons of a real or hypothetical woman and man to a wider perspective of looking at the 'posture and condition' of women as a group, compared to men as a group.[28] Thus the tribunal must look at the general characteristics of women which prevent them from complying with what are seemingly neutral conditions or requirements such as their child-bearing biological role, their socially ascribed child-rearing obligations, as well as other features such as social stereotyping in education and training. These aspects which relate to women's private domestic responsibilities are ignored in economic individualism but significantly affect labour-market participation.

In cases of dismissal for pregnancy the condition or requirement that is being imposed on the complainant is non-pregnancy. All men and some women can comply, but the proportion of women who can comply is smaller. Therefore it would seem that a *prima facie* case of indirect discrimination can be made out. This point has not yet been argued in a British case. Evidence of the proportion of women pregnant in the population at any given time would be required to support the claim.

In the United States pregnancy as a source of discrimination has also not been recognised. The Supreme Court's majority opinion in *Gilbert* v. *General Electric* was that the exclusion of pregnancy and pregnancy-related disabilities from risks covered under an employee-disability insurance plan was not sex discrimination. The reasoning was that although all pregnant persons are women, because pregnancy is unique but not universal to women exclusions based on pregnancy could not be discriminatory, as they are not 'based on sex'.[29] But a physical condition found only in one sex, although admittedly not constant or universal in that sex, has been recognised in another case as giving rise to discrimination. The reasoning in this latter case of *Nashville Gas* v. *Satty* was that a policy of denying accumulated seniority to women returning from pregnancy leave was sex discrimination because seniority was retained by other employees who took leave for disability or illness. But the denial of sick pay during pregnancy leave was not considered discriminatory, and as with the *Gilbert* case the illness-compensation scheme was considered neutral as it did not affect all women.[30]

The United States Supreme Court recognised in *Griggs* v. *Duke Power* that a policy neutral in itself can have a 'disproportionate impact' in practice, due to social conditions independent of the parties and the law.[31] This acknowledgement of socially created inequality seems to have been confined to cases on race discrimination. Yet there seems no reason why it should not be extended to pregnancy-related discrimination.

Many women on entering the labour market do not leave the private world of biology and family completely behind, as economic theory might suggest they should. In the impersonal world of work this may be seen as a nuisance, and accounts for some of the prejudice against women. The policy of anti-discrimination law is to counteract this. But legislation on factory hours and conditions of work designed to protect women points up the dilemma for policy-makers and for women. Protective legislation applies to women regardless of the contingencies of their lives. It assumes that all women have reproductive and childcare responsibilities. The concept of indirect discrimination attempts to modify market requirements to meet the needs of a considerable number of women who cannot conform to the male model. Yet the dilemma for these women continues. Should they try to adapt to the market or will the market meet them? If the market is to be modified, does it have to be through policies such as protective legislation which appear to reinforce not only female stereotypes but also male hegemony?

Equal to Whom?

Even the disabilities which the wife lies under are for the most part intended for her protection and benefit: so great a favourite is the female sex of the laws of England.[32]

It is generally assumed that Blackstone was essaying a little irony in the above passage from the *Commentaries*, for he had just described the common law system which divested the married woman of her legal personality. Yet closer examination of the context in which he wrote reveals that there were legal safeguards to mitigate the harshness of the common law and to protect the wife from the excesses of her husband's power. In effect what Blackstone describes is an assumption by the law that a wife may have been compelled by her husband to commit a felony or to perform some civil legal act such as a contract or conveyance. She can therefore be excused or protected from the legal effects of her actions.

A rational reaction to such a system would be to suggest that no protection would be necessary were it not for the disabilities created by law. The advocacy of formal equality of rights in liberal political thought has been largely realised through the removal of *de jure* barriers to women's participation in the public world of education, employment and politics. The object of the Equal Pay Act 1970 and of the Sex Discrimination Act 1975 is to complete the process by the removal of *de facto* barriers. These reforms have been designed to enable women to compete with men in the market-place on equal terms.

Arguments for formal equality assume that the free-market ideal can be improved through equal access for women. Anti-discrimination policies can be justified as integrating women into the market. Indeed this had been the reasoning behind the European Economic Community's espousal of the principle of equality in education, employment and social security laws. 'Thus, requiring market actors to abandon their irrational biases against women or their misplaced, altruistic inclinations to protect women, family life, or men can be seen as a way of forcing these actors to behave as rational profit maximisers.'[33]

Liberal arguments are committed to creating similarities between women and men where possible and to minimising differences between them. This leads to assimilation of women to men in the public world and to a denial of needs and responsibilities arising from the private. Acceptance of a distinction between public and private also results in the limitation of liberal measures to the public. It would seem therefore that differential treatment of women, such as that contained in protective legislation, should be eliminated. It is often said that the assimilationist position ignores biological or gender differences between persons and offers a model based only on rights achieved by men and on a male lifestyle. This is the source of

*Teorisky — said elsewhere has law
function to should/create/re-inforce private
attitudes.' See p. 182

disagreement over reform of protective legislation.

The Equal Opportunities Commission has advocated the repeal of protective legislation because 'the hours of work legislation constitutes a barrier – often an artificial one – to equal pay and job opportunities for women. So long as this legislation remains as it is at present, women as workers will be disadvantaged.'[34] The problem with this, as with all statements of formal equality, is that it presupposes a freely negotiated bargain between women and their employers without any constraints of inequalities of power, restraints arising from family duties and trade-union intervention. In any case the contract of employment is no longer freely negotiated. Employers are bound by a system of legislative controls placing considerable limits on their autonomy. State intervention takes place to even up the balance of power between employee and employer and to prevent exploitation. So why should the state not continue to intervene to protect women?

It is the view of the British Trade Union Congress that the state should continue its present policy of differential treatment of women workers. The language in which the repeal of protective legislation has been opposed deserves analysis:

a large proportion of working women are married with not only a house to look after, they have in effect a multiplicity of jobs. Thus the pressures to which they are subject are likely to cause them to overwork against their better judgement. They may not only damage their health and increase the risk of accidents, but have serious effects on the well being of the family. In the interests of society generally . . . the state must intervene to protect women against the combined effect of social and economic pressure.[35]

If this rhetoric is a plea for state recognition that private duties and responsibilities affect the amount of time and energy employees can expend in their public role at work, then one must sympathise. But why should this be linked to sex or gender? This debate continues in Britain but has been resolved in the United States after fifty years of argument. There, social reformers opposed the repeal of protective legislation in the hope of improving conditions for all workers by extending to men the legislation that applied to women, and also because of the needs of families of women workers. This meant opposition to the Equal Rights Amendment, which was first introduced in 1923. Recently, however, the historic opposition by American social reformers and trade unionists has been withdrawn. It is generally agreed that protective legislation reinforces women's lowly position in the labour market and at home. A society divided on sex or gender lines is believed to reinforce male hegemony and to preserve the status quo. This might seem an argument in favour of formal equality, but would it not be possible to devise legislative policies which recognise parental or family responsibilities but which do not result in sexual stratification? The recognition that what happens in private affects the public is to be welcomed. It is the assumption that only women are affected that is objectionable.

Equality Reconsidered

Nineteenth- and early-twentieth-century reforms to ensure the equality of women and men before the law concentrated on the removal of *de jure* barriers which prevented access to education, employment and politics. Since the 1970s further *de facto* barriers have been removed through anti-discrimination and equal-pay legislation. It might therefore be concluded that there is equality of the sexes. In one sense this is true. If equality means equal access to the courts, to education, to employment, to goods and services, full legal personality, then the statement can be sustained. It is sustainable only in a formal fashion.

Freedom of contract, as conscious decisions of free individuals, was a standard liberal legal shibboleth in the nineteenth century. It was thought that the egalitarian ideas of the late eighteenth century were safeguarded in the notion of equality of opportunity which was carried forward by freedom of contract. Allied to a legal system which exalted process over outcome, ideas of freedom and equality of opportunity permitted empirical evidence of inequality to be ignored. The law presupposed a formal equality between free persons. Just as the courts have moved from classical notions of freedom of contract to considerations of inequality of bargaining power, so theories of equality of opportunity have been revised to take account of *de facto* barriers to equal access to benefits. By the 1970s policy-makers realised that opening the gates of the market to women would not, by itself, create free competition between the sexes. Women's socialisation and aspects of their personal lives such as home and family responsibilities precluded real equality of participation. Women, it seemed, did not have equality of opportunity because they did not get an equal start with men. One answer was the introduction of the concept of indirect discrimination in s.1(1)(b) of the Sex Discrimination Act.

To show a *prima facie* case of indirect discrimination, statistical evidence of the proportions of women and men who can comply with a seemingly neutral condition or requirement for employment or access to other benefits such as education, goods or services must be shown. If there is disproportionate inequality then the case has been made out. In *Price* v. *Civil Service Commission* the applicant complained that women in their twenties, engaged in child-bearing and rearing, have greater difficulty than men in complying with a requirement that candidates for the post of executive officer in the civil service must not be over twenty-eight years old. The Industrial Tribunal which first heard the case held that the words 'can comply' must be strictly construed and that a woman can comply with a requirement if it is physically possible for her to do so. In other words, responsibility for children in one's personal life is irrelevant. Furthermore, if home responsibilities are discounted, the proportion of women in the population between seventeen and a half and twenty-eight, and therefore eligible to apply for the post, was not considerably smaller than the proportion of men. Therefore it was held that indirect discrimination had not been shown.[36]

On appeal the Employment Appeal Tribunal rejected the finding that the words 'can comply' must be construed narrowly.

In one sense it can be said that any female applicant can comply with the condition. She is not obliged to marry, or to have children, or to mind children; she may find somebody to look after them, and as a last resort she may put them into care. In this sense no doubt counsel for the Civil Service Commission is right in saying that any female applicant can comply with the condition. Such a construction appears to us to be wholly out of sympathy with the spirit and intent of the Act.[37]

The Appeal Tribunal went on to comment that knowledge, experience and some of the statistical evidence confirmed that a considerable number of women between their mid-twenties and mid-thirties are engaged in child-bearing and rearing, and that therefore the condition imposed by the Civil Service Commission is one which is in practice harder for women to comply with than it is for men. However, since the legislation required a finding that the proportion of women who can comply with a condition is considerably smaller than the proportion of men, that question was remitted to a new tribunal which was to hear the complaint afresh.

At the rehearing the Civil Service Commission conceded that 'the upper age limit of 28 years for direct entry into the Executive Officer grade is a requirement or condition which is such that the proportion of women who can comply with it is considerably smaller than the proportion of men who can comply with it.'[38] The only question which remained was whether the age bar was justifiable. Applying the test that the requirement or condition must be necessary and not merely convenient, and that consideration must be given to achieving the object in a non-discriminatory way, the tribunal found that the age bar was not justifiable.

The childcare obligations of a lone mother who asked her employers to permit her to return to work on a part-time basis after the birth of her second child formed the basis for a complaint of indirect discrimination in *Holmes* v. *Home Office*. The refusal of the employer to substitute part-time for full-time work gave rise to a complaint of sex discrimination. Both the tribunal which heard the case initially and the Employment Appeals Tribunal found that the requirement of full-time service in the employee's contract of employment amounted to a condition within the definition of indirect discrimination. This condition was such that the proportion of women who could comply with it was smaller than the proportion of men who could comply. 'Despite changes in the role of women in modern society it was still a fact that the raising of children placed a greater burden on women than on men.'[39] The Tribunal's finding that the employer had unlawfully discriminated against the complainant was upheld on appeal.

What these cases suggest is that the concept of indirect discrimination contained in s.1(1)(b) of the Sex Discrimination Act will force market actors to take account of women's experiences prior to market entry. This is undoubtedly an advance on the position in which women had achieved the right to be 'equally regarded as a self-sufficient monad'.[40] It illustrates a new approach to equality in which empirical evidence is taken into account, and it is therefore more than merely formal. As Christopher McCrudden explains:

The principle on which the concept of indirect discrimination is based differs from the simple non-discrimination principle (which underlines the idea of direct discrimination) in being positive as well as negative in its requirements and in taking into account some of the prior existing disadvantages which black and women workers bring to the marketplace. The employer must, if he is not to be in breach of his duty, so operate his recruitment and promotion procedures, etc., as positively to offset the group related disadvantages which adversely affect a black or woman worker's chances of being hired or promoted. Also unlike the simple non-discrimination principle, it requires questions to be asked not only about the precise basis on which the good being distributed is deserved but also about the nature of the good being distributed.[41]

Indirect discrimination is concerned with procedures and not with outcomes or results. It makes no assumption that a particular distributive pattern should result from these procedures; it limits its concern to procedural justice. Nevertheless the recognition, in the case of women, that the demands of the private realm influence and even determine access to the opportunities of the market is important.

Recent evidence from the Central Statistics Office confirms again the effect of motherhood on women's employment status. Seventy-three per cent of married mothers of children under five were not employed in 1980–2, the period under survey. For lone mothers the figure was 77 per cent. Part-time work predominated for those in employment. Where the youngest child was under ten, 41 per cent of married mothers and 45 per cent of lone mothers were not in employment. For those in paid work, part-time work predominated. Of married mothers of children over ten but under sixteen, 30 per cent were economically inactive, 38 per cent worked part-time and 33 per cent worked full-time. Of lone mothers 41 per cent were not employed, 29 per cent worked part-time and 31 per cent worked full-time. From this we can conclude that as the children grow up their mothers become freer to take up paid employment and to move from part-time into full-time employment.[42]

Part-time work remains characteristic of women's market partici-pation. The 1981 census shows that whereas there are 100 men to 60 women in the workforce, 39 per cent of the women are part-timers, whereas only 2 per cent of the men are. This reinforces the view that women's paid employment is chosen to fit in with their work at home. Furthermore the kind of work these women part-timers engage in is predominantly an extension of their domestic roles. Out of nearly 3½ million part-time women employees, 2 million are nurses, cleaners, domestic and school helpers, secretaries, shop and other assistants. And women's wages have not caught up with men's. In 1981 the female full-time wage was 67 per cent of the male full-time wage.[43]

Advocating legal reforms which make the individual the basis for social security, pensions and family income overlooks the effect of the demands of their families on women's access to an independent income. Individualism is seen by some feminists as an answer to women's economic dependence but it involves a denial of the claims of the private and therefore does not meet the conditions of many women's lives. As one spirited woman explained to a researcher: 'a lot of women are much better off married and at home . . . . So when they hear some feminist writers or lawyers or something like that say jobs are so terrific, they know that for the average woman that's a lot of baloney.'[44]

Is the answer then to maintain special treatment of women as exemplified by protective legislation whilst at the same time modifying the free market through the use of legal concepts such as indirect discrimination? An objection to this might be that not only is male hegemony maintained in such a system, but it is also condescending to women. Examination of the proposal and this objection reveals the difficulty of offering a prescription.

In liberal discourse individuals are self-interested and it is assumed that they act for their own benefit. It can be argued that a woman's decision to have children is freely made in the knowledge of the consequences. For the law to make special provision to deal with the results of this free choice appears as a special favour. The problem with this argument and with the argument that protective legislation is paternalistic is that policy options are presented as a choice between 'equality' and 'protection'. But if equality only means adapting to the male model of the life-cycle and lifestyle then its limitations are clear. The trouble with the liberal position is that women are expected to accept the rules of a game created by and for different players.

Conclusion

Behind the arguments in this chapter lie contrasting views of persons. The liberal person is an individualist with freedom to make choices about her life. The feminist, be she fierce or woolly, recognises that the liberal inhabits only the public world. Procedural equality as exemplified in the concept of indirect discrimination is the beginning of an acknowledgement of the ties and values of private life. As yet outcome equality has not been incorporated in anti-discrimination law.

If equality is to be taken seriously measures which deal only or primarily with the market-place will not be enough. Nor is individualism the answer. A more fundamental answer is given by those who advocate the reuniting of the public and the private, which would no longer be seen as split but part of each other. This will be investigated in the final chapter.

8

Reforming the Private: Why Can't a Man Be More like a Woman?

'The private strife of man and wife
Is useful to the notion
It is a harmless outlet for
Emotions that could lead to war
Or social agitation.'

RICHARD WILBUR

The thesis that has been advanced in this book is that the dichotomy between market and family reflects a distinction between public and private. Private has been shown to mean non-intervention by the law, in many instances. The problem which has been posed is of place, activities, relationships and feelings, which are termed personal, private and subjective and therefore outside the law. Concepts of privacy mask patriarchal domination. 'In feminist translation, the private is a sphere of battery, marital rape, and women's exploited labour; of the central social institutions whereby women are deprived of (as men are granted) identity, autonomy, control, and self-determination.'[1] What is to be done?

The family and sexual relations have been the locus of law reform, particularly in the twentieth century. Various strategies have been adopted. These can be summarised as regulation, legalisation, informal justice and privatisation.

Regulation

Bringing the law into the home to regulate marital and personal relations therein is a strategy which has been tried in some jurisdictions. English policy has been resistant to intervention during marriage, leaving conflict-resolution to take place on dissolution. When this occurs through divorce or death, statutory provisions are called upon by applicant or court to determine the outcome of the conflict. Yet even here there is no clear code of rights. It is up to the court to use its discretion to decide the outcome. This is generally done in accordance with the judicial view of deserts or needs.

The special nature of the marital relationship as creating rights and obligations is recognised on divorce by the provisions of the Matrimonial Causes Act 1973. Sections 23, 24 and 25 confer on the court the discretion to transfer property or assets from one spouse to the other. Thus, although there is no legal intervention during marriage to impose a régime of community of property, the nature of the relationship is recognised at the time of its dissolution. So it is with death. The intestacy rules acknowledge the special status of a spouse, as does the Inheritance (Provision for Family and Dependants) Act 1975. If dissatisfied with provision made by will or intestacy rules, an applicant can rely on the status of spouse to make a claim. Again the court has discretion to apply notions of justice based on deserts or needs to determine the outcome.

During marriage, as shown in Chapter 5, there are wide areas of the marital relationship that are unregulated. It is true that violent behaviour can now be controlled by court application under statute.[2] Occupation of the matrimonial home is protected by statutory registration and by recent case-law.[3] Financial support, although not laid down as a general principle, can be obtained through court application.[4] But no community-of-property régime exists; there is no right to a share of earnings; occupation and other property rights in the home can be upset by bankruptcy, death or third-party claims; and court application for every problem of violence or financial stringency may be impractical.

The argument for greater regulation of the marital relationship is that the law, by laying down general principles, can influence attitudes and behaviour. By expressing in its content general community beliefs concerning interpersonal justice it exhorts spouses to behave with justice towards one another. Through regulation of matters such as marital property, finances, sexual conduct and behaviour, the law acknowledges the special nature of the relationship and the value of sharing and equality. Without this legal recognition the individualistic path is clearly laid down.

The form of marriage constituted by state policies is a union of the partners, with economic dependency during the years of child-bearing and rearing. Material conditions of dependency can only be addressed by recognition of a special relationship, and therefore by regulation. In a pluralist society law is seen as the arbiter of justice, and the failure of law to regulate is as significant as its provisions are when it does intervene.

Liberals are opposed to increased legal intervention in the private. The realm of family, home, intimacy – the private – is believed to be a bulwark against an intrusive state. As Steven Lukes defines it: 'privacy in its modern sense – that is a sphere of thought and action that should be free from "public" interference – does constitute what is perhaps the central idea of liberalism.'[5] To Isaiah Berlin this idea of 'negative privacy' involves a 'sense of privacy . . . of something sacred in its own right'. It is a modern conception of liberty which 'springs from this individualistic and much disputed conception of man'.[6] Preserving a demarcation between private and public, the zone of freedom and that of regulation, is to maintain an area of life for individual autonomy. Feminist argument that women do not experience their lives as compartmentalised, that they are not free in the private sphere but are regulated by patriarchy, that the personal is political, is countered by pragmatic argument on the unenforce-ability of interventionist legislation.

In the debate which followed the Wolfenden Report[7] liberals emphasised a limited role for law as the arbiter of morality. A pluralist society in which there are divergent moralities must relegate questions of morals to the private to enable differing viewpoints to coexist. The withdrawal of the state from morality is a recognition of pluralism and avoids conflict, enforcement problems and the flouting of the law which brings it into disrepute. With the lack of consensus about desirable norms of personal behaviour which has followed the breakdown of religious ideology the allocation of such matters to the unregulated private zone was inevitable. Privacy permits people to act in ways that would have unpleasant consequences if done in public.

These arguments against regulation are a mixture of liberalism, pragmatism and social observation. At their heart lies a debate about law, its potential and its limitations. Anti-interventionists not only wish to preserve a zone free from state intrusion but argue that law weakens and undermines the family. If the promotion of stability within and support for the family is the law's goal then it should be aloof. It is said that the realistic trend for law reform in the future is to limit itself to practical problems of families and to be 'less ambitious in promoting any given set of values about how family life should be organised . . . the disappearance of some of the traditional private law of the family is in part merely a long overdue reaction against the excessive ambitions entertained in the past for legal regulation of human behaviour.'[8]

One of the arguments the liberal anti-interventionist must counter is that in relation to marriage she is not just dealing with morality but also with justice. In every marriage there is a potential conflict and if that occurs the parties may look to the law for resolution. It is true that in a pluralist society the same solution may not apply to all cases. But the law is nevertheless seen as the embodiment of social values and its failure to provide a remedy on an issue between spouses where it does so between strangers is interpreted as a statement of its position. Not legislating contains a value judgement just as legislating does. Law cannot be neutral; non-intervention is as potent an ideology as regulation.

The feminist critic countering the liberal in the above terms must admit several difficulties. Advocating regulation of marriage because law can adopt an hortatory role in laying down general principles and cannot be neutral has various consequences. The dichotomy between private and public is maintained; the law is merely thrust forward as arbiter for marital conflicts. Women are being asked to turn to the state for protection against patriarchy but what is the nature of the state in feminist theory? Is it protector or oppressor?

The debate in English law on the issue of financial support on divorce crystallises the above dilemma. Individualistic arguments posit that economic dependency in marriage should not be continued through legal requirements of payment of maintenance after divorce. It is in the interests of both ex-spouses that they should be independent of one another. A period of rehabilitative maintenance might be justified but the goal must be a complete break. If there is a residual need, then it is for the state through public law to take care of it. This individualistic argument is premised on the separation of private and public law. It is believed by many participants in the debate, from both left and right, that the state must take charge.

Arguments based on the values of community posit that economic dependence in marriage is socially and legally constructed. House-work and childcare do not earn money, pension or savings. Private responsibilities preclude or diminish market participation. The law does not adequately recognise private claims which spouses have on one another. Transferring these responsibilities from private to public law is a reification of a dichotomy that does not exist in many women's experience and substitutes state control for patriarchy. The source of these difficulties is the separation of public from private. Moving a problem such as women's economic dependence from one zone to the other is a cosmetic exercise.

Regulation of marriage-type relationships by the state through a family code is one possible reform. Codes lay down the general principles which have been lacking in English law, contain a consensus on society's view of justice in personal relationships, and provide an alternative to individualistic modes of family regulation. In those jurisdictions, such as the European civil law systems, where a family code has been adopted, there is a much greater degree of regulation by law of the marital relationship. As Rheinstein and Glendon put it: 'Codes and statutes of the Continental European type, in contrast with Anglo-American law, traditionally dealt elaborately with allocation between husband and wife of powers of decision in family life.'[9] The examples which follow are taken from West German and French law.

The West German constitution of 1949 proclaims the principle of the equality of the sexes in article 3. Court interpretation of this principle has resulted in the repeal of statutes which give greater power to the husband in marriage. The West German Civil Code provides for equality in marriage and in the concept of *Berufstätigenehe* states the freedom of marriage partners to choose their own occupation.[10] Under S1353 of the Civil Code 'the spouses are obliged to live together in marital community of life', but if there is disagreement an action can be brought 'to bring about the marital life' and the court can make a declaration that the behaviour of one of the parties is wrong.[11] Both spouses have a duty to contribute to the charges of the household and of family life, but the code makes clear that contribution can be either in work or in money, and that either spouse can satisfy this by running the household.[12] The duty to live in marital community covers such matters as polite behaviour, fidelity, attention to children and sobriety.[13]

The French Civil Code proclaims the equality of the spouses who 'are mutually bound to a community of life'.[14] Residence is chosen by common accord and the spouses are equally responsible for the support of the family.[15]

Both France and West Germany offer their citizens a choice in the way they hold their matrimonial property. If they make a marriage contract then, provided the contract is not contrary to the code, it will be enforced. But in the absence of contract a community-of-property régime will be imposed.[16] The French conception of marriage as a union of the couple in all respects means that there is community of all property acquired during marriage. Management of this community was traditionally under the husband but this is under revision in order to create complete equality, as exists in certain community-of-property jurisdictions in the United States.[17]

The new French system requires the co-operation of both spouses in transactions of major significance. The wife must consent if the husband wishes to deal with the community funds. There is responsibility for fault committed under the management of the husband. The wife can claim against the community funds for reasonable household expenses. She has a veto power over important transactions, such as sale or mortgage. Either spouse may be held responsible to the community for mismanagement of their own separate property.[18] There is special protection for the matrimonial home and its contents, whether owned or leased. Various devices protect the community fund from dissipation, including nullity actions and actions prohibiting one spouse from dealing with community or personal property.[19]

Article 214 of the Civil Code provides: 'If the matrimonial contract does not regulate the contribution of the spouses to the expenses of the marriage, they will contribute to them in proportion to their respective abilities.' Failure to observe this duty can result in an attachment of earnings by the other spouse, even where the couple are still living together.[20] On termination of the marriage by death or divorce, the basic principle of the matrimonial régime is dissolved and the fund divided equally between the two spouses.

West Germany has a matrimonial property régime known as deferred community of property. What this means is that the spouses can deal separately with their personal assets during marriage but that there is community of property on termination of marriage. There are also consent requirements from the other spouse. All European property systems have faced the problem of 'finding a viable way of combining the ancient features of community property – fusing the wealth of both parties or giving to the housewife a share in the wealth or the savings of the breadwinner – with greater powers of management and disposition in the wife'.[21] Since 1958 the concept of *Zugewinn* has been the principal basis of the German matrimonial property régime. At the time of termination of the régime a calculation is made of the increase in the spouses' assets that has occurred during the existence of the régime. The increase of one spouse's estate is compared to the increase in the other spouse's estate. The gains (*Ausgleichsforderung*) are then equalised.[22]

Consent of the other spouse is needed for certain transactions such as disposition of estate or of household goods.[23] A decree of premature equalisation of increase can be obtained to bring the matrimonial property régime to an end where one spouse acts in a manner contrary to the interests of the marital régime, or where the parties have lived apart for three years.[24] Examples of behaviour contrary to the marital relationship are failure to perform economic duties arising from the relation of marriage, transactions affecting the estate, dissipating the estate, and refusing to give information about financial affairs to the other spouse.[25]

In relation to children English legislation does provide, like French and West German law, that the parents have equal powers and can apply to a court for dispute-resolution.[26] It is worth noting, however, that when this principle was introduced into the French Civil Code in 1970, marriage as a joint enterprise was emphasised. The *exposé de motif* stated that

The Civil Code can fulfil an educational function by encouraging the spouses to exchange their points of view on all the important questions which arise in connection with the running of the household and the education of the children, as well as to come to agreement, before marriage, concerning a common ethic.[27]

The discussion of the new law in the National Assembly and the Senate showed faith in law as both symbol of the ideal state of marriage and also as educator of couples planning to marry.[28]

Legalisation

The common law rule of the unity of the spouses precluded the allocation of a separate legal personality to the wife, who could not hold property, make contracts, sue or be sued until Victorian and twentieth-century reforms. Legalisation of their relationship has meant that the wife holds her property as an independent individual. She can act in contract or tort and sue in the courts.[29] Her rights are enforceable, even against her husband as between strangers in the market-place. With regard to property transactions the law treats the spouses as legal individuals, with the exception of statutory rights of occupation of the matrimonial home.

Reforms based on legalisation deny recognition to the special relationship of the spouses. In this individualistic mode marriage and cohabitation are regarded as being (desirably) based on voluntary agreement and not on any state definition of marriage. Divorce is the result of individual contract. The marital régime, issues of sexual conduct, behaviour of spouses to one another, finances, roles, economic activities and children are embodied in personal agreements.

Legalisation has attracted many scholars to its charms. Dissatisfaction with state-regulated marriage and with the ambivalence of the law towards those who cohabit without marrying has led to advocacy of the benefits of contract. Marjorie Shultz suggests that the optimum model for the governance of marriage, and presumably other personal relationships, is one where 'the state could leave most substantive marital rights and obligations to be defined privately, but make the legal system available to resolve disputes arising under privately created legislation.'[30] This would mean that the state had decided to defer to and to enforce private choices about relationships. It is stipulated that the parties must have the capacity to plan and to make decisions in their own interests. Therefore the negotiations must be fair, free of fraud and duress, and there must be meaningful freedom of choice.

Examples are given of areas for negotiation: (a) income production and support, e.g. one partner shares an income with the other for educational, child-rearing or other reasons; (b) domestic services, e.g. one spouse pays the other a salary for domestic services; (c) marital property, e.g. the state requires the couple to file a copy of their agreement concerning property rights at the time of applying for a marriage licence; (d) the marriage relationship, e.g. the couple specify how much time they have during the week and at weekends away from each other; (e) domicile and residence, e.g. in a dual-career marriage the partners take turns in specifying where the couple will live.

Shultz recognises that, at present, the state does not permit couples to write their own marriage contracts or to vary the terms for marriage laid down by legislation or precedent. Courts have refused to enforce agreements not to cohabit during marriage, agreements on payment of one spouse to another for domestic, childcare or other services in the home, unwritten maintenance agreements, planned termination of the marriage after a given period of time, alteration of statutory duties of support, and provision in advance for breakdown of marriage.[31] However, a number of American states do permit spousal contracts concerning property rights (e.g. California, Massachusetts, South Dakota). Separation agreements are enforced in common law jurisdictions generally, provided there is no fraud, mistake, duress or other form of lack of consent.

Objections to marriage contracts have been raised on the ground that it is for the state to define the nature of marriage. American comment suggests that private choice would create a wide variety of marriages and that this would be an undesirable goal for public policy. Shultz says:

For many years, a single behavioural model of acceptable marriage has been enshrined in domestic relations law. Underlying that legal policy are the beliefs that (1) there is a particular marital structure that, as a matter of policy, is best for the individuals involved, or for the society, or for both, and (2) people will make unwise decisions if they are allowed to structure their intimate relationships.[32]

This may be true of American law, but it can hardly be said of English law with its ideology of privacy. There is a major distinction to be made here between English and American family law. American courts, in the past, have been much more open about their assumptions concerning traditional marriage and their imposition of its terms in private law. The English judiciary, being imbued with beliefs in privacy, have been less inclined to intrude on marital life. And previously, their judgements on matrimonial conduct were made *ex post facto*. This is not true in public law, however, as was shown in Chapter 6.

Interest in contract as a means to regulate intimate relations stems from a variety of sources. There are the pluralists, such as Weitzman, who see existing marriage law as a state-dictated contract 'based on outmoded assumptions about the family, assumptions often contradicted by the reality of [spouses'] own experience but nevertheless applied to them by law'. Her case, in relation to American law, is that this unwritten contract, to be found in legislation and case-law, is tyrannical. It is an unconstitutional invasion of marital privacy, it is sexist in that it imposes different rights and obligations on husband and wife, and it flies in the face of pluralism by denying heterogeneity and diversity and imposing a single model of marriage on everyone.

The model assumes that all marriages are first marriages for the young, that it is a sexual relationship, that there will be children, that the marriage will last a lifetime, that the husband will work to support the family, and that the wife will perform childcare and domestic services.

Weitzman shows the discrepancy between reality and ideology. In analysing traditional legal marriage she measures doctrine against its social and economic consequences and against the reality of how people live. Looking to matters such as age, marriage, name, domicile, consortium, maintenance obligation, matrimonial property, succession and the maternal preference role in custody cases, she makes out a convincing case against American marriage laws: 'The cumulative effect of the restrictions embodied in traditional legal marriage is to enforce the notion that one man and one woman will find happiness if they commit themselves to each other for life.'[33] The result is 'a form of tyranny that rules out individual choice'. Conscious of a pluralist society, where serial polygamy is well established, and where many individuals have personal relationships which do not fit the heterosexual monogamous form established in law, Weitzman considers it 'reasonable for people in close personal relationships to consider writing a contract that fits their individual needs and life-style'.[34]

In English law there is less direct prescription of how couples are to live out their marriages. The law confines itself to dealing with breakdown or dissolution. There is a strong belief in privacy, that 'in a happy marriage the intervention of the courts is unnecessary.'[35] Nevertheless the mixture of legislative provisions, judicial pronouncements in private law, and state policy in public law combine to provide unwritten terms which are to some extent analogous to those in American law. Proponents of marriage contracts as the solution to problems in English family law have also emerged.

Shultz advances arguments for contracts on reformist grounds. She believes that the process of bargaining and planning would increase information about marriage and clarify goals and expectations. Communication and voluntary compliance would improve, and disputes could be resolved non-adjudicatively. The divorce rate might even go down. Others are interested in contracts as permitting regulation of households or relationships that do not conform to the heterosexual dyad. In England Freeman and Lyon favour contract for heterosexual cohabitation as an escape from the confines and sexual stereotyping of legal marriage and as a realisation of the values of freedom of choice and individualism, which they espouse.[36] Reformers believe that a process of negotiation prior to marriage may permit a couple to shape their relationship to accommodate the needs of both partners. It is true that not only is the law out of touch with the partners' view of marriage, but very often the couple do not share the same perspective. Jessie Barnard has pointed to discrepancies in marriage expectations by analysing 'his' as opposed to 'her' marriage.[37] The emphasis in marriage on individual fulfilment and happiness may mean inevitable conflict if an agreement is not worked out.

Legalisation, argue the proponents of contracts for the solution to family conflict, will enable individuals to order their intimate relationships in accordance with personal choice. Private ordering is seen as conferring autonomy and independence on the partners who approach one another as strangers agreeing on a market-place contract. The example for this contract is the classical model which raised freedom of contract to its apogee in the nineteenth century. In its mature form the classical model had two characteristics: a model of contract based on a model of free market transactions; and a model of contract seen as an instrument of market planning containing a promise for future execution. In the twentieth century this model has declined, partly in recognition of a lack of freedom of choice because of inequality of bargaining power.

Professor Atiyah suggests that classic doctrines of freedom of contract have been replaced by a concern with justice and fairness and by a results-oriented approach.[38] An example of this is the concern of the courts to ensure that the parties approach their bargain as material equals and not just as formal equals. Through the development of unconscionability doctrine in the United States, and ideas of inequality of bargaining power in England, courts are attempting to do justice between the parties. In a series of cases courts have also shown their interest in the knowledge the parties have of the terms of the contract and their effects.

Looking to commercial contracts as an example of how to order personal relations shows a preference for individualism and personal autonomy. If the competitive spirit of the market-place is to inform the negotiation of intimate relationships, it seems likely that both parties will attempt to maximise their own advantage. The theory of freedom of contract presupposes that negotiators approach their exchanges as equals free to choose consciously the terms of their agreement. If the available choices open to the contracting parties are predetermined by law, convention, the market, gender roles or personal power then it is doubtful whether there is true freedom. In classical contract theory the exceptions to the enforcement of agreements which are made for cases of fraud, duress and incapacity are considered constitutive of the concept of freedom. In the twentieth century this has been further developed to include inequality of bargaining power. There is disagreement as to whether this is part of the decline in the classical mode of contract along with a continuous weakening in the values involved in individual freedom of choice, or whether this is merely an extension of freedom of contract to take account of situations of inequality where consent is vitiated.[39] However, under either explanation a possible outcome is a subsequent claim by one partner that the contract is unconscionable because of lack of equality at the time of agreement.

Weitzman admits to some doubts about the equality of bargaining power of the parties to a marriage contract. Her answer is that partners who share an egalitarian ideology will not think it just to impose an exploitative contract on someone they love. Putting one's views in writing is more likely to lead to implementation. On the issue of protecting the weaker partner, Weitzman's view is that it is better for her to know the terms of the relationship at the beginning 'instead of blindly trusting the goodwill of her intended partner'.[40] Romantic illusions of being looked after for life will be dispelled.

Flexibility is held up as one of the virtues of contract; that is, the parties could write a planning instrument which was tailored to their own needs. But a contract that may be intended to govern thirty or forty years of a person's life would have to be very flexible indeed if it is to cover child-bearing and rearing, withdrawal from the employment market and unforeseen eventualities. Conditions and interests later in married life might be quite different from those at its beginning. Contract as an instrument of marriage regulation, containing freedom and choice, presupposes a number of factors. These are knowledge, equality of bargaining power, legal information and advice, cool judgement, foresight, education, articulation, lack of state interference, and perhaps lack of trust of the other party. There is the danger that the use of contract will be confined to the articulate middle class. Perfect knowledge equals complete competition in the market-place. But the achievement of perfect knowledge for an intimate contract might be impossible. In other areas of contract, for instance the contract of employment, the state has intervened through legislation to impose terms on employer and employee. This has occurred in recognition of the inequality of the parties.

Concern with unconscionability in American contract law and with inequality of bargaining in English law is a feature of judicial approaches to contract in the latter half of the twentieth century. Although the demand for equality of bargaining power is procedural, it signals the courts' concern with substantive justice. Courts are looking to the outcome of particular suits to ensure that the result is fair to the particular parties.[41] The indications are that contracts for personal relations will be closely scrutinised to ensure that procedural safeguards have been observed. Where this is not so the agreement will be avoided. This has happened on divorce agreements.[42]

Procedural safeguards will, in general, be satisfied if independent legal advice has been obtained. How likely is it that those planning to marry will consult a lawyer? Studies of the use of legal services indicate that the clientele is middle class and that, for a variety of reasons, working-class people are reluctant to see solicitors.[43] Unless independent attendance at a lawyer's office were made a precondition to the issuing of a marriage licence, procedural objections to the way in which a marriage contract had been negotiated would always be a potential ground for avoidance.

The advantages of contract in clarifying goals and improving communication are desirable but the issue of enforcement is problematical. Firstly, there are the problems alluded to already of ignorance and inequality, which could lead to non-enforcement. Secondly, even if an action for breach of contract is successful, what view is the court to take of the measure of damages? Should damages be measured according to the reliance interest, on a theory of contract as reliance-based? Or should the court look to liabilities and benefits and calculate these? Would third parties, such as children, also be privy to the contract? How would the court assess the benefits and liabilities associated with children? *and the affluent!*

Since marriage or cohabitation contracts are likely to be the preserve of the well-informed and self-assertive, what of those who make no contract or whose contract is avoided? In these cases, presumably, the court will have to imply a contract, based on the parties' intentions and behaviour. There is then the danger that the implied contract will be imbued with exactly the patriarchal terms of traditional marriage from which the parties are attempting to escape. Thus if the court recognises inequality of bargaining power, there is the danger that in so doing it will be acting in a paternalistic fashion. If it then implies new terms which take account of inequality, it may stand accused of paternalism a second time.

Shultz suggests that under the American model most marriage agreements would not come before the courts for dispute-resolution, partly because compliance with the obligations would be high, and partly because, as with commercial contracts, private arbitration would be used. 'The bulk of contract law's impact on marriage thus would be of the indirect type . . . a background influence on conduct and private dispute settlement, a vague threat keeping the parties reliable, a legitimation of certain ideologies, and a lever allowing the powerless to influence the powerful.'[44] When disputes occur, aside from any positive effect they may have in increasing communication, mediation and conciliation may be used prior to adjudication. There is a place for adjudication, for 'if marital obligations are to be taken seriously, they need some form of enforcement and dispute resolution other than divorce.'[45]

Legalisation increases individualism and a market mentality. It discourages those selfless values so necessary to personal relations. Using the law is regarded by most people as a sign of caution and a lack of trust. Although legalisation confers individual rights it does not necessarily create equality. As Marjorie Shultz admits: 'A particularly troublesome problem of "wrong" choices arises from the tendency of private ordering to reflect and reinforce power disparities in existing relationships.'[46] As the example of property rights gained by married women under the Married Women's Property Acts 1870 to 1882 shows, an individualistic system does not benefit those who have dedicated themselves to others. To benefit from that particular reform it was necessary to be a market-place actor and not a homeworker. Permitting women who have no means of acquiring property to own it is to suggest that they change their philosophy of life from altruism to individualism.

The major problem with legalisation is that it will not affect existing inequalities. As Roberto Unger explains: 'the hierarchies that affect most directly and deeply the individual's situation are those of the family, the workplace and the market. These inequalities are neither undone nor effectively redressed by the commitment to formal equality before the law.'[47]

Informal Justice

Dissatisfaction with legal institutions and with legal methods in controlling conduct and handling conflict has led to their substitution by informal justice. In the sphere of personal relations this manifests itself as a change from formal judicial processing of family conflict to informal mediation and conciliation by the family court and other officials of the state. The advantages of informal mechanisms for coping with family disputes are said to be that they are inexpensive, discretionary, personalised, voluntary, consensus-oriented and therapeutic, and that, unlike formal methods, they empower the participants.

Informal institutions increase state control. Agencies dealing with the person can permeate society, being both dispersed and all-encompassing. There is a strong possibility that informality will stabilise social relations and reinforce existing inequalities as 'no dramatic change can be expected from institutions or settings that must be oriented to consensus and harmony because of the limits on their coercive powers.'[48] By inducing the parties to submit voluntarily to mediation and by involving them in working out a solution informal justice increases their acquiescence in the outcome.

The term 'family court' is used to convey a collection of differing and conflicting proposals for the reform of existing family jurisdictions. Such tribunals have been established in Australia and New Zealand and in some jurisdictions in the United States. Arguments supporting similar reform of English law range from economic efficiency to the advantages of combining therapy with adjudication. Thus it is argued that a family court system which unified the jurisdictions of magistrates' courts, county court and High Court would save money, time and paper. However, these arguments are taken further in criticisms not only relating to efficiency but also of traditional legal methods. At the forefront is a critique of the adversarial nature of proceedings in English courts which are said to be unsuited to family disputes. It is claimed that, instead of the court playing a part in reconciling or conciliating the parties, the adversarial method escalates conflict and creates lasting bitterness. Furthermore, family courts could offer welfare and counselling services, investigating and dealing with medical, mental, financial, child-delinquency, child-abuse and custody problems. The desirable outcome, as seen by advocates of this change, would be the replacement of the adversarial system and its polarised participants by a therapeutic inquisitorial approach. Reorienting the parties to accept a compromise solution to their dispute is an essential part of this process. The emphasis on therapy is combined with the virtual elimination of judicial process and its substitution by administrative and welfare services. The dangers to civil liberties of such an approach are self-evident.

Conciliation and mediation on divorce are forms of negotiation in which the disputants attempt to arrive at a compromise to their dispute with the aid of a third party. This may be done privately or through a state-provided mediator. It is to state involvement in this informal process that this section addresses itself. Arguments in favour of conciliation are that it empowers the parties, it enables them to structure their dispute, it supports their reinterpretation of what is fair, it enables them to consider the welfare of the family as a whole, and it creates an avenue of communication for the future.

The state becomes involved in mediation by the provision of welfare conciliation services prior to divorce or through in-court pre-trial review. State involvement in England has taken the official form of in-court mediation by registrars and court welfare officials. The focus has been on property and child-custody issues. A major problem that has emerged from conciliation proceedings on child-custody disputes is whether the line between the duty to the court of the welfare officer to safeguard the interests of the child, and the welfare officer's role as mediator, is being blurred. Under the legislation the court, prior to granting a divorce where there are minor children, must be satisfied that arrangements for their welfare 'are satisfactory or are the best that can be devised in the circumstances'.[49] One of the ways in which the court ascertains whether the arrangements are satisfactory is by requiring an independent report from the court welfare officer, although this is done only in a minority of cases. Thus the court welfare officer on the one hand may be involved in investigating the adequacy of the parties as parents in order to advise the court on a judicial dispute, and on the other hand may be helping the parents to come to a private agreement over custody. An example of failure to maintain this boundary comes from a court welfare officer:

In Leicestershire the divorce court welfare officer's report which was once a request for information has now become an opportunity to mediate. The parties are drawn together to work jointly on their responsibility for their children's future, the work goes on during the 'enquiries' and ideally the welfare report merely becomes a retrospective summary of what has been achieved.[50]

The lawyer, familiar with the adversarial process, can easily see the implicit threat to the interests of the parties in the blurring of this boundary. In judicial proceedings privilege, confidentiality and individual freedom are carefully safeguarded. There are dangers that mediation may be used to gain more information for a welfare report which is then used in criminal or adversarial proceedings.

A conciliated outcome to a disputed divorce may achieve the advantages claimed for it, but what is lost? It is suggested that three other features stand out. These are the maintenance of inequality, the containment of anger, and privacy. Informality stabilises power and the status quo. Demands by the powerless made through formal legal procedure acquire a legitimacy; if made in the privacy of a mediation session they may appear unreasonable. In containing anger, aggression and hostility, conciliation offers a strategy of conflict-avoidance.

Avoidance, surely, is the ultimate in individualism – severance of a dyadic relationship even before conflict has flowered . . . . Informal institutions encourage a limited voicing of grievances in place of precipitate avoidance by offering some continuing anonymity (through privacy) and, more importantly, protection from revenge. Yet the consequence is not to direct anger outward – at the respondent, much less at the more fundamental causes of the grievance – but rather to turn it inwards on the grievant himself.[51]

Informal meetings with a mediator take place in complete privacy. The compromise is individual. It does not form a precedent for the future, nor constitute a public statement of justice. On the contrary it embodies a private, personal view or acquiescence.

Privatisation

Privatisation of intimate relationships without state interference, supervision or agreement-enforcement would be an extension of the system prevailing in English law at present. During marriage or cohabitation there is no special régime to deal with many aspects of the relationship; it is for the partners to resolve their own problems. On breakdown or dissolution, however, the law intervenes. At present this is done through the liberal rule of law. The state by legislation provides rights and remedies which can be asserted through the courts. Although divorce has become an administrative process, matters of child custody and property allocation remain substantive legal issues which are handled through formal procedures. This is not to deny that the judiciary have a considerable leeway of discretion in deciding these issues. Nevertheless standards have been enunciated and are open to scrutiny. Cases are reported and are looked to as precedents. Procedural formality and the laying down of standards for decision and review provide the disputants and their advisers with guidelines for settling the dispute.

It is otherwise with privatised conflict settlement. Not only do the state and legal institutions regard personal relations as unjusticiable but their termination also becomes a private matter outside the law. It is for the parties to settle their differences, by using a private mediator, by personal unenforceable bargain, or by the imposition of a solution by the more powerful. Some commentators believe that this is the way of the future.

A major distinction between a completely privatised approach and other forms of private ordering such as contract or informal institutions is the absence of legal principles and court enforcement. In some versions of private ordering, bargaining over personal relations takes place against a legal backdrop; it is a 'process by which parties to a marriage are empowered to create their own legally enforceable commitments'.[52] Legal provisions which give guidance to the negotiators as to how to order their affairs are crucial to the compromise that is reached. The outcome is influenced by 'legal rules that allow the imposition of a particular allocation if the parties fail to reach agreement'.[53] Thus each party's bargaining position depends on their beliefs about the content of legal principles and how the matter would be resolved in court. The role of the law in providing general rules representing the community's views of what is fair continues. But in the case of absolute privatisation there would be no legal standards to which to turn. In the first three instances the law retains its hortatory and symbolic function as a statement of social justice. With privatisation there is total autonomy. Is it an exaggeration to suggest that this would be governed by the law of the jungle?

Legal Withdrawal?

The withdrawal of law from the ordering of personal relations has been described as 'a return to forms of social control other than legal rules concerning the formation, dissolution and organisation of married life'.[54] This has been supported on the pragmatic grounds that law is unsuited to the regulation of family matters and that it is unenforceable in this area. Behind this is a theory of the limitations of law and a particular view of the family. The role of law is confined to adversarial proceedings and trouble-shooting. The family is believed to be best left in private. It is suggested that these views represent a narrow conception both of law and of family relations.

In answering these points a distinction must be drawn between regulating existing relationships and patching up the consequences of termination. Some critics argue that although law has a function on dissolution it has no previous role to play. They would confine law to a pragmatic role and exclude its hortatory function. This is based on a value judgement that the family is better off without legal intervention; 'as little law as possible . . . . It is for living without families that many laws are required.'[55] This further presumes that no relationship will continue after dissolution, but where there are children this may not be so.

The counter argument is being advanced here that law has a function not only to catch marriage fall-out in its safety net but also to provide statements of justice for those in existing personal relationships. It is doubtful whether it is either possible or desirable for the state to withdraw completely from the regulation of marriage, directly or indirectly. In the American models of private ordering the symbolic significance of law and its ultimate role in adjudication remain crucial. In the English welfare state public law continues to constitute and regulate the family indirectly. 'The influence of legal symbols is indirect but powerful. Legal values condition perceptions, establish role expectations, provide standards of legitimacy,' observes Shultz on marriage contracts.[56]

If law's role as standard bearer, symbol and community arbiter of justice is recognised then the pragmatic account is insufficient to confront law as ideology. Discussion of law's ideological function takes place on a variety of levels. I suggest that pragmatic arguments concerning the unsuitability and unenforceability of law in family affairs contain an ideology as does the law's abstinence from intervention in the private. This point is illustrated in the account of eighteenth-century criminal law in England by Douglas Hay. During that period Parliament enacted one of the bloodiest criminal codes in Europe with the penalty of death for crimes against property. Despite this the numbers of executions were lower than in the seventeenth century and executions did not match convictions. Increased use of the royal pardon and transportation and acquittals on technical grounds are part of the explanation, but Hay is concerned with the apparent contradiction that the gentry resisted proposed reform of the law which would have made its enforcement more certain. He explains Parliament's determination to retain all capital statutes and to continue to create new ones, even when both were ineffective, as a concern with authority. 'The criminal law was critically important in maintaining bonds of obedience and deference, in legitimising the status quo, in constantly recreating the structure of authority which arose from property and in turn protected its interests.'[57] Law's importance as ideology, analysed by Hay through concepts of majesty, justice and mercy, was that it was internalised by the people through consent and submission. It represented authority outside and above the power of the ruling class, even though class interest was merely disguised.

An ideology endures by not being wholly enforced and rigidly defined. Its effectiveness lies first in its very elasticity, the fact that men are not required to make it a credo, that it seems to them a product of their own minds and their own experience . . . . The second strength of an ideology is its generality. Provided that its depths are not explored too often or by too many, it remains a reservoir of belief throughout the society.[58]

Thus, although the law was not enforced in many instances, it nevertheless was a potent symbol of justice which was internalised by the masses.

It is important that law, if it is to be effective as ideology, be seen as independent and fair. As Edward Thompson observes, 'the essential precondition for the effectiveness of law, in its function as ideology, is that it shall display an independence from gross manipulation and shall seem to be just.'[59] If we now reconsider the pragmatic arguments for law's withdrawal from the regulation of personal relations we can see how its absence is as significant as its presence.

Other arguments for law's withdrawal are that the private should be inviolable and that personal relations are governed by morality which in a pluralist society must be left to individual judgement. These points raise again the liberal view of society as split between public and private. The functionality of such a split to the liberal state cannot be denied, but as has been previously argued, this overlooks power relations within the private and law's function as ideology. In other words the liberal view of the world is as much a product of epistemology and ideology as the feminist view. To this can be added the point made in Chapter 7 that the law is not neutral in its absence from the private since it has already defined and constituted the sex/gender order in the public. 'Rather than transcending the private as a predicate to politics, feminism politicizes it. For women, the private necessarily transcends the private. If the most private also most "affects society as a whole", the separation between public and private collapses as anything other than potent ideology.'[60]

The argument I am advancing here is that law in its presence or deliberate absence has an ideological function, that it embodies principles and standards considered just in the community, and that its absence from the sphere of personal relations is highly significant. It might therefore appear that I am advocating increased legalisation or regulation of the private. Although I concede that as an intermediate strategy this has its merits, the problem remains that such a strategy accepts and reinforces existing dichotomies. Allied to this are technical problems of law's form which illustrate the wider problem. A major legal technical problem, that of a choice between a discretionary system and a rule-bound system, presents itself particularly acutely in relation to the family. There is a current view that this can be overcome through a principled approach.

A System of Principles or Market-Place Values?

Decision-making in English law about relationships during marriage and after divorce has been characterised for over a decade by an *ad hoc* or 'palm tree' justice approach. General provisions in legislation, such as s.25 of the Matrimonial Causes Act 1973, enable the decision-maker to take account of a wide variety of factors. This is a parliamentary recognition that there are a wide variety of factual situations to be encompassed. General rules cannot be devised to cover the complexities. This leads to an *ad hoc* balancing of interests by courts which have discretion. As discretions have become widespread, rules and principles are no longer emphasised. In certain areas of family law, such as division of property and other financial consequences of divorce, it is no exaggeration to say that there are no rules left at all. This is true also of custody decisions and of succession, where there is an application under the Inheritance (Provision for Family and Dependants) Act 1975. Discretion permits the judge to do as he pleases, within very wide limits. The result, as far as divorce is concerned, has been an enormous increase of work for the courts in deciding matters of child custody, property and maintenance.

Unhappiness with law's role in dealing with termination of personal relations comes from criticism of judicial discretion. Patrick

Atiyah has argued that the law now deals with the infinite variety of circumstances which give rise to a suit on matrimonial property by the individualised *ad hoc* approach of discretion. This undermines the rule of law as it abandons its hortatory function. He advocates a return to principles, which he sees as a rule of some generality giving guidance for future conduct. Criticising the limitation of law to a mere patching-up role, he nevertheless admits that this has the advantage of obscuring the values which are informing discretionary decisions. If general principles are enunciated it is harder to conceal the values underlying them.

Although Atiyah believes that a return to principles is possible, it seems more likely that his present analysis points up a central dilemma in liberal society: 'there has been a profound shift away from the belief in the hortatory function of the law, a shift from principles to pragmatism, a shift from the desire to lay down general rules for future application to the desire to do justice according to the particular circumstances of the case.'[61] It is not possible to return to Atiyah's principles unless a consensus can be engendered which speaks of values such as sharing and equality. At present the liberal version of the dichotomy between public and private is imbued in law and public discourse. This has led to the problem identified by Atiyah.

The combination of the belief in privacy of ongoing marriage and the use of discretion to resolve disputes on breakdown or termination of marriage results in a kind of anarchy. There are managerial problems for the courts, hence the current popularity of private ordering on divorce. Undoubtedly the courts have created some of the problems for themselves. Given the breadth of their discretion, the object for the courts is to adjust the conflict and to reach a fair solution. No thought is given to the ideological content of the pronouncements made. In any case, the courts do not see their primary function as being that of laying down rules for future conduct or guidance to the married. In their confining of their function to deciding a particular case the judiciary take a limiting view of their relationship to Parliament and to future litigants. They also ignore the ideological content of their decisions.

A system of principles governing private relations is an attractive alternative to the present combination of privacy and discretion. The major principle would be that of equality. From equality would stem other norms such as work-sharing, property-sharing, income-sharing, non-violence and recognition of the dignity of the other. The elaboration of the principle and consequent norms would be highly significant. It might be said that the enunciation of general principles governing marriage is a purely idealistic exercise and that it is of no practical significance. This type of pragmatic argument, so often raised by common lawyers, overlooks or refuses to recognise the ideological aspect of law. Only its dispute-resolution function is recognised. The lack of consensus about equality as a value in marriage could be raised against equality as a principle. This is the crux of the issue whether the state is to lay down standards for personal relations. But, as I have already made explicit, the absence of state regulation of the private does not mean that no state view exists. It does. Both private and public law are suffused with the ideology of the family, which operates on gendered subjects.

If a system of principles is to operate in family law it will have to be based on a consensus about a common moral position. In the absence of this it is not surprising that individual negotiations have been advocated as a way of dealing with intimate relations. This is an inevitable development in the history of the personal. No one should be surprised to find that the values of the market-place have entered the private sphere. The very unregulated nature of the private has meant that those with the greater power in the public sphere have dominated the private. The idea of marital privacy which the courts have upheld has been another form of the theory of the unity of husband and wife. As already shown, unity of the spouses has been a source of legal discrimination against women.

The emergence and expansion of personal life for the masses of people in the twentieth century has meant the upholding of the self as an autonomous realm outside society. Personal feelings and inner needs are to be realised on an individual basis, and yet within the family. Subjectivity yet co-operation with other family members is the goal of contract. This is a potent mixture which is likely to blow apart. The individual's search for warmth, intimacy and mutual support is directed towards intimate relations, in direct contrast with social relations in the public world, which are characterised by anonymity, coercion, alienation and anomie. In the public world the individual is reduced to an economic unit. People are valued in financial terms – how much they earn, how much they own, how much they are worth. The private sphere was seen as an escape from all that. But since the values of the public sphere dominated, the very unquantifiable character of the private sphere made it seem valueless.

The work performed in the private sphere of childcare and

housework is regarded as having no monetary value and therefore as worthless. The location of these activities in the private sphere has obscured their existence and nature and rendered them invisible. The paradox is that, if these activities are to be valued in terms of the public world, they must lose their personal quality and must move into the public sphere. Under the logic of capitalism the private sphere has no value. Yet this is contrary to the everyday experience of those who might say that their relations in the public sphere are priceless. In order to value the personal it must become impersonal.

The ideology of gender and the division of labour which pre-dated capitalism ensured that, when work and home were separated in the course of industrialisation, women became primarily identified with the home. Engels saw this private sphere as based on the private appropriation of communal property. 'The wife became the first domestic servant pushed out of participation in social production.' The answer was to abolish private property and for women to take part in production on a large scale. But whether these changes would abolish personal service or the personal life is doubtful. The 'freedom' sought in a separate sphere of personal life is, to a large extent, a reaction to the public world. Should the values of the market-place intrude, this could mean the destruction of the private.

The idea that there are no public criteria for choice amongst preferences for ordering private relations must be resisted. This is the consequence of the privatisation of personal morality, with the basis for consensus appearing groundless. But society does maintain certain moral beliefs through both public and private law. Violence against others, however personal, is considered wrong. Even if the legal order represents a balance among competing groups, there is a certain agreement about fundamentals.

Private ordering during marriage and on breakdown or termination may have an important role to play. After all, the will as a legal document is a form of private ordering recognised for centuries. But for a society to hand over completely to the private sphere the ordering of personal relations would be an important step along the road of signalling the end of the rule of law. This development would also involve an acknowledgement of the disintegration of consensus on personal morality, an outcome of the liberal distinction between public and private. Yet, as already shown, the distinction between public and private, whether in terms of morality or spheres, is in no way immutable. It varies at different historical times and under different economic and social conditions. The particular form of private life experienced in twentieth-century Western society is the product of a particular set of relations between the economic system and its effect on individuals. The resulting idealisation of privacy ignores its oppressive effects on those confined to the private sphere, just as it ignores the inequality that results from being apart from the public world whose values, however hated, dominate not only the public but also the private lives of all.

It is an inevitable feature of liberal society that the rule of law is undermined in its dealings with personal relations. It is not just that moral and religious ideals have lost consensual support. The rule of law is characterised by its commitment to generality, by its autonomy and by its neutrality. Individualised justice, as under a discretionary system, is the opposite. Since, in liberal society, the law's role in personal relations is under attack it must retreat into discretion. At the same time the law's claim to objectivity is most suspect in this sphere, since it is here that it is most evidently dealing with gendered subjects.

What Are the Alternatives?

So far we have considered legalisation, regulation, dejuridification and privatisation as alternatives to traditional legal liberalism.[62] It has also been shown that the challenge to liberalism comes not only from informal institutions but from within through the use of discretion. Abel explains the rise of informal justice as a means of avoiding challenge to the status quo. He points out that:

informalism helps to legitimize the legal system by distracting attention from problems of formal institutions. These, it is argued, are not defective; they are simply being asked to do too much and to do the wrong kinds of things. The solution, therefore, is not to reform the core of the legal system . . . but rather to create alternative institutions at the periphery.[63]

The problem for the upholders of the status quo is that individualised justice through the use of discretion undermines the generality of the rule of law and therefore its legitimacy. Finally, I have suggested that sources of these problems are to be found in legal definition and constitution of dichotomies between women and men, between private and public.

There are a number of alternative strategies that can be put forward to alter this. Legalisation and regulation have already been discussed as intermediate moves. But even these reforms require a recognition that law operates on gendered subjects, that formal equality masks gender inequality when applied within a system of sexual stratification. So long as the law and its interpreters claim to be neutral and objective when operating within a liberal framework, no objectivity is possible. Epistemological issues of the placing of the private, which is central to women's experience, beyond the law must be confronted. Once this happens reforms through legalisation and regulation, useful though they may be, will be perceived to be inadequate. The collapse of the distinction between public and private must follow. It is clear that this is not just a matter of epistemology and the way in which law is produced or interpreted but a fundamental question of how human beings live.

Afterword

'The formal legal framework of modern democratic societies is the guardian of the abstract individual. It provides for formal equality (before the law) and formal freedom (from illegal or arbitrary treatment). These are crucial and indispensable gains but, if we are to take equality and liberty seriously, they must be transcended.'[1] Transcendence from the abstract individual – which conception takes little account of the specificity of women's maternal and domestic roles – to what?

Respect for persons requires us to go beyond the liberal conception of the individual as a bundle of aims, motives and desires. We owe other human beings 'an effort at identification', so that we do not regard them 'as the surface to which a certain label can be applied'; rather we should try to see the world from their point of view.[2] That this point of view is determined largely by forces outside the individual should not deter us. We need to recognise that selves and self-conceptions are constituted by our roles within the communities we inhabit. The freely choosing individual depicted by rights-based liberalism may in life have her choices limited by family and responsibility to others. Her conception of the good is shaped not only by her situation as parent or family member, but also by her moral beliefs in the rightness of her conduct of her role. Throughout this book it has been argued that beliefs about the good within the family lead many women to reject the various forms of individualism and to embrace selflessness and self-abnegation.

We cannot justify arrangements in private, or even in public, without reference to an agreed view of the good. This good is not the utilitarian aggregation of preferences, but an agreement about values. The power of one member of a community to impose his individual views is a denial of the common purpose of all the members. Insofar as legal institutions support this power they are involved in a denial of equality.

If equality is to be more than merely formal, if it is to be taken seriously, then we must look at individuals in their particular situations. Rights-based liberalism, whilst providing some of the conditions for respect for persons, fails to recognise the morality of communitarian values. Family responsibility, care and obligation – this is not only the language of domestic concern, it is also a morality of concern for others. It will not be enough however to affirm such values as private. It is in their extension to the public sphere that transcendence will be achieved.

References

Foreword

1. Milsom, S. F. C., 'Introduction', in F. Pollock and F. W. Maitland, *The History of English Law*, 2nd edn (Cambridge U.P., reissued 1968), p. xxvi.
2. This book addresses itself primarily to English law, with some comparative references to American law. However, I believe that the analysis presented applies to Western societies in general.
3. See the article by Richard Abel, 'Law Books and Books About Law', 26 *Stanford L. Rev.* 175 (1973), in which he distinguishes law books which declare the law from books about law containing discussion and criticism.

Chapter 1: Divisions and Dichotomies

1. Mill, J. S., *On Liberty* (London: Dent, 1910), p. 9.
2. *Ibid.*
3. Constant, B., *De L'Esprit de Conquête* (1814), cited by Lukes, S., *Individualism* (Oxford: Blackwell, 1973), p. 65.
4. Lukes, *ibid.*, p. 66.
5. *Ibid.*, p. 62. The account of individualism in this book is largely drawn from Lukes.
6. Smith, D., 'Women, the family and corporate capitalism', in M. Stephenson (ed.), *Women in Canada* (Toronto: New Press, 1974), p. 6.
7. Ehrenreich, B., and English, D., *For Her Own Good* (London: Pluto Press, 1979), p. 9.
8. Kamenka, E., 'What is justice?', in E. Kamenka and A. E. S. Tay (eds.), *Justice* (London: E. Arnold, 1979), p. 7.
9. See Rudden, B., 'Real Property?', 2 *Oxford J. of Leg. Studs.* 238 (1982).
10. Prosser, W. L., 'Privacy', 48 *Calif. L. Rev.* 383 (1960).
11. (1848) 2 DeG & Sm. 652 at 697.
12. [1967] Ch. 302.
13. (1979) 129 *N.L.J.* 636.
14. Report of the Committee on Privacy, Cmnd. 5012 (1972), para. 78.
15. Anderson, M., 'The Relevance of Family History', in C. Harris (ed.), *The Sociology of the Family* (Keele: Soc. Rev. Monograph No. 28, 1979), p. 67.
16. Horwitz, M., 'The History of the Public/Private Distinction', 130 *U. Penn. L. Rev.* 1423 (1982), p. 1424.
17. Unger, R., *Knowledge and Politics* (N.Y.: Free Press, 1975), p. 59.
18. Mill. J. S., *On the Subjection of Women* (London: Dent, 1929), p. 263.

19. Cmd. 247 (1957), para. 13.

20. *Ibid.*, para. 61.

21. [1973] 1 All E.R. 512.

22. *Ibid.*, p. 524.

23. *Ibid.*

24. *Ibid.*, p. 516.

25. *Balfour* v. *Balfour* [1919] 2 K.B. 571 at 579.

26. Aries, P., *Centuries of Childhood* (London: Jonathan Cape, 1973), p. 385.

27. *Semayne's Case* (1604) 77 E.R. 194.

28. *In re Agar-Ellis* (1883) 24 Ch.D. 317 at 335.

29. Hansard (H.L.), vol. 405 (1980), col. 147.

30. Hansard, vol. 191 (1908), col. 279.

31. Lord Evershed, 'Foreword' to R. H. Graveson and F. R. Crane (eds.), *A Century of Family Law* (London: Sweet & Maxwell, 1957), p. xv.

32. *Balfour* v. *Balfour* [1919] 2 K.B. 571.

33. Eekelaar, J., *Family Security and Family Breakdown* (Harmondsworth: Penguin, 1971), p. 76.

34. Kahn-Freund, O., and Wedderburn, K. W., 'Editorial Foreword' to J. Eekelaar, *op. cit.* note 33, p. 7.

35. Pinchbeck, I., and Hewitt, M., *Children in English Society*, vol. 2 (London: Routledge, 1973), p. 357.

36. 39 Eliz. 1, c.3 (1597); 43 Eliz. 1, c.2 (1601). See TenBroek, J., 'California's Dual System of Family Law', Part 1, 16 *Stanford L. Rev.* 257 (1964).

37. See e.g. Freeman, M. D. A., *The Rights and Wrongs of Children* (London: Frances Pinter, 1983), p. 245; Goldstein, J. *et al.*, *Beyond the Best Interests of the Child* (London: Free Press, 1973), pp. 49–52.

38. Collier, J., Rosaldo, M., and Yanagisako, S., 'Is There a Family?', in B. Thorne and M. Yalon (eds.), *Rethinking the Family* (N.Y.: Longman, 1982), p. 35.

39. Rosaldo, M. Z., 'Women, Culture and Society', in M. Z. Rosaldo and L. Lamphere, *Women, Culture and Society* (Stanford U. P., 1974).

40. Rosaldo, M. Z., 'The Use and Abuse of Anthropology', 5 *Signs* (1980), p. 401.

41. Rosaldo, *op. cit.* note 39, p. 20.

42. *Ibid.*, p. 39.

43. Firestone, S., *The Dialectic of Sex* (N.Y.: Bantam Books, 1970), p. 5.

44. E.g. *Reed* v. *Reed*, 404 U.S. 71 (1971); *Frontiero* v. *Richardson*, 411 U.S. 677 (1973).

45. In Britain the Equal Pay Act 1970 and the Sex Discrimination Act 1975 made up an 'equality package'. In the US the equal protection clause of the Fourteenth Amendment to the Constitution has been the basis for court litigation. Title VII of the Civil Rights Act 1964 and the Equal Pay Act 1963 also form part of American anti-discrimination legislation.

46. Barrett, M., *Women's Oppression Today* (London: Verso, 1980), p. 212.

47. Marx, K., *Economic and Philosophical Manuscripts of 1844* (London: Lawrence and Wishart, 1973), p. 110.

48. MacKinnon, C. A., 'Feminism, Marxism, Method, and the State: Toward Feminist Jurisprudence', 8 *Signs* 635 (1983), p. 655.

49. *Ibid.*, p. 656.

50. See Powers, K., 'Sex Segregation and the Ambivalent Directions of Sex Discrimination Law', 1979 *Wis. L. Rev.* 55; Olsen, F., 'The Family and the Market: A Study of Ideology and Legal Reform', 96 *Harv. L. Rev.* 1497 (1983); Taub, N., and Schneider, E. M., 'Perspectives on Women's Subordination and the Role of Law',

in D. Kairys (ed.) *The Politics of Law* (N.Y.: Pantheon Books, 1983). I discovered most of this literature when my own work was largely completed.

51. Carol Smart's book, *The Ties that Bind* (London: Routledge, 1984), was published after I had finished writing.
52. Summers, R. S., 'The Technique Element in Law', 59 *Calif. L. Rev.* 733 (1971).
53. See Minow, M., 'The Properties of Family and The Families of Property', 92 *Yale L. J.* 376 (1982).

Chapter 2: From Feudalism and Patriarchy to Market Society

1. This chapter has been summarised from long and detailed chapters which covered the ground in descriptive detail.
2. Laslett, P. (ed.), *Patriarcha* by Sir R. Filmer (Oxford: Blackwell, 1949).
3. Miller, D., *Social Justice* (Oxford: Clarendon, 1976), p. 286.
4. Goody, J., *Production and Reproduction* (Cambridge U.P., 1976), p. 92.
5. Early battles in the royal courts where landholders attempted to alienate their land and the overlord tried to prevent this, ended in victory for underlord.
6. Pollock, F., and Maitland, F. W., *The History of English Law*, vol. II (Cambridge U.P., 1968), p. 307.
7. Hajnal, J., 'European Marriage Patterns in Perspective', in D. V. Glass and D. E. C. Eversley (eds.), *Population in History* (London: Edward Arnold, 1965), p. 124.
8. Homans, G. C., *English Villagers of the Thirteenth Century* (N.Y.: Norton, 1975), p. 110.
9. Bracton, *On the Laws and Customs of England*, vol. II (Harvard U.P., 1968), p. 265.
10. Coulton, G. G., *Medieval Panorama* (Cambridge U.P., 1938), p. 88.
11. Coulton, G. G., *Medieval Village, Manor and Monastery* (N.Y.: Harper Torchbrooks, 1960), p. 101.
12. Le Roy Ladurie, E., 'Family Structures and Inheritance Customs in Sixteenth Century France', in J. Goody, J. Thirsk and E. P. Thompson (eds.), *Family and Inheritance* (Cambridge U.P., 1976), p. 55.
13. Pollock, F., and Maitland, F. W., *op. cit.* note 6, vol. II, p. 281.
14. Goody, J., *op. cit.* note 4, p. 55.
15. Postan, M. M., *Medieval Economy and Society* (Harmondsworth: Pelican, 1975), p. 37.
16. *Ibid.*, p. 163.
17. Hilton, R., *The English Peasantry in the Later Middle Ages* (Oxford: Clarendon, 1975), p. 103.
18. Coulton, G. G., *op. cit.* note 10, p. 619.
19. Middleton, C., 'Property and Patriarchy among the Peasantry of Medieval England', paper given at Women's Studies Seminar, University of Kent (1979), p. 58.
20. Glanvill, vol. VI (London: Nelson, 1965), p. 3; Bracton, *op. cit.* note 9, vol. IV, p. 166.
21. Bailey, S. J., 'Warranties of Land in the Thirteenth Century', 8 *Cambridge Law Journal* 274 (1942), p. 275.
22. Bailey, S. J., 'The Countess Gundred's Lands', 10 *Cambridge Law Journal* 84 (1948), p. 91.
23. Bracton, *op. cit.* note 9, vol. IV, p. 166.

24. Glanvill, *op. cit.* note 20, vol. VI, p. 3.

25. Bracton, *op. cit.* note 9, vol. II, p. 25.

26. See Sachs, A., and Wilson, J. H., *Sexism and the Law* (Oxford: Martin Robertson, 1978).

27. Pollock and Maitland, *op. cit.* note 6, vol. II, p. 401.

28. *Ibid.*, p. 402.

29. Holdsworth, W. S., *A History of English Law*, vol. III (London: Methuen, 1942), p. 520 *et seq.*

30. Pollock and Maitland, *op. cit.* note 6, vol. II, p. 432.

31. Sheehan, M. M., 'The Influence of Canon Law on the Property of Married Women in England', 25 *Medieval Studies* 109 (1963), p. 118.

32. MacFarlane, A., *The Origins of English Individualism* (Oxford: Blackwell, 1978), p. 131.

33. Engels, F., *The Origin of the Family, Private Property and the State* (London: Lawrence and Wishart, 1972).

34. Boserup, E., *Woman's Role in Economic Development* (London: Allen & Unwin, 1970), p. 50.

35. Scammell, J., 'Freedom and Marriage in Medieval England', 27 *Economic History Review* 523 (1974), p. 526.

36. Searle, E., 'Freedom and Marriage in Medieval England: An Alternative Hypothesis', 29 *Economic History Review* 482 (1976).

37. Bracton, *op. cit.* note 9, vol. III, p. 374.

38. Clark, A., *The Working Lives of Women in the Seventeenth Century* (London: Routledge, 1919), p. 196.

39. Maine, H., *Ancient Law* (London: John Murray, 1930), p. 180.

40. Donzelot, J., *Policing the Family* (London: Hutchinson, 1979), p. 50.

41. *Ibid.*, p. 69.

42. TenBroek, J., 'California's Dual System of Family Law', 16 *Stanford L. Rev.* 257 (1964), p. 286.

43. 18 Eliz. 1, c.3, 1575.

44. Hair, P. E. H., *Before the Bawdy Court* (London: Elek, 1972), p. 236.

45. Laslett, P., 'Introduction', in P. Laslett *et al.* (eds.), *Bastardy and its Comparative History* (London: Edward Arnold, 1980), p. 23.

46. Quaife, G. R., *Wanton Wenches and Wayward Wives* (London: Croom Helm, 1979), p. 91.

47. Wrightson, K., and Levine, D., *Poverty and Piety in an English Village, Terling 1525–1700* (N.Y.: Academic Press, 1979), p. 128.

48. *Ibid.*, p. 133.

49. Wrightson, K., and Levine, D., 'The Social Context of Illegitimacy in Early Modern England', in P. Laslett *et al.* (eds.), *op. cit.* note 45, p. 162.

50. Quaife, G. R., *op. cit.* note 46, p. 61.

51. Helmholz, R. H., *Marriage Litigation in Medieval England* (Cambridge U.P., 1974), p. 27.

52. *Ibid.*, Ch. 2.

53. For the history of Lord Hardwicke's Act, see Manchester, A., *Modern Legal History* (London: Butterworths, 1980).

54. Laslett, P., *The World We Have Lost*, 2nd edn (London: Methuen, 1971), p. 153.

55. *Parliamentary History of England*, vol. 15 (1813), col. 3.

56. *Ibid.*, col. 17.

57. Lord Barrington, *ibid.*, col. 24; Solicitor-General Murray, *ibid.*, col. 75.

58. Gillis, J., 'Resort to Common Law Marriage in England and Wales 1700–1850', in *Law and Human Relations* (Past and Present Society, 1980), p. 5.

59. Jackson, J., *The Formation and Annulment of Marriage*, 2nd edn (London: Butterworths, 1969), gives a good account.

60. Gillis, *op. cit.* note 58, p. 8.

61. Pinchbeck, I., *Women Workers and Industrial Revolution* (London: Virago, 1981), p. 285.

62. Hill, C., *The World Turned Upside Down* (Harmondsworth: Penguin, 1973), p. 312.

63. *Ibid.*, p. 319.

64. Gillis, *op. cit.* note 58, p. 12.

65. *Op. cit.* note 51, p. 31.

66. Mayhew, H., *London Labour and London Poor*, vol. 1 (London: Griffin, 1864), p. 22.

67. Hardy, T., *The Mayor of Casterbridge* (London: Macmillan, 1920), p. 9. I have explored wife sale further in 'Wife Sale and Desertion as Alternatives to Judicial Marriage Dissolution', in J. Eekelaar and S. Katz (eds.), *The Resolution of Family Conflict* (Toronto: Butterworths, 1984), pp. 41–51.

68. Kenny, C., 'Wife Selling in England', 45 *Law Quarterly Review* 494 (1929); Rot. Parl. I, p. 140.

69. Peyton, S. A. (ed.), *The Church Wardens' Presentments in the Oxfordshire Peculiars of Dorchester, Thame and Banbury* (Oxford Records Society, 1928), p. 184; quoted by Thomas, K., 'The Double Standard', *Journal of the History of Ideas* (1959), p. 213.

70. Anon., *The Laws Respecting Women*, reprinted from the J. Johnson edition (London: 1777; N.Y.: Oceana, 1974), p. 55.

71. See Menafee, S. P., *Wives For Sale* (Oxford: Blackwell, 1981).

72. *Notes and Queries*, 2nd Series, vol. 8 (1859), p. 258.

73. *Notes and Queries*, 6th Series, vol. 4 (1881), p. 133.

74. (1763) 3 Burr. 1434, 96 E.R. 234.

75. Rubin, G., 'The Traffic in Women', in R. Reiter (ed.), *Toward an Anthropology of Woman* (N.Y.: Monthly Review Press, 1975), p. 157.

76. *Notes and Queries*, 3rd Series, vol. 3 (1863), p. 486.

77. See Cott, N. F., *The Bonds of Womanhood* (Yale U.P., 1977); Degler, C. N., *At Odds* (N.Y.: Oxford U.P., 1980); Ehrenreich, B., and English, D., *For Her Own Good* (London: Pluto, 1979).

78. *Ibid.*, p. 28.

79. Cited in Strachey, R., *The Cause* (London: Virago, 1978), p. 58.

80. Minor, I., 'Working-Class Women and Matrimonial Law Reform, 1890–1914', in D. Martin and D. Rubinstein (eds.) *Ideology and the Labour Movement* (London: Croom Helm, 1979), pp. 103–24.

81. *Op. cit.* note 40, p. 103.

82. The social purity movement discussed in Chapter 4 concerned itself with sexual matters such as prostitution. It also arose from women's domestic sphere. See Strachey, *op. cit.* note 79.

83. Shanley, M. L., 'One Must Ride Behind: Married Women and the Divorce Act of 1857', 25 *Victorian Studies* 355 (1982).

84. Backhouse, C., 'Shifting Patterns in Nineteenth Century Canadian Custody Law', in D. H. Flaherty (ed.), *Essays in the History of Canadian Law*, vol. 1 (U. of Toronto P., 1981), pp. 212–48.

85. Adultery by the wife was sufficient ground for the husband to divorce her, but the

wife had to prove adultery plus incest, bigamy, cruelty, or desertion for two years, or the offences of rape, sodomy or bestiality.

86. Cited by Brophy, J., 'Parental Rights and Children's Welfare: Some Problems of Feminists' Strategy in the 1920s', 10 *International Journal of the Sociology of Law* 149 (1982).

87. Mill, J. S., *On the Subjection of Women* (London: Dent, 1929), p. 263. See also Holcombe, L., *Wives and Property* (Oxford: Martin Robertson, 1983).

Chapter 3: Legal Construction of Sex and Gender

1. Births and Deaths Registration Act 1953, s.2. S.I. 1968, No. 2049, reg. 16.

2. Smith, D. K., 'Transsexualism, Sex Reassignment Surgery and the Law', 56 *Cornell L. Rev.* 969 (1971).

3. Stoller, R., *Sex and Gender* (N.Y.: Science House, 1968).

4. Oakley, A., *Sex, Gender and Society* (London: Temple Smith, 1975).

5. Bowman, K., and Engle, B., 'Sex Offences: The Medical and Legal Implications of Sex Variations', 25 *Law and Contemp. Problems* 292 (1960), p. 293.

6. Money, J., and Tucker, P., *Sexual Signatures* (London: Abacus, 1977).

7. Archer, J., and Lloyd, B., *Sex and Gender* (Harmondsworth: Penguin, 1982), Ch. 9.

8. *Op. cit.* note 6, p. 75.

9. Money, J., 'Ablato Penis: Normal Male Infant Sex-Reassigned as a Girl', 4 *Archives of Sexual Behaviour* 65 (1975), p. 69.

10. [1971] P. 83 at 105.

11. *Ibid.*, at 107.

12. (1979) F.L.C. 90–636; (1975) 53 A.L.J. 659 (note by R. Bailey).

13. Fraser, Sir K., O'Reilly, M. J. J., and Rintoul, J. R., 'Hermaphroditus Versus, with Report of a Case', 1 *Med. J. of Aus.* 1003 (1966), p. 1006.

14. *Op. cit.* note 12, at 78–327.

15. *Op. cit.* note 6, p. 69.

16. *Op. cit.* note 10, at 104.

17. *Ibid.*, at 106.

18. *Baxter* v. *Baxter* [1948] A.C. 274.

19. Bartholomew, G. W., 'Hermaphrodites and the Law', 2 *Univ. of Malaya L.J.* 83 (1960), p. 108; Finlay, H. A., 'Sexual Identity and the Law of Nullity', 54 *Aus. L.J.* 115 (1980), p. 125.

20. On Germany see Horton, K. C., 'The Law and Transsexualism in West Germany' (1978) *Fam. Law* 191; on France see Pace, P. J., 'Sexual Identity and the Criminal Law', (1983) *Crim. L. Rev.* 317; on Switzerland see *In Re Laber*, Neuchatel Cantonal Court, July 2, 1945, cited by Kennedy, I., 2 *Anglo-American L. Rev.* 112 (1973); on the US see Walz, M. B., 'Transsexuals and the Law', 5 *J. of Contemp. L.* 181 (1979).

21. *Van Oosterwijck* v. *Belgium* 3 E.H.R.R. 557 (1980), at 584. Before the European Court of Human Rights it was held that, by reason of the failure to exhaust domestic remedies, the Court was unable to take cognisance of the merits of the case.

22. Bartholomew, *op. cit.* note 19, p. 84.

23. *Op. cit.* note 21, at 584.

24. *Ibid.*, at 585.

25. *Op. cit.* note 10, at 106.

26. *The Times*, 15 February 1983.
27. Sexual Offences Act 1959, s.1; Sexual Offences Act 1956, s.32.
28. Sexual Offences Act 1956, s.6.
29. [1977] I.R.L.R. 121 at 123.
30. Under the Factories Act 1961, s.89, women are prohibited from working in factories on Sundays.
31. Sex Discrimination Act 1975, s.1.
32. In the United States it has been held that anti-discrimination provisions of Title VII of the Civil Rights Act 1964 do not cover transsexuals: *Sommers* v. *Budget Inc.* 667 F 2d. 748 (8th Cir. 1982). See 24 *Bost. Coll. L. Rev.* 266 (1982). See generally Wein and Remmers, 'Employment Protection and Gender Dysphoria', 30 *Hastings L.J.* 1075 (1979).
33. *Op. cit.* note 29.
34. *Op. cit.* note 10, at 105.
35. Dec. CP 6/76 (Nat. Ins. Comm.).
36. Bem, S. L., 'Probing the Promise of Androgyny', in A. G. Kaplan and J. P. Bean, (eds.), *Beyond Sex-Role Stereotypes* (Boston: Little Brown, 1976).
37. *Op. cit.* note 7, Ch. 2.
38. Mead, M., *Male and Female* (Harmondsworth: Penguin, 1962), p. 81.
39. *Ibid.*, p. 108.
40. *Ibid.*, p. 107.
41. Mead, M., *Sex and Temperament in Three Primitive Societies* (New York: Morrow, 1935), p. 280.
42. Ortner, S. B., 'Is Female to Male as Nature is to Culture?', 1 *Feminist Studies* 5 (1972), p. 7.
43. *Ibid.*, p. 11.
44. *Jex-Blake* v. *Senate of the University of Edinburgh* (1873) 11 M. 784.
45. *Bradwell* v. *Illinois*, 83 U.S. (16 Wall) 130; 21 L. Ed. 442 (1873).
46. Hansard, vol. 175, 4th Ser. (1907), col. 1355.
47. *Ibid.*, col. 1362. The speaker was Lord James of Hereford.
48. *Muller* v. *Oregon*, 208 U.S. 412 (1908).
49. *Hoyt* v. *Florida*, 368 U.S. 57 (1961).
50. Sachs, A., and Wilson, J. H., *Sexism and the Law* (Oxford: Martin Robertson, 1978), p. 9.
51. MacKinnon, C. A., *Sexual Harassment of Working Women* (Yale U.P., 1979), p. 155.
52. Jagger, A., 'On Sexual Equality', 84 *Ethics* 275 (1974) at p. 276.
53. Yates, G. G., *What Women Want* (Harvard U.P., 1975), p. 35.
54. Wasserstrom, R., 'Racism, Sexism and Preferential Treatment', 24 *UCLA L. Rev.* 581 (1977), p. 606.
55. Brown, B., *et al.*, 'The Equal Rights Amendment', 80 *Yale L.J.* 871 (1971), p. 889.
56. *Ibid.*, p. 904.
57. Wolgast, E., *Equality and the Rights of Women* (Cornell U.P., 1980), p. 28.
58. *Duchesne* v. *Duchesne* [1950] 2 All E.R. 784 at 791.
59. *H.* v. *H. and C.* [1969] 1 All E.R. 262 at 263.
60. *Re L. (infants)* [1962] 3 All E.R. 1 at 4.
61. *Re C.* [1978] 2 All E.R. 230.
62. *Wachtel* v. *Wachtel* [1973] Fam. 72 at 94.
63. *Op. cit.* note 42, p. 17.

Chapter 4: The Boundary Between Private and Public

1. Padgug, R. A., 'On Conceptualising Sexuality in History', 20 *Radical History Review* 3 (1979), p. 6.
2. MacKinnon, C. A., 'Feminism, Marxism, Method, and the State: Toward Feminist Jurisprudence', 8 *Signs* 635 (1983), p. 657.
3. Himes, N. E., *Medical History of Contraception* (N.Y.: Gamut Press, 1963), p. 214.
4. *R.* v. *Bradlaugh and Besant* (London: Freethought Publishing Co., 1877), p. 251. See Chandrasekhar, S., *A Dirty Filthy Book* (U. of California P., 1981).
5. (1878) L.R. 3 Q.B. 607 and 625.
6. Box, M., *The Trial of Marie Stopes* (London: Femina Books, 1967).
7. Sanger, M., *My Fight for Birth Control* (London: Faber, 1932).
8. Ministries of Health and Home Office, *Report of the Inter-Departmental Committee on Abortion* (London: HMSO, 1939), paras. 187 and 188.
9. 381 U.S. 479 (1965).
10. 405 U.S. 438 (1972) at 464.
11. 97 Sup. Ct. 2010 (1977) at 2016.
12. *Gillick* v. *West Norfolk and Wisbech Area Health Authority* (1984) *The Times*, 21 December 1984.
13. f. 268, pl. 263 (1516).
14. Dalton, M., *Countrey Justice* (1619), p. 213.
15. *Commentaries*, vol. IV (1775), p. 196.
16. Hale, M., *History of the Pleas of the Crown* (1736), p. 429.
17. Llewellyn-Davies, M., *Maternity* (London: Virago, 1978), p. 89.
18. *Ibid.*, p. 169.
19. *Op. cit.* note 8, para. 26.
20. (1939) 1 K.B. 687.
21. Dickens, B. M., *Abortion and the Law* (London: MacGibbon & Kee, 1966), pp. 77–83.
22. Greenwood, V., and Young, J., *Abortion in Demand* (London: Pluto Press, 1979), p. 33.
23. *Roe* v. *Wade*, 410 U.S. 113 (1973) at 154.
24. [1978] 2 All E.R. 987 at 991.
25. *Ibid.* at 992.
26. 3 EHRR 408 (1981).
27. *Brüggeman and Scheuten* v. *Federal Republic of Germany* 3 EHRR 244 at 258.
28. *Planned Parenthood of Missouri* v. *Danforth* (1976) 428 U.S.52; 49 L.Ed.788.
29. Helmholz, R. H., 'Infanticide in the Province of Canterbury during the Fifteenth Century', 2 *Hist. of Childhood Quart.* (1974), 379 at p. 387.
30. Lecky, W. E. H., *History of European Morals*, vol. 2 (London: 1869), p. 27.
31. Malcolmson, R. W., 'Infanticide in the Eighteenth Century', in J. S. Cockburn (ed.), *Crime in England 1550–1800* (London: Methuen, 1977), p. 196.
32. *Commentaries*, vol. IV (1775), p. 198.
33. Langer, W. L., 'Infanticide: A Historical Survey', 1 *Hist. of Childhood Quart.* (1974), 353 at p. 360.
34. British Parliamentary Papers, vol. 21 (1866), Keating J. at p. 625.
35. *Ibid.*, at p. 291.
36. (1927) 20 Cr. App. R. 132.
37. Cmnd. 6244 (1975), paras. 19, 23.

38. Cmnd. 7844 (1980), para. 103.
39. *Ibid.*, para. 105.
40. *Ibid.*, para. 109.
41. Cmnd. 247 (1957), para. 13.
42. *Ibid.*, para. 255.
43. *R.* v. *Ford* [1978] 1 All E.R. 1129.
44. [1966] 2 Q.B. 81.
45. Home Office, *Working Party on Vagrancy and Street Offence* (Working Paper, 1974), para. 268.
46. *Op. cit.* note 41, para. 285.
47. *Ibid.*, para. 289.
48. Cited in Pinchbeck, I., and Hewitt, M., *Children in English Society*, vol. 2 (London: Routledge, 1973), p. 622.
49. Hansard (H.L.), vol. 125 (1903), col. 822.
50. Hansard, vol. 191 (1908), col. 279.
51. Walmsley, R., and White, K., *Sexual Offences, Consent and Sentencing* (Home Office Research Study No. 54, HMSO, 1980), pp. 41–2.
52. CLRC, Working Paper on Sexual Offences 1980 (HMSO, 1980), paras. 118–20.
53. Gorham, D., 'The "Maiden Tribute of Modern Babylon" Re-Examined', *Victorian Studies*, vol. 21 (1978), 387.
54. *Report on the Age of Consent in Relation to Sexual Offences* (London: HMSO, 1981), Cmnd. 8216, para. 28.
55. 25 Hen. VIII c.6.
56. *Commentaries*, vol. IV, 217.
57. Weeks, J., *Sex, Politics and Society* (London: Longman, 1981), p. 99.
58. Foucault, M., *The History of Sexuality*, vol. 1 (London: Allen Lane, 1979), p. 101.
59. *Dudgeon* v. *United Kingdom* 4 EHRR 149 (1982).

Chapter 5: The Private Relationship of Marriage

1. See Barrett, M., *Women's Oppression Today* (London: Verso, 1980), Ch. 5; Green Paper, *The Taxation of Husband and Wife* (London: HMSO, 1980), Cmnd. 8093; Law Com. No. 103, *Family Law, The Financial Consequences of Divorce: The Basic Policy*, Cmnd. 8041 (1980).
2. Ehrenreich, B., and English, D., *For Her Own Good* (London: Pluto Press, 1979), p. 10.
3. The phrase originates with Lasch, C., *Haven in a Heartless World* (N.Y.: Basic Books, 1977). I do not agree with his thesis.
4. *Balfour* v. *Balfour* [1919] 2 K.B. 571 at 577.
5. *Ibid.* at 579.
6. Under the Domestic Proceedings and Magistrates' Courts Act 1978, s.1, the spouses have a mutual duty of financial support. However, there are no cases of enforcement of the duty where the spouses are cohabiting.
7. Land, H., 'Poverty and Gender: The Distribution of Resources Within the Family', in M. Brown (ed.), *The Structure of Disadvantage* (London: Heinemann, 1983), p. 55.
8. Tilly, L. A., and Scott, J. W., *Women, Work and Family* (N.Y.: Holt, Rinehart and

Winston, 1978).

9. Tebbutt, M., *Making Ends Meet* (Leicester U.P., 1983), p. 39.

10. Select Committee on Pawnbrokers, Parliamentary Papers (1870).

11. *Op. cit.* note 9, p. 66.

12. Todd, J., and Jones, L., *Matrimonial Property* (London: HMSO, 1972).

13. Occupational Pensions Board, *Equal Status for Men and Women in Occupational Pension Schemes*, Cmnd. 6599 (London: HMSO, 1976), para. 14.4.

14. Pahl, J., 'Patterns of Money Management Within Marriage', 9 *J. of Soc. Pol.* 313 (1980); Gray, A., *The Working Class Family as an Economic Unit*, Univ. of Edinburgh, Ph.D. thesis (1974).

15. Land, H., *op. cit.* note 7, p. 52.

16. Barrett, M., and McIntosh, M., *The Anti-Social Family* (London: NLB, 1982), p. 69.

17. Todd and Jones, *op. cit.* note 12, at p. 38; Manners, A. J., and Rauta, I., *Family Property in Scotland* (London: HMSO, 1981).

18. The Matrimonial Homes Act 1983; *Williams and Glyn's Bank Ltd* v. *Boland* [1981] A.C. 487.

19. See Law Com. No. 115, *Property Law: The Implications of Williams and Glyn's Bank Ltd* v. *Boland*, Cmnd. 8636 (London: HMSO, 1982).

20. Prager, S. W., 'Sharing Principles and the Future of Marital Property Law', 25 *UCLA L. Rev.* 1 (1977), p. 2.

21. Glendon, M. A., 'Is there a Future for Separate Property?', 8 *Fam. L. Quart.* 315 (1974), p. 323.

22. Kahn-Freund, O., 'Matrimonial Property and Equality Before the Law: Some Sceptical Reflections', 4 *Hum. Rts. J.* 49 (1971), p. 51.

23. See Scottish Law Commission, Consultative Memorandum No. 57, *Matrimonial Property*; Law Com. No. 115, *op. cit.* note 19; Law Com. No. 86, *Family Law: Third Report on Family Property: The Matrimonial Home* (London: HMSO, 1978).

24. *The Times*, 23 January 1969.

25. Bruch, C., 'Of Work, Family Wealth and Equality', 17 *Fam. L. Quart.* 99 (1983), p. 103.

26. *Op. cit.* note 12, p. 101.

27. Scottish Law Commission, *op. cit.* note 23.

28. Matrimonial Property Act 1976 (N.Z.).

29. *Gissing* v. *Gissing* [1971] A.C. 886, *per* Lord Reid at 896, 897; *per* Lord Pearson at 903.

30. *Cowcher* v. *Cowcher* [1972] 1 W.L.R. 425 at 437.

31. *Kowalczuk* v. *Kowalczuk* [1973] 1 W.L.R. 927 at 933 (quoted by Lord Denning).

32. *Kokosinski* v. *Kokosinski* [1980] 1 All E.R. 1106 at 1110.

33. *Falconer* v. *Falconer* [1970] 1 W.L.R. 1333.

34. *Cowcher* v. *Cowcher* [1972] 1 W.L.R. 424 at 441.

35. *Hargrave* v. *Newton* [1971] 1 W.L.R. 301 at 304. But see *Burns* v. *Burns* [1984] 1 All E.R. 244.

36. Hale, Sir M., *History of Pleas of the Crown* (1736), p. 636.

37. *R* v. *Clarence* (1888) 22 Q.B.D. 23.

38. *R.* v. *Miller* [1954] 2 Q.B. 282; Freeman, M. D. A., 'But If You Can't Rape Your Wife, Whom Can You Rape?', 15 *Fam. L. Quart.* 1 (1981).

39. *R.* v. *Hornby* [1978] *Crim. L. Rev.* 298; Gelles, R. J., *Family Violence* (Beverley Hills: Sage, 1979), Ch. 7; Faulk, 'Sexual Factors in Marital Violence', 11 *Med. Aspects of Human Sexuality* 30 (1979).

40. *Holborn* v. *Holborn* [1947] All E.R. 32.
41. *Foster* v. *Foster* [1921] 152 T.L.R. 70.
42. Bromley, P., *Family Law*, 5th edn (London: Butterworths, 1976), p. 189.
43. Smith, J., and Hogan, B., *Criminal Law*, 4th edn (London: Butterworths, 1978), p. 403.
44. CLRC, *Working Paper on Sexual Offences* (London: HMSO, 1980), p. 12. Since this section was written, the CLRC has published the Fifteenth Report on Sexual Offences, Cmnd. 9213 (London: HMSO, 1984). The Committee is divided on marital rape, although a narrow majority would not recommend extending the offence of rape to all marriages.
45. *Ibid.*, p. 13.
46. *Ibid.*, p. 15.
47. H.C., *Select Committee on Violence in Marriage*, Report (1975).
48. *Op. cit.* note 44, p. 15.
49. *R.* v. *Jackson* [1891] 1 Q.B. 671.
50. *Place* v. *Searle* [1932] 2 K.B. 497 at 500.
51. *Op. cit.* note 47, p. 366.
52. *Hoskyn* v. *Metropolitan Police Commissioner* [1979] A.C. 474. This rule has been changed by the Police and Criminal Evidence Act 1984, s.80.
53. *Ibid.* at 488.
54. *Ibid.* at 495.
55. *Ibid.* at 494.
56. *Ibid.* at 507.
57. *Coke Upon Littleton* (1629), section 6b.
58. Bentham, J., *Rationale of Judicial Evidence*, vol. 5 (London, 1827), p. 344.
59. *Wigmore on Evidence*, 3rd edn, vol. 8 (Boston: Little Brown, 1940), p. 232.
60. Gilbert, G., *The Law of Evidence* (London, 1801), p. 136.
61. *Op. cit.* note 52, at 495.
62. *Ibid.* at 500.
63. *Ibid.* at 507.
64. Boyle, C., 'Violence Against Wives', 31 *NILQ* 35 (1980), p. 50.
65. *Op. cit.* note 47, p. 418.
66. Bromley, P., *Family Law*, 6th edn (London: Butterworths, 1981), p. 112.
67. *Ibid.*
68. *Dunn* v. *Dunn* [1949] P. 98 at 103.
69. *Potter* v. *Potter* 5 *Fam. Law* 161 (1975); *B.(L.)* v. *B.(R.)* [1965] 3 All E.R. 263.
70. *Argyll* v. *Argyll* [1967] Ch. 302 at 322.
71. *Ash* v. *Ash* [1972] Fam. 135 at 140.
72. *Ibid.*
73a. S. 25 Matrimonial Causes Act 1973 as amended by the Matrimonial and Family Proceedings Act 1984.
73. *Le Marchant* v. *Le Marchant* [1977] 3 All E.R. 610 at 612.
74. See above, Chapter 3, note 62.
75. Barrington-Baker, W., *et al.*, *The Matrimonial Jurisdiction of Registrars* (Oxford: Socio-Legal Centre, 1977), para. 2.21.
76. *Ibid.*, para. 2.23.
77. *Ibid.*, para. 2.5.
78. *Trippas* v. *Trippas* [1973] Fam. 134 at 141.
79. *Ibid.* at 144.
80. *H.* v. *H.* [1975] Fam. 9 at 11 and 16.

81. *Kokosinski* v. *Kokosinski, op. cit.* note 32, at 1117.
82. *Eves* v. *Eves* [1975] 3 All E.R. 768 at 770.
83. *Cook* v. *Head* [1972] 2 All E.R. 38 at 40.
84. McIntosh, M., 'The Welfare State and the Needs of the Dependent Family', in S. B. Burman (ed.), *Fit Work for Women* (London: Croom Helm, 1979), p. 154.
85. Bott, E., *Family and Social Network* (London: Tavistock, 1957; revised 1971), p. 54.
86. Young, M., and Willmott, P., *The Symmetrical Family* (London: Routledge & Kegan Paul, 1973); Oakley, A., *The Sociology of Housework* (London: Martin Robertson, 1974).
87. Pahl, J., and Pahl, R., *Managers and Their Wives* (London: Allen Lane, 1972), p. 236.
88. Harris, C. C., *The Family and Industrial Society* (London, Allen & Unwin, 1983), p. 226.
89. *Ibid.*, p. 231.
90. Edgell, S. R., *Middle Class Couples* (London: Allen & Unwin, 1980), p. 68.
91. *Ibid.*, p. 70.
92. *Ibid.*
93. *Op. cit.* note 88, at p. 198.
94. Leonard, D., 'Legal Regulation of Marriage – Repressive Benevolence', in G. Littlejohn *et al.* (eds.), *Power and the State* (London: Croom Helm, 1977), p. 239.
95. *Ibid.*, p. 242.
96. Weitzman, L., *The Marriage Contract* (N.Y.: Free Press, 1981), p. xxi.
97. Ortner, S. B., 'Is Female to Male as Nature is to Culture?', 1 *Feminist Studies*, No. 2, 5 (1972) at p. 5.

Chapter 6: Public Law from the Private Perspective

1. I deliberately use the word men. The reasons why are clear from the text.
2. Lukes, S., *Individualism* (Oxford: Blackwell, 1973), p. 127.
3. *Ibid.*, p. 129.
4. Benn, S. I., and Gaus, G. F., 'The Liberal Conception of the Public and the Private', in S. I. Benn and G. F. Gaus (eds.), *Public and Private in Social Life* (London: Croom Helm, 1983), p. 56.
5. Rousseau, J. J., *The Social Contract*, Bk. 1, Ch. 5, trans. Benn and Gaus, *ibid.*, p. 49.
6. Green Paper, *The Taxation of Husband and Wife* (London: HMSO, 1980), Cmnd. 8093, p. 58.
7. Equal Opportunities Commission (G.B.), *With All My Worldly Goods* (1979), p. 2.
8. *Op. cit.* note 6, p. 59.
9. *Ibid.*, p. 7.
10. *Ibid.*, p. 5.
11. Meade, J. E., *et al.*, *The Structure and Reform of Direct Taxation*, IFS (London: Allen & Unwin, 1978), p. 377.
12. Equal Opportunities Commission (G.B.), *Income Tax and Sex Discrimination* (1977), p. 21.
13. *Op. cit.* note 6, p. 16.
14. Barr, N. A., 'The Taxation of Married Women's Incomes', (1980) *British Tax Review* 398 and 478, at p. 487.
15. Pahl, J., 'Problems of Money Management Within Marriage', 9 *J. of Soc. Pol.* 313 (1980), p. 313.
16. Cullivier, R., 'The Housewife: An Unjustifiable Financial Burden on the

Community', 8 *J. of Soc. Pol.* 1 (1979).

17. *Op. cit.* note 6, p. 11.
18. Lister, R., *Social Priorities in Taxation* (Child Poverty Action Group, 1981).
19. *Report of the Committee on Social Insurance and Allied Services*, Cmnd. 6404 (London: HMSO, 1942) (Beveridge Report), p. 49.
20. *Ibid.*
21. *Ibid.*
22. *Ibid.*
23. Commission of the European Communities, *A New Community Action Programme on the Promotion of Equal Opportunities for Women, 1982–85*, Com. (81)758.
24. Vredling, H., speech at EEC/EOC Conference on Equality for Women, Manchester, 28–30 May 1980.
25. Department of Health and Social Security, *Social Assistance* (1978), p. 96.
26. Supplementary Benefits Comm., *Annual Report 1976* (London: HMSO, 1977), Cmnd. 6910, para. 1.17.
27. *Op. cit.* note 25.
28. *Ibid.*, p. 96.
29. EEC, Official Journal 1977, C180/38.
30. Occupational Pensions Board, *Equal Status for Men and Women in Occupational Pension Schemes* (London: HMSO, 1976), Cmnd. 6599, para. 6.
31. *Ibid.*, table 11.
32. *Ibid.*, para. 4.19.
33. *Ibid.*, para. 12.4.
34. CSO, *Social Trends* 14 (1984), p. 34.
35. Glendon, M. A., *The New Family and the New Property* (Toronto: Butterworths, 1981), p. 138.
36. CSO, *op. cit.* note 34, p. 37.
37. CSO, *Social Trends* (1975), table 1.12.
38. Land, H., 'Poverty and Gender: The Distribution of Resources Within the Family', in M. Brown (ed.), *The Structure of Disadvantage* (London: Heinemann, 1983), p. 67.
39. Seccombe, W., 'The Housewife and Her Labour Under Capitalism', 38 *New Left Review* 3 (1974), p. 11.
40. Oakley, A., *Housewife* (Harmondsworth: Penguin, 1976), p. 8.
41. *Steer* v. *Basu* (1968), reported in Kemp and Kemp, *The Quantum of Damages*, 4th edn, vol. 1 (London: Sweet & Maxwell, 1968), p. 318.
42. *Op. cit.* note 34, p. 111.
43. House of Commons, Select Committee on Employment 1981, H.C.P. 39, 1981–82, para. 4.
44. A particular similarity is that both work in the home and that both are privatised. Neither is covered by public law.
45. Hakim, C., 'Homework and Outwork', *Employment Gazette*, January 1984, p. 10.
46. *Ibid.*, p. 11.
47. *Op. cit.* note 43, para. 6. This picture is confirmed by Hakim, C., 'Employers' Use of Homework, Outwork and Freelances', *Employment Gazette*, April 1984, p. 144.
48. *Op. cit.* note 45, p. 11.
49. Ewing, K. D., 'Homeworking: A Framework for Reform', 11 *I.L.J.* 94 (1982), p. 100.
50. [1978] I.C.R. 1210 at 1215.
51. *The Times*, Law Report, 4 May 1984.

52. In *Spinks* v. *McLaren Ltd*, I.T. 11168/79, because of the irregularity of the work pattern the outworker was denied her redundancy pay. In other cases there were occasions when the outworkers did not work for several weeks.

53. CSO, *Social Trends* 13 (1983), p. 52.

54. *Op. cit.* note 38. Workers with wages under £30 a week do not make social security payments and neither do their employers on their behalf. The overall increase in the numbers of married women doing part-time work may account for the increase in the numbers outside the national insurance scheme.

55. Unger, R., *Law in Modern Society* (N.Y.: Free Press, 1976), p. 144.

Chapter 7: Reforming the Public: Why Can't a Woman Be More Like a Man?

1. Baker, E., *The Politics of Aristotle* (Oxford: Clarendon Press, 1946), p. 3.

2. Elshtain, J. B., *Public Man, Private Woman* (Princeton U.P., 1981), p. 47.

3. Wollstonecraft, M., *A Vindication of the Rights of Women* (London: Dent, 1929), p. 63.

4. Mill, J. S., *On the Subjection of Women* (London: Dent, 1929), p. 263.

5. *Ibid.*

6. Engels, F., *The Condition of the Working Class in England* (St Albans: Panther, 1969), p. 172.

7. Humphries, J., 'Protective Legislation: The Case of the 1842 Mines Regulation Act', 7 *Feminist Review* 1 (1981).

8. Pinchbeck, I., *Women Workers and Industrial Revolution* (London: Routledge, 1930), p. 312.

9. *Muller* v. *Oregon*, 208 U.S. 412 (1908).

10. Brown, B. A., *et al.*, 'The Equal Rights Amendment', 80 *Yale L.J.* 871 (1971), p. 837.

11. Chester, R., 'A Social Agenda: Policy Issues Relating to the Family', OPCS, *British Society for Population Studies, Occasional Paper 31* (1983), p. 102.

12. The Sex Discrimination Act 1975 covers employment, training, education, goods, facilities, services, premises, advertisements, that is discrimination in the market-place. It does not cover state rules or actions on taxation and welfare.

13. Land, H., *Parity Begins at Home*, E.O.C. (G.B.) and S.S.R.C. (1981).

14. *Muller* v. *Oregon*, *op. cit.* note 9, at 422.

15. Engels, *op. cit.* note 6, p. 174.

16. [1981] 1 All E.R. 394.

17. *Ibid.* at 398.

18. *Frontiero* v. *Richardson*, 411 U.S. 655 (1973) at 684.

19. Locke, *The Second Treatise of Civil Government*, Ch. ix, Sec. 123, p. 62. This account is based on Lukes, S., *Individualism* (Oxford: Blackwell, 1973), Ch. 19.

20. Macpherson, C. B., *The Political Theory of Possessive Individualism* (Oxford: Clarendon Press, 1962).

21. Mill, J. S., *On Liberty* (London: Dent, 1910), p. 73.

22. [1977] IRLR 121.

23. Coyle, A., 'The Protection Racket?', 4 *Feminist Review* 1 (1980).

24. Trade Union and Labour Relations Act 1974, Sched. 1, para. 10(a) (unfair dismissal); Employment Protection (Consolidation) Act 1978, ss.31A; 33–36, 45–48, 56, 60(1) (maternity leave, pay, etc.); unfair dismissal (variation of quali-fication period) order 1985, S.I. 782.

25. [1978] IRLR 427 at 428.

26. [1980] ICR 66 at 70.

27. Although both women and men can complain of sex discrimination under the legislation, and indeed there is evidence of more complaints by men than by women, I choose to use women as my example.

28. *Griggs* v. *Duke Power Co.*, 401 U.S. 424 (1971).

29. *Gilbert* v. *General Electric Co.*, 429 U.S. 125 (1976).

30. 98 Sup. Ct. 347 (1977).

31. *Op. cit.* note 28.

32. Blackstone, W., *Commentaries*, vol. 1 (1765), p. 433.

33. Olsen, F. E., 'The Family and the Market', 96 *Harv. L. Rev.* 1497 (1983), p. 1549.

34. OEC Report, *Health and Safety Legislation: Should We Distinguish between Men and Women?* (London: HMSO, 1979), p. 92.

35. Dept. of Employment, *Papers* (1969), para. 20.

36. [1976] IRLR 405.

37. [1878] ICR 27 at 31.

38. [1978] IRLR 3 at 5.

39. *The Home Office* v. *Holmes* [1984] IRLR 299 (EAT).

40. Marx, K., 'On the Jewish Question', in *Early Writings* (Harmondsworth: Penguin, 1975), p. 230.

41. McCrudden, C., 'Changing Notions of Discrimination', paper delivered at ALSP Conference, London, 8 April 1984, p. 3.

42. CSO, *Social Trends* 14 (1984), p. 34.

43. OPCS, *Census 1981*, 'Economic Activity in Great Britain'.

44. Anonymous houseworker in 1970, quoted by Louise Howe, *Pink Collar Workers* (N.Y., 1977), p. 200.

Chapter 8: Reforming the Private

1. MacKinnon, C. A., 'Feminism, Marxism, Method, and the State: Toward Feminist Jurisprudence', 8 *Signs* 635 (1983), p. 657.

2. Domestic Violence and Matrimonial Proceedings Act 1976.

3. Matrimonial Homes Act 1983; *Williams and Glyns Bank* v. *Boland* [1981] A.C. 487.

4. Domestic Proceedings and Magistrates' Courts Act 1978, s.1.

5. Lukes, S., *Individualism* (Oxford: Blackwell, 1973), p. 62.

6. Berlin, I., *Four Essays on Liberty* (Oxford U.P., 1969), pp. 129, 128.

7. Cmd. 247 (1957).

8. Glendon, M. A., *The New Family and the New Property* (Toronto: Butterworths, 1981), p. 108.

9. Rheinstein, M. and Glendon, M. A., *International Encyclopedia of Comparative Law*, vol. iv: *Persons and Family* (1980), Ch. 4, paras. 4–14.

10. Civil Code, West Germany, art. 1356.

11. German C. C. Proc., art. 606, para. 1.

12. C.C., art. 1360.

13. Rheinstein and Glendon, *op. cit.* note 9, p. 17.

14. French Civil Code, art. 215.

15. *Ibid.*, para. 2.

16. According to Mazeaud and Mazeaud, *Leçons de Droit Civil*, vol. iv, 3rd edn (1967),

p. 74, about 20 per cent of French couples draw up marriage contracts.

17. Rheinstein and Glendon, *op. cit.* note 9, p. 80.

18. C.C., arts. 1421; 220; 1424; 1403, para. 2.

19. C.C., arts. 215 and 1751; 220–221.

20. C.C. Proc., art. 864. See Revel, J., 'L'article 214', *Rec. Dalloy Sirey Heb.*, No. 4 (1983).

21. Rheinstein and Glendon, *op. cit.* note 9, p. 47.

22. Beitzke, *Familienrecht*, 17th edn (Munich, 1974), 72 SS.

23. West German Civil Code, art. 1364.

24. *Ibid.*, arts. 1385–1389;

25. *Ibid.*, art. 1386, paras. 1, 2 and 3.

26. Guardianship Act 1973; French Civil Code, art. 372; West Germany, B. Verf. G., 29 July 1959.

27. Quoted in Rheinstein and Glendon, *op. cit.* note 9, p. 27.

28. Colombet, 'Commentaire de la loi du 4 juin 1970 sur l'autorité parentale', *D.S.* (1971), Chr. 1–29.

29. Married Women's Property Acts 1870–1882; Law Reform (Husband and Wife) Act 1962.

30. Shultz, M., 'Contractual Ordering of Marriage', 70 *Calif. L. Rev.* 204 (1982), p. 212.

31. *Brodie*, 1917 p. 271; *Youngberg* v. *Holstrum*, 252 Iowa 815, 108 N.W. 2d 498 (1961); *Balfour* [1919] 2 K.B. 571; *Davis* 191 A.2d.138 (D.C. 1963); Foote, *Cases on Family Law* (1976), pp. 896–9; *Westmeath* (1830) 1 Dow and Cl. 519.

32. *Op. cit.* note 30, p. 241.

33. Weitzman, L., *The Marriage Contract* (N.Y.: The Free Press, 1981), p. 3.

34. *Ibid.*, p. 225.

35. Law Com. No. 25 (1969), para. 3.

36. Freeman, M. D. A., and Lyon, C., *Cohabitation Without Marriage* (Aldershot: Gower, 1983).

37. Bernard, J., *The Future of Marriage* (N.Y.: Bantam Books, 1972), Ch. 1.

38. Atiyah, P., *The Rise and Fall of Freedom of Contract* (Oxford: Clarendon Press, 1979), p. 681 *et seq.*

39. See Kennedy, D., 'Distributive and Paternalist Motives in Contract and Tort Law', 41 *Maryland L. Rev.* 563 (1982).

40. *Op. cit.* note 33, p. 248.

41. *A. Schroeder Music Publishing Co.* v. *Macaulay* [1974] 3 All E.R. 616; *Lloyds Bank* v. *Bundy* [1974] 3 All E.R. 757.

42. *Camm* (1983) 13 Fam. Law 112; *Backhouse* [1978] 1 All E.R. 1158.

43. Zander, M., *Legal Services for the Community* (London: Temple Smith, 1978), Ch. 9.

44. *Op. cit.* note 30, pp. 315–16.

45. *Ibid.*, p. 327.

46. *Ibid.*, p. 332.

47. Unger, R. M., *Law in Modern Society* (N.Y.: The Free Press, 1976), p. 179.

48. Santos, B. de S., 'Law and Community', in R. Abel (ed.), *The Politics of Informal Justice*, vol. 1 (N.Y.: Academic Press, 1982), p. 260.

49. Matrimonial Causes Act 1973, s.41(1)(b).

50. Francis, P., 'Divorce and the Law and Order Lobby', 11 *Fam. Law* 69 (1981), p. 72.

51. Abel, R., 'The Contradictions of Informal Justice', in R. Abel (ed.), *op. cit.* note 48, p. 290.

52. Mnookin, R., 'Bargaining in the Shadow of the Law', (1979) *Current Legal Problems*, p. 65.

53. *Ibid.*, p. 76.

54. Glendon, M. A., *State, Law and Family* (Amsterdam: North Holland Publ., 1977), p. 321.

55. Carbonnier, J., cited by Glendon, *op. cit.* note 8, p. 138.

56. Scheingold, S., *The Politics of Rights* (Yale U.P., 1974), p. xi.

57. Hay, D., 'Property, Authority and the Criminal Law', in D. Hay *et al.* (eds.), *Albion's Fatal Tree* (Harmondsworth: Penguin, 1977), p. 25.

58. *Ibid.*, p. 55.

59. Thompson, E. P., *Whigs and Hunters* (Harmondsworth: Penguin, 1977), p. 25.

60. MacKinnon, C. A., *op. cit.* note 1, p. 657.

61. Atiyah, P. S., *From Principles to Pragmatism* (Oxford U.P., 1978), p. 10.

62. For another form of analysis, from which I benefited in rewriting this chapter, see Olsen, F., 'The Family and The Market', 96 *Harv. L. Rev.* 1497 (1983).

63. Abel, R., *op. cit.* note 51, p. 306.

Afterword

1. Lukes, S., *Individualism* (Oxford: Blackwell, 1973), p. 153.

2. Williams, B., 'The Idea of Equality', in P. Laslett and W. G. Runciman (eds.), *Philosophy, Politics and Society* (second series) (Oxford: Blackwell, 1979), p. 117.

Suggestions for Further Reading

The following is a guide to writings not referenced in the text which were used as sources.

Chapter 1

As this chapter brings together a variety of perspectives, there is no one work which covers the same ground. General discussions of privacy are contained in volume 33, no. 3, of the *Journal of Social Issues* (1977). Suggestions for an historical approach to the privacy of the family are contained in Laslett, P., 'The Family as a Public and Private Institution: An Historical Perspective', *Journal of Marriage and Family* 480 (August 1973). The distinction between privacy as a concept and the issue of a right to privacy is made in MacCormick, D. N., 'Privacy: A Problem of Definition?', 1 *B.J. of Law and Society* (1974). Legal accounts of privacy can be found in Gavison, R., 'Privacy and the Limits of Law', 89 *Yale L.J.* 421 (1980); O'Brien, D. M., *Privacy, Law and Public Policy* (Praeger, 1979); Wacks, R., *Protection of Privacy* (Sweet & Maxwell, 1980). The distinction between public and private, and the multiguous references involved, are elaborated in volume 130 *University of Pennsylvania L. Rev.* (1982); in Benn, S. I., and Gaus, G. F. (eds.), *Public and Private in Social Life* (Croom Helm, 1983); and in two works by Roberto Unger: *Law in Modern Society* (Free Press, 1976) and *Knowledge and Politics* (Free Press, 1975).

On the feminist critique of the private see Ehrenreich, B., and English, D., *For Her Own Good* (Pluto Press, 1979); Eisenstein, H., *Contemporary Feminist Thought* (Allen & Unwin, 1984); Elshtain, J. B., *Public Man, Private Woman* (Princeton U.P., 1981); Pateman, C., in

Benn and Gaus (eds.), *Public and Private in Social Life* (Croom Helm, 1983); Power, K., 'Sex Segregation and the Ambivalent Directions of Sex Discrimination Law', 1979 *Wisconsin L. Rev.* 55; Taub, N., and Schneider, E. M., 'Perspectives on Women's Subordination', in D. Kairys (ed.), *The Politics of Law* (Pantheon Books, 1983); Dahl, T. S., and Snare, A., 'The Coercion of Privacy', in C. Smart and B. Smart (eds.), *Women, Sexuality and Social Control* (Routledge, 1978); Wolff, R. P., 'There's Nobody Here But Us Persons', in C. C. Gould and M. W. Wartofsky (eds.), *Women and Philosophy* (Putnam, 1976). For the argument that the distinction between work and the personal life is created and constantly reinforced by capitalism, see Eli Zaretsky, *Capitalism, The Family and Personal Life* (Pluto Press, 1976).

Chapter 2

In order to write this chapter the author consulted a large number of works on social and legal history. What follows is a selection of those not referenced in the text. There has been a controversy among feminist writers over the use of the concept of patriarchy: see Beechey, V., 'On Patriarchy', 3 *Feminist Rev.* 66 (1973), and Robotham, S., 'The Trouble With Patriarchy', *New Statesman* (21 December 1979). See further Polan, D., 'Toward a Theory of Law and Patriarchy', in D. Kairys (ed.), *The Politics of Law* (Pantheon, 1982). For a study of women in medieval England see Power, E., *Medieval Women* (Cambridge U.P., 1975). An account of the changing role of women in the seventeenth century is contained in Hamilton, R., *The Liberation of Women* (Allen & Unwin, 1978); see further Thompson, R., *Women in Stuart England and America* (Routledge, 1974). For the Victorian period a good collection of essays is Vicinus, M. (ed.), *A Widening Sphere* (Indiana U.P., 1977), and a general collection is Carroll, B. A. (ed.), *Liberating Women's History* (U. of Illinois P., 1976). On access to land see Goody, J., *Production and Reproduction* (Cambridge U.P., 1976); Goody, Thirsk and Thompson (eds.), *Family and Inheritance* (Cambridge U.P., 1976); MacFarlane, A., *The Origins of English Individualism* (Blackwell, 1978).

Various accounts of married women's property exist. Lee Holcombe has undertaken a thorough investigation of the Victorian reforms in *Wives and Property* (Martin Robertson, 1983). See also Minor, I., 'Working-Class Women and Matrimonial Law Reform, 1890–1914', in D. Martin and D. Rubinstein (eds.), *Ideology and the*

Labour Movement (Croom Helm, 1979); Kahn-Freund, O., *Selected Writings*, Chs. 7 and 8 (Stevens, 1978); Ullrich, V., 'Reform of Matrimonial Property Law in England During the Nineteenth Century', 9 *Vict. U. of Wellington L. Rev.* 13 (1977).

There has been a resurgence of interest in family history: examples are Flandrin, J-L., *Families in Former Times* (Cambridge U.P., 1979); Laslett, P., and Wall, R., *Household and Family in Past Time* (Cambridge U.P., 1972); Outhwaite, R. B. (ed.), *Marriage and Society* (Europa, 1981); Shorter, E., *The Making of the Modern Family* (Fontana, 1977); Stone, L., *The Family, Sex, and Marriage in England 1500–1800* (Weidenfeld, 1977). There has also developed an interest in the history of bastardy: see Hair, P. E. H., 'Bridal Pregnancy in Rural England in Earlier Centuries', 20 *Population Studies* 233 (1966) and 24 *Population Studies* 59 (1970); Helmholz, R. H., 'Bastardy Litigation in Medieval England', XIII *Am. J. of Legal Hist.* 360 (1969); and Laslett, P., *et al.* (eds.), *Bastardy and its Comparative History* (Edward Arnold, 1980).

For accounts of forms of marriage and divorce, see Mueller, G., 'Inquiry into the State of a Divorceless Society', 18 *Univ. of Pitt. L. Rev.* 545 (1979); O'Donovan, K., 'Wife Sale and Desertion as Alternatives to Judicial Marriage Dissolution', in J. Eekelaar and S. Katz (eds.), *The Resolution of Family Conflict* (Butterworths, 1984), and 'Legal Marriage – Who Needs It?', 46 *Modern L. Rev.* 111 (1983) and references therein; Couch, H., 'The Evolution of Parliamentary Divorce in England', 52 *Tulane L. Rev.* 513 (1978); McGregor, O., *Divorce in England* (Heinemann, 1957); Harrison, R., and Mort, F., 'Patriarchal Aspects of Nineteenth Century State Formation', in P. Corrigan (ed.), *Capitalism, State Formation and Marxist Theory* (Quartet Books, 1980); Shanley, M. L., ' "One Must Ride Behind": Married Women and the Divorce Act of 1857', 25 *Victorian Studies* 355 (1982); Stetson, D. M., *A Woman's Issue, The Politics of Family Law Reform in England* (Greenwood Press, 1982). For discussions of ideology, separate spheres, the cult of domesticity and individualism, see Perkin, H., *The Origins of Modern English Society 1780–1880* (Routledge, 1969), Ch. 7; Cott, N., *The Bonds of Womanhood* (Yale U.P., 1980); Degler, C., *At Odds* (Oxford U.P., 1980); George, M., 'From Goodwife to Mistress: The Transformation of the Female in Bourgeois Culture', *Science and Society* 152 (Summer, 1973); Thomas, K., 'The Double Standard', *Journal of the History of Ideas* 195 (1959).

Chapter 3

General works on biology and gender identity are Archer, J., and

Lloyd, B., *Sex and Gender* (Penguin, 1982); Money, J., and Tucker, P., *Sexual Signatures* (Abacus, 1977); Money, J. (ed.), *Sex Research: New Developments* (Holt, Rinehart and Winston, 1965); Stoller, R., *Sex and Gender* (Science House, 1968). For legal writings on sex determination and on transsexualism see Bartholomew, G. W., 'Hermaphrodites and the Law', 2 *Malaya L.J.* 83 (1960); Bowman, K. M., and Engle, B., 'Sex Offences: The Medical and Legal Implications of Sex Variations', 25 *Law and Contemp. Pbs.* 292 (1960); Green, D. A. R., 'Transsexualism and Marriage', 120 *N.L.J.* 210 (1970); Finlay, H. A., 'Sexual Identity and the Law of Nullity', 54 *Australian L.J.* 115 (1980); Lupton, J. L., 'The Validity of Post-Operative Transsexual Marriages', 93 *South African L.J.* 385 (1976); Ormrod, R., 'The Medico-Legal Aspects of Sex-Determination', 40 *Medio-Legal J.* 78 (1972); Smith, D. K., 'Transsexualism, Sex Reassignment Surgery and the Law', 56 *Cornell L. Rev.* 963 (1971); Taitz, J., 'The Legal Consequences of a Sex Change', 97 *South African L.J.* 65 (1980); Walz, M. B., 'Transsexuals and the Law', 5 *J. of Contemp. Pbs.* 181 (1979); Thompson, J. M., 'Transsexualism, A Legal Perspective', 6 *J. of Medical Ethics* 82 (1980). For a personal account of transsexualism see Morris, J., *Conundrum* (Signet, 1974); Fallowell, D., and Ashley, A., *April Ashley's Odyssey* (Arena, 1983).

For a feminist argument that a society that produces sex-role stereotyping also produces transsexualism, see Raymond, J., *The Transsexual Empire* (Women's Press, 1980). On sex determination in sex-discrimination cases see Pannick, D., 'Homosexuals, Trans-sexuals and the Sex Discrimination Act', [1983] *Public Law* 279; Wein and Remmers, 'Employment Protection and Gender Dysphoria', 30 *Hastings L.J.* 1079 (1979). On social category and stereotypes see Bem, S. L., 'The Measurement of Psychological Androgyny', 42 *J. of Consulting and Clinical Psychology* 155 (1974); Eichler, M., *The Double Standard* (Croom Helm, 1980); Mead, M., *Male and Female* (Penguin, 1962); Oakley, A., *Sex, Gender and Society* (Temple Smith, 1972).

Chapter 4

On boundary theory see Katz, A., 'Studies in Boundary Theory', 28 *Buffalo L. Rev.* 383 (1979). On the history of the birth-control movement in Britain and the United States see Fryer, P., *The Birth*

Controllers (Secker & Warburg, 1966); McLaren, A., *Birth Control in Nineteenth Century England* (Croom Helm, 1978) and 'Contraception and the Working Classes', 18 *Comp. Studies in Society and History* 236 (1976); Langer, W., 'The Origins of the Birth Control Movement in the Early Nineteenth Century', 5 *J. of Interdisciplinary History* 669 (1975); Gordon, L., *Woman's Body, Woman's Right* (Penguin, 1977). For arguments linking social change and feminism to a reduction in the birth rate, see Banks, J. A., *Prosperity and Parenthood* (Routledge, 1954); J. A. and Olive Banks, *Feminism and Family Planning in Victorian England* (Liverpool U.P., 1965).

On the history of abortion see Knight, P., 'Women and Abortion in Victorian and Edwardian England', *History Workshop J.* 57 (Autumn, 1977); McLaren, A., 'Abortion in England, 1890–1914', xx *Vict. Studies* (Summer, 1977). Means, C. C., 'The Phoenix of Abortional Freedom', xvii *New York Law Forum* 335 (1971). On the history of infanticide see Greaves, G., 'On the Laws Referring to Child-Murder and Criminal Abortion', *Transactions of the Manchester Stats. Soc.* 19 (1863–64); Hair, P. E. H., 'Homicide, Infanticide, and Child Assault in Late Tudor Middlesex', 9 *Local Population Studies* 43 (Autumn, 1972); Hanawalt, B., *Crime and Conflict in English Communities, 1300–1348*, (Harvard U.P., 1979); Langer, W. L., 'Infanticide: A Historical Survey', 1 *Hist. of Childhood Quart.* 353 (no. 3, 1974); Kellum, B. A., 'Infanticide in England in the Later Middle Ages', 1 *Hist. of Childhood Quart.* 367 (no. 3, 1974); Malcolmson, R. W., 'Infanticide in the Eighteenth Century', in J. Cockburn (ed.), *Crime in England 1550–1800* (Methuen, 1977); Wrightson, K., 'Infanticide in Early Seventeenth Century England', 15 *Local Population Studies* (1975). For modern studies of infanticide see Seaborne Davies, D., 'Child Killing in English Law', 1 *Modern L. Rev.* 203 and 269 (1937); O'Donovan, K., 'The Medicalisation of Infanticide', (1984) *Crim. L. Rev.* 259; Walker, N., *Crime and Insanity in England* (Edinurgh U.P., 1968), Ch. 7.

On the regulation of sexuality see Weeks, J., *Sex, Politics and Society* (Longman, 1981); Edwards, S., *Female Sexuality and the Law* (Martin Robertson, 1981). For a fascinating account of the Victorian Contagious Diseases Acts, see Walkowitz, J., *Prostitution and Victorian Society* (Cambridge U.P., 1980); see also McHugh, P., *Prostitution and Victorian Social Reform* (Croom Helm, 1980). For an account of prostitution law see Sion, A., *Prostitution and the Law* (Faber, 1977). Feminist accounts of and arguments for decriminalisation of prostitution are available from McLeod, E., *Women Working, Prostitution Now* (Croom Helm, 1982) and 'Man-made Laws for Men?', in B. Hutter and G. Williams (eds.), *Controlling Women* (Croom Helm, 1981); McIntosh, M., 'Who Needs Prostitutes?', in C. Šmart and B. Smart (eds.), *Women, Sexuality and Social Control* (Routledge, 1978); Sumner, M., 'Prostitution and the Position of Women: A Case for Decriminalisation', in A. Morris (ed.), *Women and Crime* (Cambridge U.P., 1981). On the history of incest as a crime, see Bailey, V., and Blackburn S., 'The Punishment of Incest Act 1908', (1979) *Crim. L. Rev.* 708; Bailey, V., and McCabe S., 'Reforming the Law of Incest', (1979) *Crim. L. Rev.* 749. The Wolfenden Report provoked academic debate about private morality and the limits of law. See Devlin P., *The Enforcement of Morals* (Oxford U.P., 1968); Hart, H. L. A., *Law, Liberty and Morality* (Oxford U.P., 1963), and 'Social Solidarity and the Enforcement of Morality', 35 *Univ. of Chicago L. Rev.* 1 (1967).

Chapter 5

This chapter is based on the author's own knowledge of family law. For an excellent textbook on the subject which takes a broad approach, consult Cretney, S. M., *Principles of Family Law*, 4th edn (Sweet & Maxwell, 1984); see further Eekelaar, J., *Family Law and Social Policy*, 2nd edn (Weidenfeld, 1984). On family property see Gray, K., *The Reallocation of Property on Divorce* (Professional Books, 1977), and Gray, K., and Symes, P. D., *Real Property and Real People* (Butterworths, 1981). There is an enormous literature on violence in marriage and wife abuse: see Dobash, R., and Dobash, R., *Violence Against Wives* (Open Books, 1979); Freeman, M. D. A., 'Violence Against Women: Does the Legal System Provide Solutions or Itself Constitute the Problem?', 7 *B.J. of Law and Soc.* 215 (1980), and *Violence in the Home* (Saxon House, 1979). Borkowski, Murch and Walker recognise that privacy might increase the likelihood of marital violence in Ch. 7 of *Marital Violence* (Tavistock, 1983).

For a review of the literature on women's and men's work in the home and its effects on their paid employment, see Land, H., *Parity Begins At Home* (EOC/SSRC, 1981). A very interesting argument that individual security in Western society today is obtained through paid employment and not through the family is contained in Glendon, M. A., *The New Family and the New Property* (Butterworths, 1981).

Chapter 6

On family policy generally see Land, H., and Parker, R., 'United Kingdom', in S. B. Kamernan and A. J. Kahn (eds.), *Family Policy* (Columbia U.P., 1978); Poster, M., *Critical Theory of the Family* (Pluto Press, 1978); Land, H., 'The Family Wage', 6 *Feminist Rev.* 55 (1980). Feminists have argued for the disaggregation of the needs of the married couple in tax and social security legislation. See Land, H., 'Women Supporters or Supported', in D. L. Barker and S. Allen (eds.), *Sexual Division and Society: Process and Change* (Tavistock, 1976) and 'Sex-Role Stereotyping in the Social Security and Income Tax Systems', in J. Chetwynd and O. Hatnett (eds.), *The Sex Role System* (Routledge, 1978). Studies have been done on judicial valuation of the housewife's time: see Clarke, K. A., and Ogus, A. I., 'What is a Wife Worth?', 5 *B.J. of Law and Soc.* 1 (1978); O'Donovan, K., 'Legal Recognition of the Value of Housework', 8 *Fam. Law* 215 (1978). On liberal theory and individualism see Macpherson, C. B., *The Political Theory of Possessive Individualism* (Oxford U.P., 1962).

Chapter 7

Accounts of the history of women's demands for equality are available in Chafe, W., *Women and Equality* (Oxford U.P., 1977); Strachey, R., *The Cause* (Virago, 1978); Sachs, A., and Wilson, J. H., *Sexism and the Law* (Martin Robertson, 1978). Protective legislation is discussed in Coyle, A., 'The Protection Racket?', 4 *Feminist Rev.* 1 (1980). It is generally assumed that men wish to exclude women from employment but Jane Humphries argues that there is no evidence to support the theory that male coalminers feared female competition, 'Protective Legislation, the Capitalist State, and Working Class Men', 7 *Feminist Rev.* 1 (1981). See further O'Donovan, K., 'Protection and Paternalism', in M. D. A. Freeman (ed.), *State, Law and the Family* (Tavistock, 1984); Baer, J. A., *The Chains of Protection: The Judicial Response to Women's Labor Legislation* (Greenwood Press, 1978); John, A., *By the Sweat of their Brow* (Croom Helm, 1980). Employment protection legislation covering pregnancy is discussed in Upex, R., and Morris, A., 'Maternity Rights', 10 *Industrial L.J.* 218 (1981); Pannick, D., 'Sex Discrimination and Pregnancy', 3 *Oxford J. of Legal Studies* 1 (1983).

On paternalism see Luban, D., 'Paternalism and the Legal

Profession', (1981) *Wisconsin L.J.* 454; Kennedy, D., 'Distributive and Paternalist Motives in Contract and Tort Law', 41 *Maryland L. Rev.* 563 (1982); Dworkin, G., 'Paternalism', in R. A. Wasserstrom (ed.), *Morality and the Law* (1971). David Miller discusses different conceptions of equality in *Social Justice* (Oxford U.P., 1976). For explanations and critiques of sex discrimination legislation see McCrudden, C., 'Institutional Discrimination', 2 *Oxford J. of Legal Studies* 303 (1982); Sedley, A., 'Equal Rights', *Legal Action* 9 (January 1984); Hutton, J., 'How the SDA has Failed', *Legal Action* 10 (April 1984).

Chapter 8

In general there is little work on the area covered in this chapter. Arguments against state intervention in the family are contained in Mount, F., *The Subversive Family* (Cape, 1982). Most of the literature on the family contains the assumption that it is a universal good which will be destroyed by official supervision. For example, see Goldstein, Freud and Solnit, *Beyond the Best Interests of the Child* (Free Press, 1973); Glendon, M. A., *The New Family and the New Property* (Butterworths, 1981). Catharine MacKinnon argues that women are in a dilemma when they look to the state for protection, as the state is male-identified and law's claim to objectivity is false. See her two articles entitled 'Feminism, Marxism, Method, and the State', 7 *Signs* 515 (1982) ('An Agenda for Theory') and 8 *Signs* (1983) ('Toward Feminist Jurisprudence'). For the debate on continuation of financial support obligations of spouses after divorce, see Deech, R., 'The Principles of Maintenance', 7 *Fam. Law* 229 (1977), and O'Donovan K., 'The Principles of Maintenance – an Alternative View', 8 *Fam. Law* 180 (1978). There is a large volume of work on delegalisation and conciliation. For examples see Mnookin, R., 'Bargaining in the Shadow of the Law – the Case of Divorce', (1979) *Current Legal Problems* 65; Eekelaar, J., and Katz, S., *The Resolution of Family Conflict* (Butterworths, 1984).

Index of Cases

Airfix Footwear Ltd v. Cope [1978] I.C.R. 1210   155
Argyll v. Argyll [1967] Ch. 302   6, 126
Ash v. Ash [1972] Fam. 135   127
Backhouse v. Backhouse [1978] 1 All E.R. 1158   193
Balfour v. Balfour [1919] 1 K.B. 571   11, 13, 108–9
Bradwell v. Illinois 83 U.S. (16 Wall) 130; 21 L.Ed. 442 (1873)   75
C and D (Aus.) (1979) F.L.C. 90–636   65–6
Camm v. Camm (1983) 13 Fam. Law 112   193
Carey v. Population Service International 97 Sup. Ct. 2010 (1977)   86–7
Charter v. Race Relations Board [1973] 1 All E.R. 512   9–10
Cook v. Head [1972] 2 All E.R. 38   130
Corbett v. Corbett [1971] P. 83   64–7, 70, 72
Cowcher v. Cowcher [1972] 1 W.L.R. 424   117–18
Cook v. Edmondson [1966] 2 Q.B. 81   102
Duchesne v. Duchesne 2 All E.R. 784   79
Dudgeon v. U.K. 4 E.H.R.R. 149 (1982)   106
Dunn v. Dunn [1949] P. 98   125–6
Eisenstadt v. Baird 405 U.S. 438 (1972)   86
Eves v. Eves [1975] 3 All E.R. 768   130
Falconer v. Falconer [1970] 1 W.L.R. 1333   117
Foster v. Foster [1921] 152 T.L.R. 70   119
Frontiero v. Richardson 411 U.S. 677 (1973)   17
Gilbert v. General Electric Co. 429 U.S. 125 (1976)   172
Gillick v. W. Norfolk and Wisbech Area Health Authority (1984) *The Times*,
    Dec. 21   87
Gissing v. Gissing [1971] A.C. 886   116
Griggs v. Duke Power Co. 401 U.S. 424 (1971)   172–3
Griswold v. Connecticut 381 U.S. 479 (1965)   86
H. v. H. [1975] Fam. 9   130
H. v. H. and C. [1969] 1 All E.R. 784   79
Hargrave v. Newton [1971] 1 W.L.R. 301   118
Holborn v. Holborn [1947] All E.R. 32   119
Home Office v. Holmes [1984] 1. R.L.R. 299   178
Hoskyn v. M.P.C. [1979] A.C. 474   123–5
Hoyt v. Florida 368 U.S. 57 (1961)   76
Jex-Blake v. Senate of the University of Edinburgh (1873) 11 M. 784   75

Kokosinski v. Kokosinski [1980] 1 All E.R. 1106   117, 130
Kowalczuk v. Kowalczuk [1973] 1 W.L.R. 927   116–17
Le Marchant v. Le Marchant [1977] 3 All E.R. 610   128
Lennon v. Twist (1979) 129 N.L.J. 636   6
Lloyds Bank v. Bundy [1974] 3 All E.R. 757   193
Muller v. Oregon 208 U.S. 412 (1908)   76
Nashville Gas v. Satty 98 Sup. Ct. 347 (1977)   173
Paton v. Trustees of B.P.A.S. [1978] 2 All E.R. 987   91
Paton v. U.K. 3 E.H.R.R. 408 (1981)   91–2
Place v. Searle [1932] 2 K.B. 497   122
Price v. Civil Service Commission [1976] I.R.L.R. 405   177–8
Prince Albert v. Strange (1848) 2 De G. & Sm. 652   6
R. v. Bourne (1939) 1 K.B. 687   90
R. v. Bradlaugh and Besant (1878) L.R. 3 Q.B. 607 and 625   84
R. v. Clarence (1888) 22 Q.B.D. 23   119
R. v. Delaval (1763) 3 Burr. 1434, 96 E.R. 234   52
R. v. Jackson [1891] 1 Q.B. 671   122
R. v. Miller [1954] 2 Q.B. 282   119
R. v. O'Donoghue (1927) 20 Cr. App. 132   96
Re Agar-Ellis (1883) 24 Ch. D. 317   12
Re C. [1978] 2 All E.R. 230   79
Re L. (infants) [1962] 3 All E.R. 1   79
Reaney v. Kanda Jean Products Ltd [1978] I.R.L.R. 427   170–1
Reed v. Reed 404 U.S. 71 (1971)   17
Schroeder Music Publishing Co. v. Macaulay [1974] 3 All E.R. 616   193
Semayne's Case (1604) 77 E.R. 194   12
Trippas v. Trippas [1973] Fam. 134   129
Turley v. Allders Stores Ltd. [1980] I.C.R. 66   171
Van Oosterwijck v. Belgium 3 E.H.R.R. 557 (1980)   68–9
Wachtel v. Wachtel [1973] Fam. 72   79
White v. British Sugar Corp. [1977] I.R.L.R. 121   71

Index of Statutes

Abortion Act 1967   90–1
Civil Code (France)   185–7
Civil Code (West Germany)   185–7
Contagious Diseases Act 1864   100
Criminal Code (Canada), s.246   121–2
Criminal Justice (Scotland) Act 1980   106
Criminal Law Amendment Act 1885   103–6
Criminal Law Amendment Act 1912   106
Divorce Reform Act 1969   113, 127
Domestic Proceedings and Magistrates' Courts Act 1978   120, 126, 143
Domestic Violence and Matrimonial Proceedings Act 1976   120
18 Eliz. 1 c.3, 1575   40
Employment Protection (Consolidation) Act 1978   155
Equal Pay Act 1970   71, 144, 174
European Convention on Human Rights, Art. 8   69, 91–2
European Economic Community Directive 75/117   144
                   Directive 76/207   145
                   Directive 79/7   145–8
European Economic Community Treaty, Art. 119   144
Factories Act 1961   71
Family Income Supplements Act 1970   146
Fatal Accidents Act 1976   152
25 Henry VIII, c.6, 1533   105
Income and Corporation Taxes Act 1970   137
Infant's Custody Act 1839 (Talfourd's Act)   55
Infanticide Act 1922   95–6
Infanticide Act 1938   96–7
Infant Life Protection Act 1929   90
Inheritance (Provision for Family and Dependants) Act 1975   182, 201
Law Reform Act 1971   152
Lord Ellenborough's Act 1803   88, 94–5
Lord Hardwicke's Marriage Act 1753   44–50
Marriage Act 1653   46
Married Women's Property Acts 1870–1882   56, 112, 137, 194
    s.17 (1882 Act)   114
Married Women's Property Act 1964, s.1   109

Matrimonial Causes Act 1857   55–6
Matrimonial Causes Act 1973   114, 119–20, 127–8, 143, 182, 201
Matrimonial Proceedings and Property Act 1970   114, 128, 143
Matrimonial Property Act 1976 (New Zealand)   115
Offences Against the Person Act 1828   95
Offences Against the Person Act 1861   89, 105
Poor Law Relief Act 1601   39
Punishment of Incest Act 1908   103
Race Relations Act 1968, s.2(i)   9
Sexual Offences Act 1956   70, 102, 104, 106
Sexual Offences Act 1967   106
Sexual Offences (Amendment) Act 1976, s.1   120
Social Security (Pensions) Act 1975   148, 153
Statute of Westminster I, c.22, 1275   24
Street Offences Act 1959   7, 82, 100
Vagrancy Act 1898   106

General Index

abortion and the law, 87–92
age of consent, 104–5
aggregation
  of individuals, 136
  and social security, 142, 145, 147
  and taxation, 138–40
allowance, housekeeping, 111, 117
Aristotle, 161
assimilation, 77–8, 174
astrier, 26–7
Auden, W. H., 135

bankruptcy and marital property, 116, 117, 182
bastardy and the law, 40–2
Beauvoir, S. de, 81
Besant, A., 84–5
besom weddings, 49
Beveridge Report, 142–4
biological/biology
  and culture, 16–17, 74–5
  differences and discrimination, 75–6, 166–7, 170–3
  and infanticide, 96–9
  and marriage, 65–7, 119
  and sexual determination, 59–69
Birkett Committee, 86, 89–90
Birth Control, 84–5
birth control and the law, 83–7
Blackstone, W., 173–4
Bracton, 26, 29, 31, 35
Bradlaugh, C., 84–5
Butler Committee (on Mentally Abnormal Offenders), 97
Butler, J., 101

canon law, *see* church law
chattels, 25–6, 30, 32–4
  women as, 35
child custody, 55–6, 129, 130, 197–8

child protection, 13, 54–5, 104–5, 166, 168
childwite, 34
church law in medieval society
  abortion, 88
  homosexuality, male, 105
  infanticide, 92–3
  marriage, 40–4
Civil Code, 185–7
cluster-concept method of sex determination, 64, 67–9, 72
co-habitation
  contracts, *see* marriage contracts and social security, 144
Coke's Third Institute, 88
Commentaries, 173–4
Commission on Capital Punishment, 95, 96
common law in medieval society
  abortion, 87–8
  marriage, 42–4, 46–50, 173–4
  property, 23–35
common prostitute, 100–1
community of property, 32, 112–15, 182, 185–7
community values, *see* gemeinschaft
compellability, 123–4
Comstock law (US), 85
consortium rights, 125–6
contraception and the law, 83–7
co-parceners, 25
Council of Trent, 43
couverture, 31
Criminal Law Revision Committee, 97, 104, 121
culture as men's creation, 15–17, 74–5, 79–80

dependence, financial, *see* women, married

discretion, judicial, 128–30, 201–2, 205
discrimination, *see* sex discrimination
division of labour, *see* labour
divorce
  and conciliation/mediation, 196–7,
    205
  financial consequences, 128–30, 197,
    201–2
  no-fault, 113, 130
  and private conflict settlement, 197–8
  regulation, 50, 52–3, 55–7, 127–30
  self-regulated, 50–2, 202, 204
  and unity of spouses, 150–3
  see also child custody
'domestic' and 'public', 10
domesticity, cult of, 53–6
domestic services, valuation of, 151–3,
  188, 203–4
Donzelot, J., 37–8, 54–5
dower (dowry), 26–7, 30, 34

earning election, wife's, 138–9
ecclesiastical law, *see* church law
economic power, *see* power
Employment Appeal Tribunal, 155–6,
  168–9, 171, 177
Engels, F., 16, 33, 164, 204
equal pay, 144–5, 179
equality
  of bargaining power, 191–4
  and family code, 185–7
  formal, 17, 55, 160–3, 176, 206
  of opportunity: 167; and indirect
    discrimination, 171–3
  and social security, 144–50
  see also sex discrimination legislation
Equal Opportunities Commission, 138,
  140–1, 175
Equal Rights Amendment (US), 78
essentialist approach to sex
  determination, 64–7, 72, 75
European Commission on Human
  Rights, 68–9, 91, 106
expressive role of women, 73, 75

family
  code, 185–7
  courts, 195–7
  as economic unit, 31, 48, 56–7, 137–
    53, 157, 203
  income supplement, 146–7
  regulated, 14–15, 37–40, 44–50, 54–6

  unregulated, 11–15
  wage, 165
  see also marriage; patriarchy; power
Family and Social Network, 131
feminism
  and gender behaviour, 74–5
  and individualism, 36, 179–80
  and labour division 35–6
  and private sphere, 15–19, 82, 183–4
feudalism, 21–35
financial dependence, *see* women,
  married
Fleet Prison, 46
freedom of contract, 191–2
  for women, 169–80
Fruits of Philosophy, The, 83–4

gemeinschaft (community values), x, 2,
  4–5, 11–12, 108
gender
  and the law, 19–20, 59, 75–6, 78–9
  and sex, 60–4, 69
  and social role, 15–17, 62–8, 73–5,
    168, 176
  and status (feudal), 30–5, 37
gesellschaft (individualism), x, 5, 77, 108
Glanvill, 29, 31
Green Paper on Taxation of Husband
  and Wife, 138–42, 150

heriot tax, 34
homeworkers, women and
  discrimination, 154–6
homicide and infanticide, 92–6
homosexuality, male, regulation of, 7, 9,
  70, 102–6 *passim*
housekeeping allowance, 111, 117
housework, valuation of, 151–3, 188,
  203–4

ideology
  of law, 19–20, 112, 128, 199–203
  of love, 9, 12, 18, 109, 128
  of non-intervention, 184, 200
idiots and polis, 161
incest and the law, 13, 102–4
individualism, 33, 36–7, 113, 157–8, 203
  and marriage, 150, 153, 179–80,
    191–4
  and pensions, 148–50
  and social security, 44, 147–8
  and tax, 141–2

and see gesellschaft
Industrial Tribunal, 170
infanticide and the law, 92–9
inheritance, partible/impartible, 24–6
instrumental role of men, 73
instrumental view of law, 19
invalid care allowance, 147

judicial discretion, 128–30, 201–2, 205
jure uxoris, 29

Knowlton, C., 83–4
labour, division of (sexual)
 and family power, 9, 12–18, 55–6,
  109–12, 116, 125–6, 131–4
 and housework valuation, 151–3, 188,
  203–4
 and private/public, 9, 35–7, 53–6,
  107–8, 113, 118
 and women's work, 154–6
 and see protective legislation
Ladies' National Association, 101
land alienation, 29–30
Lane Committee, 105
law
 and adversarial process, 195–7
 and gender order, 17, 19–20
 hortatory function, 202
 as ideology, 19–20, 112, 128, 199–203
 instrumental view of, 19
 and private sphere (unregulated), 82,
  86, 102, 106, 181–4, 198–9
 private/public border areas
  abortion, 87–92
  age of consent, 104–5
  contraception, 83–7
  homosexuality, male, 7, 9, 70,
   102–6 *passim*
  incest, 102–4
  infanticide, 92–9
  prostitution, 100–2
 private/public distinction, 3–15
 and public sphere
  pensions, 148–50
  reforms proposed, 171–80
  social security, 142–8
  taxation, 136–42
 and sexual differentiation, 67–80
  anomalies in, 70–3
 'solemn mockery' of, 95–7
 see also church law; common law;
  judicial discretion

Law of Population, 84
Laws Respecting Women, The, 51
Leach, Sir E., 107
legerwite, 34
Leges Henrici, 34
lesbianism, unregulated, 7, 105
Lewis, C. S., 160
liberal philosophy and private/public
 spheres, 8–9, 38
Liber Gersumarum (of Romsey Abbey), 29
Liberty, On, 102, 169–70
Locke, J., 8, 21, 169

maritagium, 25–9
marriage
 breakdown and divorce, 52–3, 127–30
 contracts, 108–9, 188–94
 common law (spousals), 42–4, 46–50
 church law and, 40–4
 definition, 133–4
 marital behaviour, 125–7
 marital rape, 119–22
 portion, 25–8
 property, 112–18
 regulated by law, 44–50, 67, 69, 136–
  50
 reforms proposed, 181–206
 secret, 45–50
 unregulated by law, 7–8, 11, 108–34
 wife battering, 122–5, 182
 see also divorce; family; women,
  married
married couple as economic unit, 31,
 48, 56–7, 137–53, 157, 203
Married Love, 84–5
matrimonial home
 co-ownership, 12–13, 115–18
 and occupation, 112, 115, 182, 187–8
 see also community of property
Mead, M., 73–4
Meade Committee, 139
merchet, 34–5
military tenure, 31
Mill, J. S., 2, 8–9, 56, 102, 162–3, 169–
 70
Money, J., 62–3, 66
moral purity movement, 55, 101–5
motherhood
 and employment, 154–6, 166–71, 179
 idealisation of, 54, 55, 89
mund, 32

Occupational Pensions Board, 149
On Liberty, 102
outworkers and discrimination, 154–6

part-time work and married women,
    154–6, 179–80
paternalism, state and protective
    legislation, 165–76
patria potestas, 10–11
Patriarcha, 22
patriarchy
    and domesticity, 54–7
    in medieval society, 11, 21–35, 53
    and public law, 39, 44–5, 48–9, 135–
        58
    survival of, 1, 59, 82, 132–4, 157, 181
    see also family; power
pawning, secret, 110
pensions and discrimination, 148–50
'personal is political', 17–18, 82, 183
Place, F., 83
Policing the Family (La Police des familles),
    37–8
Policy Advisory Committee on Sexual
    Offences, 104
polis, 161
Politics, 161
pooling of income, 111, 116–17, 141
Poor Law Commissioners, 54
Poor Laws, 14, 39, 48, 53, 94
population and birth control, 86
power in the family, 12–18
    bargaining inequality, 191–4
    economic, 9, 33, 37, 56, 109–12, 116–
        18, 125–6, 131–4, 157, 203
    and marital violence, 119–25
    see also patriarchy; women,
        dependence of pregnancy and
        discrimination, 170–3
primogeniture, 22, 24, 35
private sphere (unregulated)
    concept of, 1, 5–8
    and the invisible, 7, 82–90, 99, 102–3,
        105, 118
    and public, ix–xi, 1–20
    see also divorce; family; marriage
property
    allocation and divorce, 112–18, 128–
        30, 197–8, 201
    community of, 32, 112–15, 182, 185–7
    see also matrimonial home; women
        and property

prostitution, regulation of, 9, 70, 82,
    100–2
protective legislation, 70–1, 75–6, 163–
    70, 173–6
public sphere (regulated)
    concept of, 3–5
    and private, ix–xi, 1–20
    see also law

Radcliffe Commission, 138
rape, marital, 119–22
regulated, *see* public sphere
retirement, earlier for women, 148–9
Royal Commission on the Taxation of
        Profits and Income, 138

Sanger, M., 85–6
scutage, 31
Secret Life, 101
Select Committee on Violence in
        Marriage, 121–2, 125
sex
    assignment, 60–2
        errors in, 62–4
    determination, legal, 64–9, 72
        application of, 70–3
        elimination of, 72, 76–80
    discrimination
        biological differences and, 75–6,
            166–7, 170–3
        direct, 170–2
        indirect, 167, 171–3, 176–80; and
            non-discrimination, 178–9
        legislation against, 17, 18, 71–2, 78,
            166–7, 174, 176
        and pay, 179
        in pensions, 148–9
        and protective legislation, 70–1,
            166–76
        and sexual crime, 70
        in social security, 142–4, 146
        in taxation, 138–41
        and women's work, 154–6
        see also homosexuality; judicial
            discretion; labour, division of;
            patriarchy; power; transsexual
            and gender 60–4
sex-neutral language, 77–9
sex-specific crime, 94–8
sexual
    behaviour
        double standard of, 101–2

in marriage, 119–22
single standard of, 55
stereotyping, 72–3, 76–7
sexuality, regulation of, 81, 99–106
Social Assistance, 146–7
Social Contract, 136
social purity movement, 55, 101–5
social security and discrimination, 142–5, 147
spousals, 42–4, 46–50
State, *see* law
statists, 38
status and gender, 30–5, 37
Stopes, M., 84–5
Subjection of Women, On the, 8–9, 162–3
succession, partible/impartible, 24–6
supplementary benefit, 146–7
Sutherland, H., 84–5
Synod of Exeter, 27

taxation and discrimination, 136–42
tenancy by the curtsey, 30
testation, freedom of, 27, 32–33
Thompson, E. P., 20
'tipping up', 111
Trade Union Congress and protective
legislation, 175
transferability of allowances, 141–2
transsexuals
and employment, 71–2
and gender, 65–6, 68, 70
and sexual crime, 70
and social security, 72
Tönnies, F., 2, 4–5

unconscionability doctrine (US), 191–4
unregulated, *see* private sphere

villeins, 26, 28, 34–5
Vindication of the Rights of Man, 161
Vindication of the Rights of Women, 161–2
violence in marriage, 119–25

wardship, 24
widows' benefits, 147, 150
wife battering, 122–5
Wilbur, R., 181
Wolfenden Report, 9, 100, 102, 106, 183
Wollstonecraft, M., 161–2
Woman Rebel, The, 85
women
and assimilation, 77–8, 174
and culture (men's), 15–17, 74–5, 79–80
and expressive role, 73, 75
and freedom of contract, 169–80
and infanticide, 93–9
lesbianism, 7, 105
and protective legislation, 70–1, 75–6, 163–70, 173–6
married
and consortium rights, 125–6
dependence, financial, 36, 39–40, 56–7, 109–12, 131–4, 150–2, 156, 184
earning election, 138–9
in feudal system, 21–35, 47, 174
gift/sale of, 50–2
as homeworkers/outworkers, 154–6, 179–80
and marriage contract, 188–94
and motherhood, 54, 55, 89, 154–6, 166–71, 179
and pensions, 148–50
and property: inherited, 23–30; rights, 12–13, 112–18, 182, 187–8
and rape, 119–22
and social security, 142–8
and taxation, 136–42
and violence, 122–5
see also divorce; equality; labour, division of; marriage; patriarchy; power; sex discrimination
single, in feudal system, 23–9

Younger Committee, 6–7